# Conversations
# with Michael Crichton

Literary Conversations Series
*Peggy Whitman Prenshaw*
*General Editor*

# Conversations
# with Michael Crichton

Edited by Robert Golla

University Press of Mississippi    Jackson

www.upress.state.ms.us

The University Press of Mississippi is a member of the Association of American University Presses.

First printing 2011

∞

Library of Congress Cataloging-in-Publication Data

Conversations with Michael Crichton / edited by Robert Golla.
    p. cm. — (Literary conversations series)
Includes index.
ISBN 978-1-61703-012-3 (cloth : alk. paper) — ISBN 978-1-61703-013-0 (pbk. : alk. paper) 1. Crichton, Michael, 1942–2008—Interviews. 2. Novelists, American—20th century—Interviews. I. Golla, Robert.
 PS3553.R48Z57 2011
 813.54—dc22                                      2010047206

British Library Cataloging-in-Publication Data available

# Books by Michael Crichton

*Odds On.* (as John Lange) New York: Signet, 1966.
*Scratch One.* (as John Lange) New York: Signet, 1967.
*Easy Go.* (as John Lange) New York: Signet, 1968.
*A Case of Need.* (as Jeffery Hudson) New York: World Publishing Co., 1968.
*Zero Cool.* (as John Lange) New York: Signet, 1969.
*The Venom Business.* (as John Lange) New York: World Publishing Co., 1969.
*The Andromeda Strain.* New York: Knopf, 1969.
*Five Patients: The Hospital Explained.* New York: Knopf, 1970.
*Drug of Choice.* (as John Lange) New York: Signet, 1970.
*Dealing: Or, The Berkeley-to-Boston Forty-Brick Lost-Bag Blues.* (as Michael Douglas; co-written with Douglas Crichton) New York: Knopf, 1970.
*Grave Descend.* (as John Lange) New York: Signet, 1970.
*Binary.* (as John Lange) New York: Knopf, 1972.
*The Terminal Man.* New York: Knopf, 1972.
*The Great Train Robbery.* New York: Knopf, 1975.
*Eaters of the Dead.* New York: Knopf, 1976.
*Jasper Johns.* New York: Abrams, 1977.
*Congo.* New York: Knopf, 1980.
*Electronic Life: How to Think about Computers.* New York: Knopf, 1983.
*Sphere.* New York: Knopf, 1987.
*Travels.* New York: Knopf, 1988.
*Jurassic Park.* New York: Knopf, 1990.
*Rising Sun.* New York: Knopf, 1992.
*Disclosure.* New York: Knopf, 1994.
*The Lost World.* New York: Knopf, 1995.
*Airframe.* New York: Knopf, 1996.
*Timeline.* New York: Knopf, 1999.
*Prey.* New York: HarperCollins, 2002.
*State of Fear.* New York: HarperCollins, 2004.
*Next.* New York: HarperCollins, 2006.
*Pirate Latitudes.* New York: HarperCollins, 2009.

# Contents

# Introduction

Michael Crichton was a renaissance man. He was a doctor, screenwriter, film director, art collector, video game pioneer, and, most famously, known to millions of readers around the world as the prolific author of bestsellers including *The Andromeda Strain, Sphere, Jurassic Park, Disclosure, Prey, State of Fear, Pirate Latitudes,* and many others. His novels have sold more than 150 million copies and have been translated into thirty-six languages. He remains the only writer to have simultaneously had the number one book, number one movie, and number one television show.

Such was the nature of Crichton's genius that he once told an interviewer, "I never want to do anything twice." Indeed, Crichton's range of interests and endeavors makes labeling impossible, though he was delighted by the monikers given by two friends: Tom Clancy famously called him "Father of the Techno-Thriller," and Steven Spielberg described him as "The high priest of high concept."

But long before he was given these laurels, he clandestinely wrote action-thrillers under an array of pseudonyms to earn his tuition for Harvard Medical School. No interviews were conducted with Crichton until the debut of *The Andromeda Strain* in 1969, the first novel published under his own name. The publication of every subsequent Crichton book became a literary event introduced to readers through a national publicity campaign. His duel career as writer and filmmaker only fueled media interest.

This collection of nineteen conversations has been carefully selected to show the arc of development that led to his nearly unequaled commercial success. The interviews were drawn from Crichton's numerous print, radio, and broadcast appearances over nearly forty years.

Perhaps the most intriguing aspect of Crichton's fiction was his unmatched prescience, his ability to anticipate public interest in emerging technologies and controversial topics. Most Crichton novels address a larger issue: medical experimentation in *The Terminal Man*, animal rights in *Congo*, evolution and DNA in *Jurassic Park*, Japanese-American economic relations in *Rising Sun*, sexual harassment and office politics in *Disclosure*, the airline industry and the media in *Airframe*, quantum teleportation in *Timeline*, nanotechnology in *Prey*, global warming and the environmental movement in *State of Fear*, and genetic research in *Next*. The conclusions that Crichton reaches may not always be shared but they are always interesting.

Crichton spent years carefully researching the intricate technical details that he included in each novel. His command of prose enabled him to blur the line between fiction and nonfiction by weaving the information seamlessly into the books without lagging the suspenseful pace. His method was to read widely on scientific and historical topics and let the concepts percolate in his mind. He often gestated an idea for years before it found its way onto the bestseller lists. In the *American Film* magazine article of 1979 interviewer Patrick McGilligan makes reference to Crichton's library's being filled with "hundreds of books on such subjects as dinosaurs, vampires, particle physics, the West in 1876, Alaska, Victorian England, Africa during World War I, insurance in the eighteenth century, and sailing ships." In 1980 Crichton's book *Congo* was set in Africa; in 1990 *Jurassic Park* featured dinosaurs; in 1999 *Timeline* discussed particle physics. McGilligan later notes that Crichton "will try to complete a long-standing book project about Caribbean pirates in the seventeenth century." *Pirate Latitudes* was released thirty years after the interview.

The most insightful conversations in the book were conducted by Charlie Rose, the consummate interviewer, who covered every aspect of Crichton's public and private life. The probing questions and searching answers reveal Crichton at his most articulate and least guarded.

Although popular success and diversity of career interests prevented him from ever being regarded as a "literary writer," Crichton was largely unconcerned with his status among reviewers and critics. "I expect to get hit because at a certain point what you do won't get reviewed anymore—you get reviewed."

He was nonetheless favorably profiled and interviewed by the most prestigious American publications. Of particular benefit to aspiring writers will be his *Playboy* interview, *Vanity Fair* profile, and interviews in *Saturday Review* and the *Los Angeles Times*, which focus on his early life, writing rituals, literary influences, and his philosophy on character development.

As customary with all books in this series, the interviews herein have not been edited from the form of their initial publication. Consequently the reader will at times encounter repetitions of both questions and answers, but it is the feeling that the significance of the same questions being asked and the consistency (or inconsistency) of responses will prove of value to readers in their unexpurgated form.

Thanks are due to all the writers and publishers who consented to have their interviews included in this project; to Walter Biggins, editor of University Press of Mississippi; and to my father for his invaluable contribution.

RG

# Chronology

| | |
|---|---|
| 1942 | John Michael Crichton born on October 23, 1942, in Chicago, Illinois. |
| 1959 | "Climbing up a Cinder Cone," a travel article for the *New York Times*, is Crichton's first published work. |
| 1960 | Graduates from Roslyn High School, Roslyn, New York. |
| 1960–1964 | Studies physical anthropology at Harvard University; graduates A.B., summa cum laude, and Phi Beta Kappa. |
| 1964–1965 | Henry Russell Shaw Travelling Fellow. |
| 1965 | Visiting lecturer in anthropology at Cambridge University. Marries Joan Radam. |
| 1966 | Publication of *Odds On*, written under pseudonym John Lange. |
| 1967 | Publication of *Scratch One*, written under pseudonym John Lange. |
| 1968 | Publication of *Easy Go*, written under pseudonym John Lange. Publication of *A Case of Need*, written under pseudonym Jeffrey Hudson. |
| 1969 | Graduates with an M.D. from Harvard Medical School. Publication of *The Andromeda Strain*. Receives Edgar Award for Best Novel for *A Case of Need*. Publication of *Zero Cool*, written under pseudonym John Lange. Publication of *The Venom Business*, written under pseudonym John Lange. |
| 1969–70 | Postdoctoral fellow at the Salk Institute for Biological Sciences in La Jolla, California. |
| 1970 | Publication of *Five Patients*. Receives Association of American Medical Writers Award for *Five Patients*. Publication of *Drug of Choice*, written under pseudonym John Lange. Publication of *Grave Descend*, written under pseudonym John Lange. Publication of *Dealing*, co-written under pseudonym Michael Douglas with younger brother Douglas Crichton. Marriage to Joan Radam ends in divorce. |

| | |
|---|---|
| 1971 | Release of the film *The Andromeda Strain*. Receives Edgar Award nomination for Best Paperback Original for *Grave Descend*, written under pseudonym John Lange. |
| 1972 | Publication of *The Terminal Man*. Publication of *Binary*, written under pseudonym John Lange. Release of the film *Dealing*. Release of the film *The Carey Treatment*, based on novel *A Case of Need*. Broadcast of ABC Movie of the Week *Pursuit*, directed by Crichton. |
| 1973 | Release of the film *Westworld*, screenplay and directed by Crichton. Release of the film *Extreme Close-Up*, screenplay by Crichton. |
| 1974 | Release of the film *The Terminal Man*. |
| 1975 | Publication of *The Great Train Robbery*. |
| 1976 | Publication of *Eaters of the Dead*. |
| 1977 | Publication of *Jasper Johns*. |
| 1978 | Release of the film *Coma*, screenplay and directed by Crichton. Marries Kathy St. Johns. |
| 1979 | Release of the film *The Great Train Robbery*, screenplay and directed by Crichton. |
| 1980 | Publication of *Congo*. Receives Edgar Award for Best Motion Picture for *The Great Train Robbery*. Television show *Beyond Westworld* airs for one season on CBS, created by Crichton. Marriage to Kathy St. Johns ends in divorce. |
| 1981 | Release of the film *Looker*, screenplay and directed by Crichton. Marries Suzanne Childs. |
| 1982 | Release of computer game Amazon. |
| 1983 | Publication of *Electronic Life*. Marriage to Suzanne Childs ends in divorce. |
| 1984 | Release of the film *Runaway*, screenplay and directed by Crichton. |
| 1985–1991 | Board of Directors, International Design Conference at Aspen. |
| 1986–1991 | Board of Trustees, Western Behavioral Sciences Institute, La Jolla, California. |
| 1987 | Publication of *Sphere*. Marries Anne-Marie Martin. |
| 1988 | Publication of *Travels*. Visiting writer, Massachusetts Institute of Technology. |
| 1989 | Daughter Taylor Anne Crichton is born. Release of the film *Physical Evidence*, directed by Crichton. |
| 1990 | Publication of *Jurassic Park*. |

| | |
|---|---|
| 1990–96 | Board of Overseers, Harvard University. |
| 1992 | Publication of *Rising Sun.* |
| 1993 | Release of the film *Jurassic Park*, screenplay co-written by Crichton. Release of the film *Rising Sun*, screenplay co-written by Crichton. |
| 1994 | Publication of *Disclosure*. Release of the film *Disclosure*, co-produced by Crichton. |
| 1994–2008 | *ER* debuts on NBC, created and co-executive produced by Crichton. The show is a production of Crichton's Constant C Productions and Steven Spielberg's Amblin Entertainment. The show wins a Peabody, BAFTA, WGA, and twenty-three Emmy Awards. |
| 1995 | Featured on cover of *Time* magazine, September 25. Publication of *The Lost World*. Receives a Technical Achievement Academy Award "for pioneering computerized motion picture budgeting and scheduling." Release of the film *Congo*. |
| 1995–2008 | Council member, the Author's Guild. |
| 1996 | Publication of *Airframe*. Release of the film *Twister*, co-produced by Crichton, screenplay co-written with Anne-Marie Martin. |
| 1997 | Release of the film *The Lost World: Jurassic Park.* |
| 1998 | Release of the film *Sphere*, co-produced by Crichton. |
| 1999 | Publication of *Timeline*. Release of the film *The 13th Warrior*, co-produced by Crichton. |
| 2000 | Release of computer game Timeline. |
| 2001 | Release of the film *Jurassic Park III*, characters by Crichton. |
| 2002 | Publication of *Prey*. A newly discovered Ankylosaur dinosaur is named Crichtonsaurus bohlini in his honor. Marriage to Anne-Marie Martin ends in divorce. |
| 2002–2008 | Board of Directors, Gorilla Foundation. |
| 2003 | Release of the film *Timeline.* |
| 2004 | Publication of *State of Fear.* |
| 2005 | Marries Sherri Alexander. |
| 2006 | Publication of *Next.* |
| 2006–2008 | Board of Trustees, Los Angeles County Museum of Art. |
| 2008 | Dies of throat cancer in Los Angeles, California, on November 4. Television miniseries *The Andromeda Strain* airs on A&E. |
| 2009 | Son John Michael Todd Crichton is born. Publication of *Pirate Latitudes.* |

# Conversations
# with Michael Crichton

# Michael Crichton
# (Rhymes with Frighten)

## Israel Shenker/1969

From the *New York Times*, June 8, 1969. © 1969 The New York Times. All rights reserved. Used by permission and protected by the Copyright Laws of the United States. The printing, copying, redistribution, or retransmission of the Material without express written permission is prohibited.

If there is a bigger literary property these days than Michael Crichton (rhymes with frighten), where will the money come from? Within the past six months, young Crichton (he is twenty-six, stands 6 feet 9 inches, and is in his fourth year at Harvard Medical School), has:

Finished *The Andromeda Strain*, which is Book-of-the-Month Club co-selection for June and has been sold to Universal for $250,000;

Written an original screenplay called *Morton's Run*, which has also been sold to Universal;

Fulfilled two-thirds of a contract for three original paperbacks;

Written a prospectus for a TV series, and a two-hour script for a pilot show;

Continued work on a nonfiction study of the Massachusetts General Hospital;

Done magazine articles;

Started four novels and two screenplays;

Steeled himself to hear the worst about his seventh book—*The Venom Business*—to be published July 15.

When the cash register clicked more slowly, during his sophomore year at Harvard College, he tried basketball as well. Crichton likes to win and Harvard usually loses, so he quit while they were behind.

Crichton writes summers, during Christmas vacations—and sometimes when he should be at class or clinic. "It's a bit like epileptic seizures," he said. "This spring I freed myself from classes and I wrote like a fiend."

Because of his height he is exempt from the draft. Since doctors, however, are drafted whatever their altitude, he will not become an intern. "Anyway," he says, "as you go on in medicine the conflict of interest grows between the demands of writing and commitment to your patients."

"At medical school a number of people find it intriguing that I write," said Crichton, "and have always been well disposed. The dean always reads my books. A few of the teachers feel I'm wasting my time, and that in some way I've wasted theirs. When I asked for a couple of days off to go to California about a movie sale, that raised an eyebrow.

"These months have been explosive, but I consider everything that happened as external to me. All I did was write a book, and the publishing bandwagon super-phenomenon has nothing to do with me. It's occasionally disturbing to meet people who can't see beyond this person who's at medical school, who's made a lot of bread writing novels, and who's famous.

"I'm not going to buy a yacht or a gold lamé suit or divorce my wife. She was working to put me through medical school, and every time the money was about to run out it was time to write another book. That gets dreary, especially because I wasn't writing good books.

"So it's of great concern to me to get some distance from this hand-to-mouth thing, although I've found that Galbraith was right: there's an enormous difference between not having enough and having enough, and no important difference between having enough and having more than enough.

"I'm interested in exposure. If there's something you want to say, no matter how wild, the best way is television. More people will see one lousy television show in a night than will see a good movie in a year. More people will see a lousy movie in a week than read a good book in a year."

That commercial message might—or might not—go down well with Crichton's father, who is president of the American Association of Advertising Agencies. At dinner the children—all keen on writing—would discuss English usage. "I remember writing scripts for puppet shows in the third grade," said Crichton, "and long short stories in the sixth grade. When I was fourteen, I sold an article to the Travel section of the *Times* and got $60. It kept me in money for a year."

He worked just hard enough at Harvard College to be graduated summa cum laude, and was awarded a $3,000 travel fellowship. Crichton left for England and found himself teaching a semester of anthropology at Cambridge University—and measuring the Elgin Marbles for anthropological purposes.

"I picked up *The Ipcress File*," he recalled, "and was terrifically impressed with it. A lot of *The Andromeda Strain* is traceable to *The Ipcress File*, in terms of trying to create an imaginary world using recognizable techniques and real people.

"Between Deighton and Fleming the spy business was booming. It appeared to me that almost any idiot could write a spy story, and I discovered that almost any idiot can—although I never finished the first one."

His fellowship forbade him to stay more than two months in a place, so he moved on to the rest of Europe. By the time he reached the Riviera he was married (a girl from back home in Roslyn, L.I.) and torn between the lures of the Cannes Film Festival and the Monaco Grand Prix. "I decided any idiot should be able to write a potboiler set in Cannes and Monaco," he said, "and it took me eleven days."

"The book was no good," he added. But N.A.L. published it as *Scratch One*, giving the author's name as John Lange. An Andrew Lang used to write fairy tales; Crichton had added an "e" to Lang and substituted his own first name (which he otherwise never used) for Andrew.

Crichton decided on a pseudonym so that future patients would not believe he was interested in them for his plots instead of their pains. He became addicted to pseudonyms when he decided his output appeared too great for a single author. His fourth book—*A Case of Need*—for example, boasted a new pseudonym: Jeffrey Hudson. The name belonged earlier to a dwarf in the court of Charles I who was served to his monarch in a pie and later captured by Barbary pirates.

The Mystery Writers of America awarded the book an Edgar—as the best mystery published in the United States last year, and film rights were purchased by Herb Alpert, whose Tijuana Brass had turned to gold.

"My feeling about the Lange books is that my competition is in-flight movies," said Crichton. "One can read the books in an hour and a half, and be more satisfactorily amused than watching Doris Day. I write them fast and the reader reads them fast, and I get things off my back."

For *The Andromeda Strain* he was willing to slow down. "The idea was in my mind for at least three years," he said, "and I was trying to write it for a year and a half, collecting newspaper clippings and research articles, and writing draft after draft. Every draft was awful. What I was up against was the very considerable absurdity of the idea of a plague from outer space.

When I finally learned that a complicated quarantine procedure really existed for the U.S. moon program, it was a considerable psychological boost, and then I knew I could do the book.

"People have compared *The Andromeda Strain* to *Fail-Safe*, but it's the exact reverse. *Fail-Safe* describes an event with great immediacy, as though it could happen at any moment. You are there and it's now. I found you could make something more believable if you pretended not that it might happen or was happening, but that it had happened. You are not there, and it's over.

"The secret of the success is that the appropriate tone was found and rigorously adhered to. And then there was an enormous amount of luck."

Crichton plans to push his luck and has even considered a third pseudonym—a woman's name—to see how amusing it would be to write from a woman's viewpoint. He may call herself Marie Antoinette (court of Louis XVI), whose goose was cooked by a cake and who was later captured by Bastille pirates.

Whether as Lange or Hudson or Antoinette, or even the essential Crichton, he has become less indulgent about his facility for generating 10,000 words each fifteen-hour working day as he heats up potboilers that are never watched very long. He would like to write seriously about: euthanasia (he favors it), abortion on demand (ditto), marijuana (he wants it legalized), and the battered baby problem (he gropes for words to express his shock). He is already serious enough about reading (three hundred books a year) and seeing other people's movies (sixty a year).

For a change of climate and scenery, he and his wife are moving to California after his graduation this month from medical school. One immediate project is a joint novel with his nineteen-year-old brother, Douglas, a junior at Harvard. "It's about youth and drugs," said the older Crichton. "I wrote it completely from beginning to end. Now he's rewriting it from beginning to end, and then I'll rewrite it completely. Eventually we'll have a book.

"Since Douglas is concerned about anonymity, we'll probably call the author *Time* magazine."

# Hollywood Gets a New Man

## Barbara Rose/1973

Michael Crichton might be the boy next door, only taller and smarter. Author of the bestsellers *The Andromeda Strain* and *The Terminal Man*, Crichton, at thirty, has just finished *Westworld*, the first movie he has both written and directed—something of a phenomenon in Hollywood. But Crichton has always been exceptional. As a wunderkind, he wrote successful mystery stories while studying at Harvard. Later he was one of Harvard's most brilliant medical students, but medicine soon took a backseat to literature. A fellowship at the Salk Institute for Biological Studies in La Jolla brought Crichton to California.

Today he seems thoroughly comfortable in his peaceful retreat on top of a remote Los Angeles canyon. The house was originally designed by Southern California's leading modern architect Richard Neutra. The glassed pavilions, reflecting pools, and groomed lawns suggest a Japanese tranquility. Inside there is Crichton's own gradually expanding art collection. Most of the artists whose work he owns—Stella, Johns, Oldenburg—are people he has met at Gemini, G.E.L., the lithography workshop directed by Crichton's friend Ken Tyler.

The first thing you realize about Michael Crichton is that he is a very nice person. This is a surprise in Hollywood. He strikes you as an obviously brilliant but otherwise not unusual young man involved in acquiring, assimilating, and processing great quantities of information at an incredible rate. His books have been called science fiction, but there is more fact in their horrifying details of where advanced technology is taking us than fiction. He won't say why he gave up medicine for literature and finally film making, but he does remark that machines can now make much more accurate diagnoses than people. Like his idol Alfred Hitchcock, Michael Crichton

7

denies being a moralist. His personal style is the studied insouciance and cool, detached, ironic stance of Hitchcock. Sharing Hitchcock's pessimistic view of human nature, Crichton also shares the British director's conviction that the most important thing is to tell a good story, keeping your audience glued to their seats through action and suspense. But just as Hitchcock's *The Birds* may be seen as a nightmare of ecological catastrophe (a warning of what may happen if we are not aware of the forces we have set in motion) so Crichton's *Westworld* is a projection of the wasteland we may be creating through our ignorant use of a directionless technology.

Although on the surface Crichton seems thoroughly conventional, one ultimately finds he breaks every stereotype. On the set he is the anti–Cecil B. DeMille: calm, understated, and soft spoken; he exhibits no signs of the temperament we associate with Hollywood directors. At home he is good-natured, introspective, candid—perhaps a trifle remote—which gives one the impression that possibly the most real parts of his life are his fantasies. An unlikely combination of scientist and artist, he promises to be one of the most exciting new talents in American film.

**BR:** Why did you decide to direct films?
**MC:** You write something and you see it made and it isn't what you thought it would be. So you start wanting more and more control over your work.

**BR:** Is directing different from writing?
**MC:** Yes. At the point when you don't know what you want to get down on paper or film, there are certain similarities between trying things out in writing and directing. But when you do know what you want, the only person you have to push to get it is yourself in writing. It's a solitary business. In directing you're prodding other people. That makes a big difference. When I'm writing, I get very involved in how I'm feeling that day—whether I'm tired, internal stuff like how my stomach is feeling. When I'm directing, the important thing is what's happening outside of myself.

**BR:** Why do so many good directors like Antonioni, Fellini, Buñuel, write their own screenplays?
**MC:** I think writing, directing, and editing are ideally part of the same job. I had one experience working on a picture where I was the director and somebody else wrote it. I felt very limited working with somebody else's script. I came out of writing into directing: I don't know what the reverse would be like.

**BR:** How did you get interested in film?

**MC:** I was always interested in film. When I applied to medical school, the doctor who interviewed me said he didn't have any feeling about me as a doctor. He asked me what I would do if I weren't applying to medical school. I thought about it for awhile and I said I'd like to be a movie director. Like all American kids, I was exposed to a lot of movies when I was very young. They impressed me; I was totally involved. That's the quality I want to get— total involvement. So many of the movies I see have no effect on me. What I want is that jump you make when you participate in the action. That's what I mean by having an effect—getting people to participate—and it isn't easy. I have to admit I'm interested in audience manipulation. Point of view is the most important thing. It's true of books, too. Joan Didion once said that the voice everyone listens to in a novel is not that of any particular character but the voice of the person telling the story. I think that's true of film.

A lot of Hollywood directors think in terms of the film's "message." A film's statement is more complicated than that. You can't tell an audience what the movie is about anymore; they have to figure it out for themselves. I think of seeing things from different points of view, different perspectives, as you would in a painting. Movies have style, too, like paintings. They can be very glossy and slick, or dark and pessimistic, or very detailed, or broadly and grossly sketched. This has a lot to do with how and what the "message" is finally understood as by the audience.

**BR:** How does a young person become a Hollywood director?

**MC:** All you can do is talk in terms of physics and say it's a rare event. For a long time nobody would hire me as a director. What I finally did was write a script for ABC television with the provision that I direct it. I was lucky because at the point I decided I wanted to direct film, *Easy Rider* had convinced studio executives to look for new talent, and it seemed as if anybody who could speak in declarative sentences—and a lot of people who couldn't— were going to get to make films. Usually these unknown young directors, who were often writers, just died. And I think the reason they died is because there's something about the job of directing they weren't prepared for. When you make a movie, it's a process of continuously committing yourself to decisions that seem irrevocable. The kind of pressure you're under making a film cracks a lot of people, especially writers because writers are used to having the option of being able to rewrite. A film production is knocking it off at nine or ten grand a day, and you just don't have those options.

**BR:** Was your medical training of any use to you as a director?

**MC:** Definitely. As a medical student, you were always tired but you had to perform anyhow. I was prepared to do my TV movie never sitting down because I had all those years on my feet as a doctor. Medicine is really terrific at teaching you to acquire new skills fast. Some guy says, "Now this is how you do an operation," shows you, and then you do five. You become quick at picking things up. You also learn a lack of embarrassment at not knowing how to do something. A medical student always is in the position of not knowing how to do something. Medicine also got you into the frame of mind of dealing with very high-pressure situations, dealing with complex factors, emergencies. You often had to act and make fast decisions: Something is always going wrong in a movie, and that kind of experience is invaluable in salvaging a situation. Directing is really hard work. Pauline Kael's right, it's a young man's game. It's very physically demanding. It falls into the general category of job where at the end of the day your feet hurt. It's also very social. You talk to a lot of people, you listen to a lot of people for hours and hours.

**BR:** Do you think the physical demands of directing account for why there are so few women directors?

**MC:** No. It's simple discrimination. Exactly the same thing occurs in medicine. There's no reason why more women aren't doctors in this country.

**BR:** Do you think of yourself as a Hollywood type?

**MC:** I think of myself as an intellectual. I guess that's not a Hollywood type. But I think there's more chance to be an intellectual in Hollywood than in Cambridge, Massachusetts. What most people mean by Hollywood is a social existence. I don't have much to do with that. I also have access to the "publishing world" which is a kind of social life, and I don't participate in that either. It's interesting that when I'm directing, I'm much more outgoing.

**BR:** How did you get the idea for *Westworld*?

**MC:** I make up little stories about how I get ideas, but I really don't know most of the time. I think I got the idea for *Westworld* because I was very interested in the astronauts. I was fascinated by the fact they were being trained to be machines. Then I was also fascinated by the animated figures at Disneyland. The two tendencies toward making people as machinelike as possible and machines as human as possible are creating a lot of confusion. That's what suggested *Westworld* to me. The tendency to make concessions to machines can only grow. ZIP codes, for example, are a concession to machines. There are advantages and disadvantages to this tendency. I don't think that people are strongly threatened by ZIP codes; it's inevitable that we accommodate ourselves to the machines we need to support our existence.

**BR:** Do you think machines are becoming more human?
**MC:** By and large the history of machines is that they are designed to duplicate some human function, to improve on something people can't do very well. They're getting more subtle; we're no longer impressed with a machine that's stronger than a person, but we're still impressed with a machine that can think faster.

**BR:** Many people feel that major technological innovation has slowed down; do you agree?
**MC:** Technology goes wherever there's a use for it. Wherever there's financial reservoir to support it. Leisure time used to be very simple; now it's very technological—there are trail bikes, campers, sophisticated hiking equipment, time-off gadgetry. Technology is going more and more into leisure. Take rock music, for example, which has really replaced the theater as the only live amusement that has any viability. It's entirely created by technology; no rock-music concert could take place without all that equipment.

**BR:** Do you think there's something perverse about such technology?
**MC:** It's better than making missiles. The areas of technological advance will be the areas the society decides to invest time and money in, and it's not altogether clear right now what these will be. For example, will we have major innovations in transportation? It would be easy to do, but who knows if society wants to put money in it.

**BR:** In other words, you mean our society is more likely to put money into *Westworld.*
**MC:** The evidence is that things like *Westworld* are very popular. We're building more resorts all the time on the Disneyland model. You know they are actually building a resort like *Westworld* right now. Apparently it's called World Park. They're building London and Paris and a few other places.

**BR:** Are there many innovations in film today?
**MC:** Movies are a funny business, very susceptible to fads. Take the redis-

covery of the dissolve, for example. Dissolves used to be used lavishly in films, but the Europeans cut them out and went to straight cuts. Now everybody is back to dissolves. Young directors without a sense of film history say ". . . look at that, I invented something, the dissolve!"

**BR:** Are you trying to do anything new in film?
**MC:** I would say no. One of the things I feel very strongly about is that the stranger your story, the straighter you tell it. If you're telling a simple love story about a suburban lawyer and his wife, you can be very bizarre, using strange camera angles and odd cutting, and be really very weird, because fundamentally you're dealing with something very understandable and straightforward and the only risk you run is being accused of jazzing up something that's boring. I think particularly with a wild story you must be very conventional. There is not, for example, a single handheld shot in the movie. The sets were deliberately chosen to look like Hollywood sets.

**BR:** Is *Westworld* a vision of the future? Is it a science-fiction film?
**MC:** I hate "science fiction." I never wanted to be called a science-fiction writer. *Westworld* is really about fantasies. Most of our fantasies are movie generated. When I was growing up, I didn't want to be a character out of Hemingway; I wanted to be Cary Grant. *Westworld* is about people living out their fantasies generated by seeing Western movies.

**BR:** Do you try to convey an attitude toward technology in *Westworld*?
**MC:** The ways that technology interests me are the ways that it traps you. *Westworld* is a personification of that situation; it's about a person pursued by a machine. In a human situation, you can always call up your friend the next day and say you didn't mean it. But you can't call up technology and say you didn't mean it. In terms of technology, you often can't change your mind. Once you set out on a given course, you can't reverse.

**BR:** Do you think the relationship between men and women has changed as a result of technology?
**MC:** I would hate to try to be very rigorous about it, but it's almost impossible to argue that Women's Liberation could have occurred prior to the introduction of the birth-control pill. Vasectomy on the other hand is like hysterectomy. It's radical. It has some odd effect on men. The man's self-image is changed.

**BR:** Suppose there were a male pill. Would that be important?

**MC:** I think so. Just as no one could have predicted that Women's Liberation would have followed five years on the heel of the birth-control pill, one can't say what will happen with the development of a male pill. For example, I don't think anyone realized that one of the consequences of the birth-control pill would be an increase in homosexuality. Suddenly the wife is no longer afraid of getting pregnant, and she decides she wants sex. Her husband, who could previously spend a substantial part of the month pressing his wife with the full knowledge that she would refuse him, can't play that game anymore. If he says "Let's go to bed, honey," she can now say "yeah." Maybe even if he didn't say let's go to bed, she'd say yeah—this is a very disturbing change in the world.

# Ready When You Are, Dr. Crichton

## Patrick McGilligan/1979

From *American Film* magazine, March, 1979. Patrick McGilligan is the author of numerous books about film including the *Backstory* series of interviews with screenwriters. He lives in Milwaukee, Wisconsin. Reprinted by permission of Patrick McGilligan.

There are no novels in Michael Crichton's library. Instead there are hundreds of books on such subjects as dinosaurs, vampires, particle physics, the West in 1876, Alaska, Victorian England, Africa during World War I, insurance in the eighteenth century, and sailing ships. There doesn't appear to be a method to his inquiry, although there is a clue in the row of shiny books about the life of Leonardo da Vinci. For wasn't da Vinci the epitome of the Renaissance man—sort of an ultradabbler?

Crichton may not be a twentieth-century da Vinci, but if there is another example of an M.D. who also writes books and directs films, history does not readily provide it. At thirty-six, Crichton is a success in both fields. His writing includes "at least" sixteen novels (allowing for a pseudonymous or two that may have slipped his memory) and such unrelated nonfiction as an art monograph, a treatise on the linguistics of medicine, and a sociological case study of hospital care. As a director, he has three movies under his belt (and another half dozen for which he provided the idea or screenplay), including *Westworld, Coma,* and now *The Great Train Robbery,* a period adventure story based on his novel. Quantity aside, the sheer range of his output is incredible. Crichton has an almost clinical urge to roam fresh territories.

"I never want to do anything twice," Crichton told me on the eve of the release of *The Great Train Robbery.* "One of the awful things about doing something once is that if you do it again, you really know how to do it. In a certain sense, having done *The Andromeda Strain,* I really knew how to do a book like that. Having done *The Great Train Robbery,* I really had a quite good idea about how to do a certain kind of historical novel. But I can't seem to do another one. I just can't seem to repeat myself. My desire is to have fresh problems."

Crichton was talking to me in the living room of his home overlooking Laurel Canyon in Los Angeles, a house designed by Bauhaus architect Richard Neutra in the fifties and tastefully furnished with a modernist art collection that includes sculpture and pieces by Rauschenberg, Oldenburg, Jasper Johns, Stella, Warhol, and Lichtenstein. It was two days before Christmas, and it seemed an appropriate time to talk to Crichton, for childhood enthusiasms have played an elemental role in his career. He is six feet nine, a height which undoubtedly qualifies him for the title of world's tallest movie director, but his body is so well proportioned, his face so boyish and unlined, that he has the appearance (a *Time* reporter once wrote) of "a fifteen-year-old boy standing on a chair."

Although his height provided him a niche on the Roslyn, Long Island, high school basketball team, sports were not as much of a lure as the literary arts. He wrote puppet shows in the third grade, short stories in the sixth grade. When Crichton was fourteen, he wrote an article for the travel section of the *New York Times*. He devoured pulp fiction and the stories of Poe, Dickens ("The miniserialist of his day"), and Sir Arthur Conan Doyle (who, incidentally, was a medical doctor). The movies of Hitchcock provided inspiration and pleasure. After graduating summa cum laude in anthropology from Harvard in 1964, Crichton did anthropological fieldwork in Europe on a fellowship. Then he applied to medical school at Harvard—even though his heart wasn't in it.

"They almost didn't let me into medical school," Crichton recalled, as he draped his frame sideways over a chair. "They kept calling me back for more and more interviews. Finally, one guy said, 'Listen, you're a nice fellow, but I just don't have the sense that you're a doctor. If you could do anything in the world, what would you do?' And I said I'd direct movies. He laughed, and I laughed. It was a very farfetched idea."

Not as things turned out. Inspired partly by Len Deighton's spy novel, *The Ipcress File*, Crichton began to crank out novels in his mid-twenties under the pseudonym of John Lange—*Odds On, Scratch One, Easy Go, Zero Cool,* and *The Venom Business*. There were other pseudonyms, too—Crichton professes to disremember how many. He wrote *A Case of Need*, about a benevolent illegal abortionist, under the nom de plume Jeffrey Hudson (taking the name from a dwarf in the court of King Charles I). Later, under yet another pseudonym, he and his brother Douglas wrote *Dealing: Or, The Boston to Berkeley Forty-Brick Lost-Bag Blues*, a hippie, dope-hustle adventure. The former became MGM's *The Carey Treatment* in 1972, while Warner Bros. brought *Dealing* to the screen the same year.

"I started writing to pay for medical school bills," explained Crichton. "I wasn't particularly eager to have people know that I was writing because it would look as though I wasn't very interested in medicine, which at that time wasn't true. Also, I was using my own experiences as background, and I felt that disguising the author was the best way to maintain confidentiality. It was very pleasurable to write under a pseudonym. It was like being Zorro. You've got to have another identity. At one point I was living in Cambridge, and I had two desks for my two selves. And I would change desks, depending on which writer I was. The whole thing just entertained me to no end."

*The Andromeda Strain*, published in May 1969, as he was completing his final year at Harvard Medical School, marked a turning point for Crichton: He dropped his pseudonyms and any plans to practice medicine. Medicine did not recede entirely from his consciousness—Crichton has since written *Five Patients: The Hospital Explained*, an account of the experience of patients at Massachusetts General Hospital in Boston, as well as a noteworthy polemic against doctors' obfuscatory language that was published by the *New England Journal of Medicine*. But both works—even the film *Coma*, with its chilling hospital milieu—are sharply critical of medical cliquishness and the often detrimental role of the American Medical Association. In that sense, Crichton is plainly a defector from the ranks.

*The Andromeda Strain*, Crichton's cautionary, think tank scenario about a returned space capsule with lethal interplanetary bacteria, had been knocking around inside his head for at least three years. When it hit the bestseller lists, one reviewer dubbed Crichton's style of plausible authenticity "knowledge fiction." Universal snapped up the motion picture rights, and Crichton wound up in Hollywood in 1970 on the set of *The Andromeda Strain*. Director Robert Wise was very helpful to the young author, allowing him to watch the filming and sit in at the dailies. Crichton couldn't figure out precisely what directing was, but it looked as though he could do it.

And he thinks that having been trained as a doctor was very helpful in directing. "For one thing, medical training is a prolonged period of time in which you acquire one new skill after another," Crichton said. "Inevitably, you become very adept at picking things up very quickly—technical procedures, jargon. When I came to California after medical school, the idea of taking on a new job with a new set of challenges was not in the least daunting. So I was completely prepared to just jump in and do it, which is what I've been doing for the last four years.

"That's one aspect. Another is that when you're doing medicine, you're thrown into contact with lots of different kinds of people. You're obliged to assess personalities rapidly, and you have to learn to get along with people and get what you want done. That kind of training is very helpful for a director. That's the only utility that medicine really had."

"That was such a long time ago," Crichton mused. "After I decided I wanted to direct, I would pick people who were directing and hang around, watching them. Jeannot Szwarc, who subsequently did *Jaws 2*, was doing a lot of *Night Gallery*'s at the time. Jeannot was terrifically organized in terms of his time, and I used to go and watch him to see how he laid out his days. Steven Spielberg was doing television pilots—this was pre-*Duel*. And I used to go and watch Steve because I thought he really had an interesting head for camera movement. Arthur Penn was working on something, too, and I'd go see Arthur because I was very interested in how he got his performances. That was an area of great concern to me, working with actors. So I went around and watched people. What I learned, in the end, was that everybody does it their own way."

*The Andromeda Strain* was followed by *The Terminal Man*, published in 1972, which drew on actual experiments for its unsettling tale of behavior modification gone berserk. Crichton, with hopes to direct, was hired to write the screenplay. He wrote what he maintains to this day was a "terrific" screenplay "designed to scare the hell out of people." But following his own maxim that once is enough, Crichton's screenplay did not follow Crichton's book. Horrified, Warners reassigned the project to writer-director Mike Hodges. Somewhat on the rebound, Crichton conceived of *Westworld*.

After directing a television movie in 1972 called *Pursuit* (based on a "John Lange" novel called *Binary*, about "a government agent who is trying to stop a madman who wants to explode nerve gas over the Republican convention"), Crichton convinced MGM to let him direct his screenplay for *Westworld*. The result was a clever science fiction fantasy about a vacationing businessman (Richard Benjamin) who pays $1,000 a day to stalk a cybernetic gunslinger (Yul Brynner) in a simulated frontier town. But, discounting *Extreme Close-Up*, a minor film about a voyeur (screenplay by Crichton), it was another four years before Crichton made a movie in Hollywood. Why? Partly because he stubbornly returned to fiction—writing *The Great Train Robbery* in 1975 and then *Eaters of the Dead* in 1976, a takeoff on *Beowulf* about Norsemen in medieval Scandinavia.

Ironically, it was a book about corpses—not written by Crichton—that brought Crichton back to the movie industry. "I didn't make another movie right after *Westworld*," he said, "and that was a mistake. I think what made me a director in the eyes of the town was doing somebody else's project." *Coma*, based on Robin Cook's novel and starring Genevieve Bujold, Michael Douglas, and Richard Widmark, was a slick slice of Grand Guignol and a box-office hit. Though Crichton now finds the movie "appalling" in some respects, *Coma* shows an improving director. There are some calculated strides that pay off—progressions in the visuals (warm colors to cold), the angles ("very sharp and literal" wide angles to claustrophobia), and music (almost none in the first half, then accelerating).

*The Great Train Robbery* is even more ambitious. Crichton's novel recounts the story of a tour de force robbery of gold bullion on the South Eastern Railway in England in 1855. Though the robbery actually happened, Crichton's version of the incident is liberally spiced with made-up facts, because, he said, "I sought to create a coherent idea about a time and a world that was internally consistent, whether or not it was objectively true; I think a lot of what people call history is invention, anyway." Of course, the movie is not as laden with supposed fact as the novel. But there is lavish Dickensian period detail, despite the relatively moderate shooting budget (ten weeks, in Ireland and England). It stars Sean Connery as the master criminal Edward Pierce, Donald Sutherland as the expert lockpick Agar, and Lesley-Ann Down as the beautiful, mysterious actress Miriam.

The film owes much of its visual elegance to cinematographer Geoffrey Unsworth, who died last year as he began shooting *Tess* in France. In *The Great Train Robbery*, his last credit, Unsworth provides a visual modernity within a period setting. Unsworth, according to Crichton, was happy to work with muted colors—the cinematographer was a master of lighting and diffusion. But there was some harrumphing about Crichton's decision to occasionally resort to a hand-held camera and outright disapproval among the crew of his decision to shoot certain scenes from a helicopter. But Crichton's visual strategy—along with the "fearless" stunts of the actors, like Connery, who did all their own locomotive hopping—was meant to give *The Great Train Robbery* the fast pace and immediacy of a thriller, regardless of the period décor.

"I told everyone involved with the physical appearance of the film," Crichton explained, "that the picture had to be as correct for the period as it could be. All costumes, all the physical settings had to be accurate. Everyone fell right in line with that. They adored finding errors in the book—I didn't bother to tell them how much I had simply made up. So we had a picture that, in its physical trappings, was going to be as accurate in the documentary sense as we could contrive it to be. All the colors were accurate, even certain things that I don't like. We built the 1852 locomotive and painted it an odd green, a color I wouldn't have painted a locomotive, but that was the color of the South Eastern Railway of that period.

"From the beginning, my plan was to create this very accurate setting and then shoot inside it as contemporary a film as I could. In line with that, I did a lot of things that I've never done before and probably won't do again. On a technical level, for example, I don't like zooms. I tend to shoot everything with prime lenses. I think there was one zoom in *Westworld* and two in *Coma*. But the camera is always zooming in the *The Great Train Robbery*. I think of the zoom lens as something that says to the audience: This is modern. I wanted to have that contrast. The use of the lenses and the fluidity of the camera are all things you don't associate with a period film."

Crichton hopes the seams of his strategy will not show, because he likes to think of himself as an "invisible" director, a minimalist and a collaborator. In this, as in most everything, he is self-effacing. When Crichton wrote his monograph on Jasper Johns for the 1977 retrospective at the Whitney Museum, *New York Times* art critic Hilton Kramer called it "one of the most ludicrous exercises in the annals of pretentious puffery." (To be fair, Mary Ann Tighe, writing the same month in the same newspaper, hailed it as "the most charming and readable art book in recent years.") But Crichton seems unruffled by such barbs and is content to describe himself as, yes, a quick study, a respectful inheritor of pulp, potboiler traditions, a popular artist. It is enough to have fun and give audiences a treat.

"I like genres," Crichton told me, "because in a genre there's a set of preconceived notions that you can play with, a set of expectations that you can meet or fail to meet. And I like to work inside an established form. It comes out of two things. On the simplest level, I remember certain books and films I read and saw when I was young, often genre and kind of pulpy stuff. I want to make things like that, that's the simple answer. I've never had a movie that's been rated anything but PG, because I think movies ought to be available for kids. I'm completely sympathetic with people who see other uses for the medium. But what I want to do is make movies kids can see, because that's what I like. A more complicated answer is that I think everyone needs limitations in which to work and I find mine within preexisting structures."

Crichton went on, "Since I have the choice of working in other forms, if I want to do something smaller and more personal, I can write a book or a journal article. There's no way on earth that any film can be as personal as a book. Nobody has anything to do with my books, except for me. I do the whole thing, from start to finish—sometimes I even make the covers. It's inconceivable to me that any film, no matter how tightly you control it, can be yours in the way a book is yours. What draws me to movies is that I want to play with the big screen and the big form and attract big audiences."

Crichton finds himself distressed about a lot of recent films, those of the last ten or fifteen years. "Even today, very often I'd rather see old movies than new ones. I got a lot of pleasure out of those old movies. I think they're better, more satisfying. Today, when I see a movie, I often sit there and say to myself, 'Whoever thought this was interesting?' They're sloppily made, sloppily written. Or else somebody got his hands on a camera and decided he was going to be so innovative that a five-hundred-year tradition of English-language dramatic structure need not apply to him."

Crichton himself aims not at art but at reaching audiences. "This town is full of directors who turned down *The Godfather* because it was a junky crime novel. I think Coppola made a work of art without any question. But I don't know what his internal frame of mind was, and I couldn't be persuaded that he sat down and said, 'I'm going to make a work of art.' My thinking is more in line with Hawks, guys like that, who just made movies. And if any one of them turns out to be of interest for more than the period of its initial run, then that's terrific. But I don't think you can work for timelessness, although some people do. My working stance is that I'm not making art."

We had been conversing for nearly three hours. Crichton was chain-smoking, his voice was fading. On the coffee table were two books: *Space, Time, and Gravity* by Robert M. Wald (about black holes, general relativity, and the big bang theory) and *Supplying War: Logistics from Wallenstein to Patton* by Martin Van Creveld. His future calendar is just as wide-ranging: Crichton will write a contemporary story set in Africa, his first novel in roughly three years; he will direct a thriller for Twentieth Century-Fox about television commercials; he will try to complete a long-standing book project about Caribbean pirates in the seventeenth century. And he will continue to read.

"When I don't know what to do, which is the awful time, I read all kinds of things. I just read and read. I'll read half a book and put it down. I'll read three books at once. I'll read several chapters of one thing in the morning, put it down, read something else in the afternoon and something else at night, look for something to do. Just all kinds of odd interests. Pretty soon, I've read a lot. I decide I want to write something. And then, I just start to write."

A book like *The Andromeda Strain* or the Caribbean project may take him three to five years of intermittent work, of note-taking and browsing. In the stretch, Crichton may put in a sixteen-hour day, producing ten thousand words of readable prose. Always, there will be the possibility of a movie of the book.

"I think it really started in college," Crichton said of this regimen, "because most of my university time was spent—certainly the part that I liked best—at Harvard with tutors. I'd go and see a tutor. He'd say, 'What do you want to write about?' I'd say this or that. He'd say, 'Well, you might start looking here,' and off I'd go. Then I'd come back in a month with a paper. I just adored that. Well, in a sense, that's what I'm still doing."

# Fact, Fiction Intertwined by Crichton

## Wayne Warga/1981

From the *Los Angeles Times*, March 1, 1981. Copyright © 1981. Reprinted by permission.

There is a passage in Michael Crichton's new novel, *Congo*, in which the author describes a group of apes fishing for termites. It relates in some detail the delicate process of extracting the termite grub, an action which requires both learning and intelligence.

Then, before one realizes the action has stopped for this brief, engrossing lecture, the adventure is off and running again. The reader has acquired some actual information to add to the fantasy now under way. Nonfiction and fiction have mixed, however briefly.

There are similar episodes, though less obvious, in his original script, *Looker*, the film of which Crichton just finished directing for release next fall. I read it with growing involvement, all the while thinking the story engagingly farfetched, though bits of interesting facts do pop up from time to time.

Highly simplified, it is about a plastic surgeon who finds he is creating perfect models for a TV-commercial organization which, in turn, is murderously protective of the secrets he discovers. Afterwards, I got the chilling notion it might all be pretty much true. It is. Crichton has once again layered nonfiction onto a work of fiction, used the one to illuminate the other.

It is not an unusual technique, but among its practitioners, Crichton is one of the best. He is also responsible about mixing the two, making it clear all along that what is being presented is indeed a fiction.

"I'm intrigued by the blurring of the lines between fiction and nonfiction, the whole concept of verisimilitude. I'm fascinated by playing with cues you take as a reader about what is real and what is not real. I've become more and more interested in nonfiction."

Crichton is a rare creator among his fellows, for he is both a successful novelist and a successful director, two forms considered, if not incompatible, at least odd by the practitioners of either. Few others come to mind: James Clavell, (*Shogun*) who has not directed since *To Sir, With Love* in 1967, and Nicholas Meyer, author of, among others, *The Seven-Per-Cent Solution* and the director of *Time After Time*. No one, however, matches Crichton for sheer productivity.

Crichton is in the living room of his Richard Neutra–designed house high in the hills above Studio City, looking out across his pool to a large, incarnadine sculpture by Claes Oldenburg. On the wall directly behind him is an elegant wood sculpture by Frank Stella. Facing him from the dining area is a row of Warhols. His home is full of the works of the other modern artists. He is a collector of note and has written a book on Jasper Johns.

His other nonfiction work is *Five Patients* and his novels are *The Andromeda Strain, The Terminal Man, The Great Train Robbery*, and *Eaters of the Dead*. There were several pseudonymous novels before he turned full-time to writing and began using his own name.

His art collection is not unlike his work, and not unlike Crichton himself. There is a precision about his writing and his speech, a slight preference for the technological, a sense of distance between the author and his characters. Some critics have accused him of a distinct coolness toward his characters, an accusation he politely protests.

"So much of how we live is made possible by technology. It has had a big impact on how we live and I'm very interested in that. I'm also very interested in how things work. I saw the pictures taken of Saturn the other day. Most people say, 'Oh, isn't that interesting,' and imagine something about being there. I sort of stop right there and ask myself, 'How did this happen? What were the problems?' then I get to the people.

"There may be a way to write what I do and have the characters and the technology equal, but it seems to me they're competing interests in the dramatic form.

"It's like detective stories. You have a very heavy plot and it's absolutely necessary. You examine it. Why not? The detective moves like a physical narrator through the landscape. When you do a story with a lot of plot you don't have a lot of character. Your story has to be about something; it can't be about everything.

"Stories focused on technology are often impersonal because that is what technology is."

Crichton is a tall, large man who is both casually friendly and reserved, a lively talker who is nevertheless thoughtful in conversation. One senses he would prefer no answer at all to one that is unclear or imprecise. He dresses as the Ivy Leaguer he is—he is a graduate of Harvard Medical School, though his writing career quickly took precedence and he has never practiced medicine. He is thirty-eight and twice divorced. In a biography he prepared for a speech at a convention of psychiatrists he listed his hobbies as "scuba diving, tennis, and getting divorced."

His father was the editor of *Advertising Age,* and Crichton spent much of his childhood in and around New York City. He thinks it was his custom of frequently visiting the Museum of Modern Art that started him off on his passion for modern art, though he confesses to be unaware of it at the time and only hazily sure of it now. He does, however, remember the writers who drew him into the world of literature.

"Conan Doyle was the first writer I really liked. Also, Poe. It's very odd in retrospect that those people should have a sort of medical orientation. I also liked Twain a lot, and he is one of the few I reread from time to time."

Part of the genesis of *Congo,* Crichton's fifth novel and seventh book, is the hangover of a youthful fascination with H. Rider Haggard's *King Solomon's Mines.*

"I like to work within existing forms," he says, "and the original impulse for *Congo* was from the nineteenth-century romantic adventures in faraway places. The difference was to do it in a contemporary way. It is not a conducive form for twentieth-century sensibilities. Whether or not the world still has secrets is up to question, but we certainly no longer perceive it as having any. It seemed to me a very great challenge to work within that form."

*Congo* also deals with primate behavior, a subject that is still much debated in academic circles. Crichton has created an ape named Amy whose ability to "sign"—communicate by sign language—makes her an object much desired by a major business organization. Amy is the heroine of the book, a loving but temperamental animal who seems mired forever in her terrible twos, and she is in the charge of a primatologist named Peter Elliot. They all come under the willful spell of Karen Ross, an ambitious, somewhat calculating woman who leads an expedition into Africa in which Amy is a critical element. Because of her, Elliot is too.

"There are people who say the signing behavior of a primate is not language, but they do not dispute hand gestures that are reproduced in response to certain contexts. Animals can indicate when they want a drink and other things like that. They can also communicate, but the level of communication is subject to much debate. Whether it is language or circus-trick training is very much up in the air. I take the position it is language."

Crichton can talk at length about primate behavior, just as he can speak with considerable expertise on the race to animate human figures by computer, forms which the viewer will be unable to distinguish from the real thing, and on the making of commercials, and the study of viewer response to commercials. These are the subjects he has researched in order to write his script for *Looker*, a subject which interested him for a number of reasons.

"My thinking about it started in 1975 or '76, at a time when everybody seemed to be talking about the future, the changes the future would bring. No one seemed to notice that they had pretty much already happened. I remember my mother, when I was a kid, asking why I was so interested in drawing rockets. She said she'd never live to see men travel in space. Well, she did. She saw men go to the moon. She not only lived to see it, she lived to see the beginning and the end of it. And all those people who used to scream that computers are going to take over our lives are now at home playing with their Atari toys. I wanted a futuristic story occurring in the present day.

"Then I made a trip to Southeast Asia, where I was shuffled through a couple of expatriate groups. They were endlessly social, and there was another difference I couldn't quite figure out. I can't believe it took me as long as it did, but it finally occurred to me that television was completely missing from their lives. They were leading pre-1950 lives, and there was an emphasis on conversation. They didn't just talk about what Mork said to Mindy, they were serious conversationalists who were also interested in people. I came back with a very strong sense of what incredible damage to the ordinary social fabric in a country can be done by television, had been done in this country.

"I chose commercials because that is ultimately why television exists and they are very expensive attempts to manipulate you. Advertisers spend up to $1 million for a few seconds to get your attention and tempt you. People spend more than one year of their lives watching commercials. We're all a little too busy for that, aren't we?"

Computer technology has, of course, impacted strongly on the making of commercials, particularly in the area of the viewer's eye fixation, the point at which the sales pitch is made. Much research has been done, and now the race is on to be able to animate the human figure in such a way as to make it impossible to tell the real from the computer-created. Computer-animated logos and symbols are now in use by all the networks, and a number of major advertisers also use them. But the human figure—control of which will increase the effectiveness of the commercial pitch beyond anything that has come before—is the supreme challenge.

"They can generate an image," Crichton says, "but they can't animate it. They can make it three-dimensional, but it's not real. When they can, look out.

"Most of the stuff in the screenplay turned out to be true. It's appalling in a way, but also funny in a way."

*Looker* is, after *Westworld, Coma,* and *The Great Train Robbery* (based on his novel), the fourth film Crichton has directed, and before it is released he will be at work as a writer again, though he is not at all sure what he will be writing, or even whether it will be a book or a screenplay.

"After sixteen years of writing books, it is not as fascinating to me as it used to be. I'm beginning to feel I don't want to write fiction any more, at least not in books. Screenplays are OK because they're blueprints, steps in the process and not the thing itself.

"In a subjective sense, I just don't want to sit there alone any more. I think what I ascribe that feeling to is that once I began making movies I found it very agreeable to be in a position to work with a lot of people in a public way. I think it is a pretty common experience to want change after you've done something for a while.

"I've been working on a pirate story set in the seventeenth century, but it has been tough work. I spent a week trying to figure out what people had for breakfast then, and I couldn't even find out if breakfast existed at that time. I'm interested in Captain Cook, a name of renown about whom almost nothing personal is known. I've been interested in him a long time.

"And I've got another movie in which the woman is the central character. She is an architect. I think what's happening to women is very interesting.

"Whatever I do, I'd like to get away from technology. Essentially I deal with my taste, and taste is the most difficult problem to discuss abstractly. Still, you can't dispute it."

# A Tall Storyteller

## Eric Sauter/1984

From *Saturday Review*, November/December 1984. Reprinted by permission of Eric Sauter.

Nothing changes.

This is the sum of all the parts that constitute Michael Crichton's view of the world in general, and the impact of technology on that world in particular. It's a big, old blanket of a philosophy that the writer-director has been toting around with him in one form or another since the early seventies, and probably even before that. It's comfortable, secure, and, like an old blanket that has been carted from room to room, possesses a few holes, but none that Crichton himself seems too worried about. His life these days is quiet and under control. He moves at evolutionary speed. Nothing changes.

He can apply this philosophy to his latest film, *Runaway*, a thriller for Tri-Star, starring Tom Selleck and some robots, which will open this December. *Runaway* is Crichton's first effort since *Looker*, his 1981 film that came and went quickly.

"*Runaway* is a cop movie," Crichton explains, "good guys versus bad guys. How can I put this? . . . Courageous cop meets . . . let's say, a very inventive villain." *Runaway* is also about—what else?—hardware. "It's about the introduction of smart weapons into civilian life—like the Exocet missile. The pilot who sunk the battleship *Sheffield* in the Falklands war never even saw the target. He just fired at it over the horizon." *Runaway* turns this back on the folks at home. "When people buy a coffeemaker these days, they expect it to have a microprocessor in it. What about when they buy a gun?"

Crichton is pleased with *Runaway* and with Selleck, a TV performer not quite yet considered a film star in some quarters. Crichton thinks of him as both a television and film star.

"Tom has not been in a film that has been perceived by the industry as a hit, but this is an industry that really begrudges success. *High Road* was a hit, it did very well overseas. The initial grosses of *Lassiter* were very strong, and that's an indication of how popular a star he is; if people will come to see him in anything. He's the most popular actor on television. When we were shooting, it was incredible, like The Beatles. We'd always know when he came on the set because we'd hear these screams. 'Well, Tom's here.'"

*Runaway* also contains robots, and they have caused Crichton an immeasurable amount of grief. "I thought people would ask about Tom," he says, puzzled, "but they want to hear about the robots. I think if you come to the film looking for robots, you'll be sorry. The robots are used peripherally, for things like diffusing bombs and sentries."

Still, at its heart, *Runaway* is a cop picture. "There are new settings and new techniques, but it's still just cops and robbers. My idea is that technology doesn't change anything." He points to an IBM computer on his office desk. "There's a new computer on my desk. It hasn't really made my life different. Not that I wouldn't shriek if you tried to take it away, but its effect just isn't that earth-shattering."

Crichton grew up in the Long Island suburbs and went to Harvard as an undergraduate and then to Harvard Medical School—a place that he claims to have hated. While at school, he began writing paperback thrillers, secretly and pseudonymously. He wrote *The Andromeda Strain* the year he graduated from medical school and moved to California ostensibly to take a postdoctoral fellowship. Soon, however, he was finished with medicine and his first marriage. Remaining in California, he came up with another high-tech bestseller, *The Terminal Man*. In 1973 he wrote and directed *Westworld*, his first theatrical film. It was a success. He was thirty years old.

Crichton leads a surprisingly private life for a successful man in a business that ranks seeking publicity with breathing as an automatic response. In the fifteen years since the publication of *The Andromeda Strain*, the book that first put him on the bestseller lists and helped ease his way into directing Hollywood films, there have probably been less than a dozen articles written about him—not even one a year.

"In some ways," he says, "you are either seeking attention or you're not, and I just don't want it. I would like people to pay attention to what I do and not to me. You have to understand, these products are, to a certain degree, excretions. I don't want to play with them once they're out."

The offices of Constant C Productions, Crichton's company, reflect this withdrawal from the light. They are in a nondescript section of Santa Monica, surrounded by a mix of buildings that might best be called eclectic. Next door is a small church mission; next to that is an auto body shop; across the street and down half a block is a small park that, on closer examination, turns out to be a cemetery.

Crichton's office is on the second floor. It is comfortably furnished: a brown leather couch and chair, both nicely worn, a pair of glass coffee tables, an oriental rug, a miniature television, a book on Porsches, a pair of Steinbergs and a Jasper Johns on the walls, a new IBM computer with a color monitor, and an Olivetti word processor on the desk.

His staff is friendly. No one seems particularly agitated by the fact that *Runaway* is due into Tri-Star at the end of the week. The film is on-time, on-budget, and there is nobody sleeping on cots and working round the clock. Crichton has time for conversation.

He curls his long frame—Crichton is 6 feet 9 inches tall—in and over the chair, hooking one leg over the arm, then, shifting, he sits up again, closes his eyes, and throws his head back. His body seems in a slow lope to catch up with his mind. He wears glasses that make him seem a decade younger than his forty-one years.

"There was a time," he says, "when I never had a bad review. Of course, if everyone likes your work, it is probably not very interesting."

Then, in 1980, there was *Congo*, a book that managed to get its share of less than favorable reviews. It was Crichton's usual mix of high adventure—an expedition into darkest Africa, lost cities, killer apes, exploding volcanoes—and high tech: transponders, lasers, computers, and satellite feeds. The book became a bestseller and the film rights sold immediately—that is, before the screenplay was even written—but then, as Crichton remembers, it got away from him.

"I discovered I was more interested in the periphery of the story than in the center. It was basically a nineteenth-century adventure story but I found myself putting in all this technology to distract the reader's eye from the basic preposterousness of the whole thing. It became a literary stretch and finally, too great a literary stretch."

Along with *Congo*'s technology came enormous amounts of pure information, some of it fictional, but all dressed up like a college text, a mini-lecture on whatever Crichton considered interesting: a history of African rivers, the behavior of volcanoes, primate language. All of it was injected into the story and the narrative style was lost. "There is a certain didactic side to me," Crichton observes. It was his last novel to date.

A movie of *Congo* was to follow but it withered, the victim of studio politics and the passage of time. Then came the film, *Looker*, a good idea about mind control through computerized television commercials gone bad, and Crichton's only certifiable flop.

"With *Looker*," he says, "no one was making the movie they wanted to make—not me, not the studio, certainly not the actors, no one. It was a very frustrating experience. But I learned some structural things about films—make certain you're in charge. They make it so you're responsible for it but you can't control it."

In contrast, *Runaway* has gone incredibly well and that is precisely why Crichton is thinking about never doing another film.

"I look at the popular movies today and they aren't the ones I want to make," he says. "I don't have much in common with the audience that seems to enjoy them.

"People's attention spans are so short now, they're almost nincompoops. I started to notice it in 1978 with *Coma*. At the preview, about twenty minutes into it, people started getting restless. I thought, 'What is all this shuffling going on?'" He smiles here, nearly a wince. "It was time for a station break. What an audience can follow, what they can hold in their minds as the dramatic intent of a film, has gone from twenty minutes to ten, and now it's down to three and a half minutes, the length of an MTV video."

If movies are becoming more like television commercials strung together—and Crichton blames that on certain directors of commercials who have jumped into film—he also sees himself as one of the people who have pushed "hardware" movies about as far as they can go.

"I may be one of the ones who helped get the ball rolling," he says, "but it's time that the ball stopped rolling."

His feelings about film and technology—"hardware"—revolve so tightly around one another now that he is not entirely certain where it will end up. But he knows that something is going on.

"I don't have an answer for it. I'm often very surprised when an episode in my life is over—like a love affair. I didn't know when I was finished with medicine but there was suddenly a moment when I knew I'd had enough of it. So, right now, I'm thinking of ending film work.

"Now, generally, I feel that way after any picture. This may have a greater significance—then again it may not. But I know that my dealing with, writing about, thinking about all this technology is finished for some time." He stops and releases a deep sigh that is like a wringing of hands. "I am so bored with hardware. I can hardly look at it anymore. I know, everybody thinks I'm Mr. Gadget, but I'm not sure I ever was."

If his fascination with technology is finished, he is leaving with a nice bang. His book, *Electronic Life*, an explanation of computers and why we shouldn't fear the new machine, is just out in paperback. "I wrote the computer book because I knew if I didn't do it now, I wouldn't ever write it. And it's easy for me, computers don't scare me. So, I figured I could write about them and that would coincide with my lack of interest in them."

This fall he will also publish Amazon, a floppy disk computer game that he has been working on with a programmer for the last year and a half. He calls it an experiment in "interactive fiction."

"I started doing it because I thought I ought to learn about these things and because I thought we could do something different. But the one thing I learned is that there's no way to get around telling a story. You've got to tell a good story. I just thought I could get away from it." He shrugs. "Nothing changes."

He was a workaholic. "I was dedicated to work performance and I performed like a son of a bitch. I don't believe in luck. I worked harder than anybody I know—literally, day and night."

"I was absolutely flattened by the success of *Westworld*," he says. "There I was at thirty. I had a divorce, money, lawsuits, fame, as much celebrity as I wanted." He did nothing. "For three years there were no books, and no films for four years. I read and I traveled."

He has a list all set. "I read about gravitation, dinosaurs, Charles II, Victorian engineering, volcanoes, Antarctica, the American West, Mark Twain, da Vinci, John Singer Sargent. I went to Malaysia and Africa." He looks up from his litany as if it has given him a new idea. "It's probably time for another one of those periods."

It was in this early fallow period that he began to study Eastern thought. Spurred by a trip he made, alone, to Bangkok in 1973, he immersed himself in a world of meditation.

"I hired a car and a driver to take me on a tour of the city. He took me to see the temples. I had never seen a Buddha up close before, so I walked into one of the temples. I stood there and looked around." He begins to smile as if he were experiencing it again. "I thought, 'I like this! This is good!'" He stops and laughs quietly. "I just liked it."

That experience moved him towards others. He talks around them at first, avoiding anything specific. "When you start talking about some of this," he says, "people start thinking you're some kind of New Age loony." He becomes genuinely uncomfortable.

"The first thing is, I have no desire to talk about it. There was no turning point, no Paul on the road to Damascus, no blinding light or revelation for me. My life hasn't been like that. I just had some experiences that I thought were impossible, or that I had always been taught were a sure sign of psychosis. I thought I must be crazy, or if I wasn't crazy, then the scientific view of the world simply wasn't enough any longer.

"So, yes, I have seen visions and heard voices—big, booming voices in my head—and no, I won't tell you what they said because what they said was so banal." He makes a face and intones, 'Brush your teeth every morning;' something as ridiculous as that."

He pauses again and closes his eyes. After he does this several times, it seems like a deliberate motion, as though he were snatching just a wee bit of meditation in the middle of speech, as though he were looking at something on the inside of those closed lids.

"When people go to the holy men of India," he says, "the first things they want to hear about are the miracles. The holy men probably say to themselves, 'Shit. Somebody else wants to know about the miracles.' The miracles—the voices and the visions—are really a by-product of something else." Again, he stops and closes his eyes.

"I got interested in 1973 and got increasingly involved in meditation-related experiences. Those are what are spiritual to me. I came to a point where I didn't think another Porsche would matter too much. I might have bought it anyway but I didn't think it would matter."

Nothing changes. Crichton's ideas and experiences aren't so "New Age loony," although the average person might have trouble relating to the idea that buying or not buying a brand-new Porsche is a metaphysical problem, and not one of how much you have in your checking account. Of course, in Crichton's business, Porsches are what the average person buys.

He is not a loon, New Age or otherwise, but he does offer a whiff of a New Age view of the world. He has a cynical, if slightly cranky, idea why the general public hasn't cottoned to the idea of thermonuclear war: "Don't tell me it's because your five year old can't sleep at night. It's because you're tired of paying for it. I'm a great believer in the economic determinism of intellectual positions."

On the other hand, he is sincerely horrified over the media-generated industry based on showing what is in store if they drop the big one. "I don't think nuclear war should be used for the purpose of entertainment," he says, possibly because he doesn't like the idea of people thinking a nuclear exchange is going to be anything like the movie.

He also has a strange New Age naiveté about the impact of his ideas on the world in general: "The balance between the rational mind and the intuitive mind was lost in the Renaissance and it's now coming back into balance. Things such as precognition are an everyday occurrence. There are evolutionary changes going on right now."

Crichton has come to this mindset from a rationalist point of view, a kind of loop-de-loop through the world of science, and through a very difficult personal period. There have been two marriages and divorces since 1980 and that clearly troubles him. *Congo* and *Looker* were, for the most part, unsatisfactory. His life has been made up of movement from one journey to another; a hunger for experience, especially of the transcendent sort, that pushes him up against his fears.

He climbed Mt. Kilimanjaro: "My idea of preparation was to quit smoking two days before the climb." Halfway up, his shoes were full of blood from the blisters. But he finished the climb.

"When the altitude, exhaustion, and the cold all hit you at once, and you can't move, you can put your mind in one area and have the energy to move on, and put it in another and not move at all. I find that interesting, an example of the interconnectedness of mind and body." In a curious way, this is why he took up running after quitting smoking last December. "I suspect running is probably not good for you physically, but I love to turn those endorphins loose." (Endorphins are the morphine-like substance produced by the brain responsible for what has become known as a "runners high.")

That same hunger for the transcendent led him to spend time with African mountain gorillas in 1981: "You're a guest in their territory. They can reach out and crush you in an instant. No other primates are like gorillas, they might as well be people. They're very hairy people. I found it troubling, the fact that they were so unexpectedly human-like. Other animals, well, elephants give me strange feelings, too."

His travels have forced him to deal with his fears; a motif that runs through his fiction. While diving around a newly discovered wreck in the Caribbean, he experienced a "feverish desire for buried treasure," he says. "I turned around and came face to face with this six-foot barracuda. I just didn't care. I went back to looking for gold. I decided then that my fear of barracudas was a great indulgence.

"I used to have lots of fears but now I'm not afraid of much," he says. If it has left him at peace, it has also left him apart. "I feel very alienated from this culture right now," he says, clearly curious about those feelings.

His world is less restricted by work, which is how he now thinks of writing. "Writing is for work—I no longer have an image of it as play. So, I started drawing in a notebook, all for me. It doesn't have to be good, because no one gets to see it."

He also does some of his art on the computer. He has produced a program to re-create a Mondrian painting called Broadway Boogie-Woogie. After receiving its instructions, its rules of behavior—"You can draw a straight line but not parallel to any other line," for example—the machine started to act like an artist. "As it searched the program, it would take time and began to behave like a thoughtful artist selecting a new place for a line.

"If you believe, as I do, that the bulk of your life springs from your unconscious, it's useful to do things that allow you to get a glimpse of that unconsciousness. So, I throw the *I Ching*, use tarot cards, keep a diary."

For the *I Ching*, he also uses the computer. "I don't throw the stones anymore; I have written a program. The interesting thing is how you interpret. That comes from yourself and isn't that what you're interested in?"

He has spent the last decade purging his life of what he has come to consider irrelevant. First medical school, now, possibly, films. This purge has been accompanied by a search for some experience that will put all of his life on one big Mobius Strip, something that will combine science and intuition into a whole.

This year he will move back to Cambridge for a few months, to use the Harvard library and to teach a freshman course in anthropology. He talks about the difference between the two coasts, finding something funny, and pertinent, even in that: "Out here we have everything for the body; the ocean, the sex. In the East, they have everything for the head. I'm still looking for the place where there's a balance—and don't tell me it's Chicago."

# Sphere

## Don Swaim/1987

Recorded on June 1, 1987, for *Book Beat*. Reprinted by permission of CBS Radio News.

**Swaim:** A lot of use of the computer in *Sphere* and I wondered what you were using?

**Crichton:** It was a Macintosh. Some of the material in *Sphere* is a code—a very simple letter substitution code—and it began to be clear that when the book is translated into different languages, all that graphic material is going to have to be reconstituted. I began to realize I didn't want to do it. A lot of it was actually done with a computer program, so I've been sending the programs to foreign publishers, saying, "You do it. This is the program. You get a Macintosh and run it through with whatever the sentence equivalents are in Norwegian and Swedish and German."

**Swaim:** So these codes have real meaning—they are not just graphics?

**Crichton:** No, no, no—if you want to go through and play the game, it all makes sense—sure, absolutely.

**Swaim:** Which is why when it goes into foreign translations it can't be faked?

**Crichton:** No, you would have to change all that. They would have to redo it for every foreign edition.

**Swaim:** . . . Well, I have to say about *Sphere*—I have to complain about it a little bit—you kept me up until two o'clock in the morning reading it, so you really cut into my sleep.

**Crichton:** Sorry about that.

**Swaim:** I just couldn't put it down. A couple of questions come to mind: One is the habitat you have created in the bottom of the Pacific Ocean—is there anything like that now, or is this something out of the imagination of Michael Crichton?

**Crichton:** I think there used to be habitats like that but habitats have, in part, gone into disfavor. There are very industrial habitats that are used, for example, in the North Sea for oil drilling operations. Divers go down there and it's a very grubby, saturated diving environment. There are not the plush habitats that are described in this book.

**Swaim:** But there could be?
**Crichton:** There could be, sure.

**Swaim:** Another question comes to mind: There was a really dramatic episode where the hero is in the submarine and he's being chased by this giant squid. The tentacle is coming up through the various decks trying to reach out at him. He looks out a porthole and sees the eye and realizes that this squid is tracking him from outside. Why doesn't the water just rush into that sub? How could the squid get the arm up there and not have the sub flooded by water?
**Crichton:** That's just the experience you would have if you take an empty glass and turn it upside down and hold it in a bathtub—the water won't fill the glass. If there's pressure inside an inverted glass, it will hold the water out and there will be just a floating water level.

**Swaim:** That's why they were able to come in and out of the airlock without any problem?
**Crichton:** Right. The atmosphere inside the habitat is pressurized to equal the outside sea water.

**Swaim:** Knowing you, I would assume all, or most, of the science in this book is pretty accurate. Isn't that right?
**Crichton:** It is pretty accurate. There's one area which is tremendously wrong [Laughs]; and there was nothing I could do about it. In order to tell the story I had to live with that.

**Swaim:** You don't want to divulge that?
**Crichton:** It's just a trivial technical point and it's not very important; but I know of one glaring error. Otherwise, my intention is to make these things pretty accurate. The fun of it for me is to do it in a very detailed way.

**Swaim:** Now you're telling about black holes and time travel, and there's a lot of dispute about things like that, isn't there?

**Crichton:** Yes, there is. The fact of the matter is that we don't even know for sure of any black hole. We think we have the locations of several of them and we think we know quite a lot about the behavior of them. There are some people who think, or at least have thought in the past, that a rotating black hole could conceivably be entered and passed through; a stationary black hole couldn't, but a rotating black hole could. The possibility exists that one could go through a black hole and come out somewhere else. That's a current speculation and it's available for use in a speculative book. I didn't make it up, is what I'm trying to tell you. I got it from someone else.

**Swaim:** You're a practical guy—you live with the sheer practicalities of putting novels together and directing motion pictures; you have an MD from Harvard—you're not one to let flights of fancy go through your mind too much. I would assume you have your feet on the ground. What are your personal opinions about going back into space and creating the kind of situation that actually happened in *Sphere*?

**Crichton:** Do you mean: Do I think the book is possible?

**Swaim:** Yes.

**Crichton:** My immediate answer is no. But my answer to almost everything I've written is: I don't think it's possible. What interested me in this, Don, was to take a book in which a very extreme situation was presented to a group of people and then to see how this group of people responded to the extreme situation. I didn't really want to spend too much time challenging the extreme situation itself—to say, "How realistic is this?" What I was trying to do the book about was just to say, "What would happen to people if they were confronted by this extreme situation? What would happen to people if they were confronted by—as a premise—the possibility of time travel, the possibility of contact with an extraterrestrial artifact, something that comes from another civilization that's very much more advanced than ours?" All I would say in defense of the extreme premise is: Take anyone from a hundred years ago—take Charles Darwin, pretty knowledgeable guy from that time—and plunk him in front of a Macintosh. The chances are he would run screaming from the room: "It cannot be anything but witchcraft." If you decide to sit down and say: "Okay, Chuck. Let me explain to you how this works"—it involves whole fields of highly developed knowledge he doesn't know anything about. The electron hasn't been discovered yet—he doesn't know what an electron is. He certainly doesn't know anything about electronics; doesn't know anything about solid-state electronics; doesn't know anything about cathode-ray tubes. This is one giant piece of magic to him, and all he can really do is sit on the outside and look at it as some very strange rectangular object that has funny black and white shifting images on it. If that's true in a hundred years, then there must be something very much like it fifty or a hundred years in the future if we could see ahead—see what kinds of things we would be doing. This is a book about people who find something from, as it turns out, our own future. It's pretty mysterious.

**Swaim:** I believe you say in *Sphere* that if you were to take a television set a hundred or two hundred years into the past it would be worthless to anybody. You couldn't turn it on.
**Crichton:** That's right; no place to plug it in.

**Swaim:** I was talking, not too long ago, with Jean-Louis Gassée, the man currently behind all the Macintoshes. I asked him to speculate on the kinds of computers we might have in the future. He said one thing that was interesting: He could see a computer that would be the size of this book, or of a notepad, but instead of typing you just write on it and the computer will translate your handwriting. I don't know if that's an advance or not, but that would be one form of computer in the future. Another form would be, of course, just having a computer you can talk to and can talk to you back; [they] do a little of that now, but it's very undeveloped. The concept for a computer was pretty well established by the mid-'40s, wasn't it?
**Crichton:** Yes.

**Swaim:** I read someplace that in order to create a computer of even the most primitive nature, it would have to use vacuum tubes; it would have to be so large that a simple computer would take up as much room as the Empire State Building.
**Crichton:** Oh, yes. In fact, even the computers in the '60s—those big IBMs that were so terrific and lived in their own little rooms and stuff—were incredibly small. Those big computers of the '60s that I remember when I was in college—they are the size of pocket calculators; they're 10k–12k machines; they're tiny. No one would own a personal computer so small, in terms of its memory, now; it's kind of a joke. And the kinds of machines that are for sale for a few thousand dollars now that everybody can have and carry around if they want them—were unimaginable twenty years ago.

A man lived up the street from me who was a computer pioneer and he once told me about programming a 256-byte machine. Not 256-k, 256 bytes. It's ridiculous. There have been extraordinary changes. I agree with you in terms of whether or not a future computer that can decipher handwriting is advantageous—I can type a lot faster than I can write. I certainly think that to have many kinds of input devices is only advantageous.

**Swaim:** *Sphere* is going to be one hell of a motion picture. Will you be directing it and writing it?

**Crichton:** At the moment I have no plans for either. It was, I think in part, a feeling I had that my tendency to become involved in the film versions of my books might not be as good an idea as I originally thought it was. For one thing, it keeps me very much involved with a limited number of projects over a longer time. For another thing, I sometimes think there's a certain amount of energy that you have available for a subject or for a story. By the time I've done the novel I don't know if I really want to do the movie, to tell you the truth. How I got to this is actually the other way around. I had done an original screenplay and the studio began to say, "Why don't you do the novel?" I said, "No, I don't want to do a novel." They said, "Well, if you do a novel you'll do the movie afterwards." I thought, "That's true—I will. Let's think about that." So my sense is: it would make a good movie and I don't think I should probably do it.

**Swaim:** It would be a hell of a movie and it requires a degree of special effects, but they've been done. It's certainly possible to do it. As I recall, the Disney movie *20,000 Leagues Under the Sea* had a giant squid, didn't it?

**Crichton:** Yes, it did.

**Swaim:** So they could probably dust that off and use it. [Laughs]

**Crichton:** [Laughs] Let's find that squid; bring it back.

**Swaim:** It was '83 that you wrote [*Electronic Life*]—that's four years. In addition to working on *Sphere*, what all have you been doing?

**Crichton:** I've written another book called *Travels*, which will be out next year. I did a movie called *Runaway* that came out in '84.

**Swaim:** Wrote it?

**Crichton:** Wrote and directed it.

**Swaim:** The new book, is that also fiction?

**Crichton:** No, the new book is nonfiction. It's an autobiographical book and it began as a series of travel pieces. I've done a lot of traveling in the last twenty years. Originally, my idea was never to write about it. My thought was that I wanted to do something that I just did for myself and wasn't work-related; it wasn't supposed to amount to anything; wasn't supposed to turn into anything. But, as time went on, so many of the really important experiences in my life occurred on those trips that it began to seem almost evasive to me that I wasn't writing about it. So I finally decided that I would. Once I was writing an autobiographical book—which certainly I never thought I'd do—I began to think about some medical stories that I'd always promised myself that I'd write, although not until enough time had gone by that they were pretty ancient history. To my amazement, enough time has gone by. It's more than fifteen years since I went to medical school, so I've put those in there, too.

**Swaim:** When you were in medical school you were writing potboilers under pseudonyms to help pay your way through. How has your writing changed over all those years, and is it easier or harder than it was way back then?

**Crichton:** It's gone through many permutations, and I've felt differently about it at different times. At this particular time I'm very enthusiastic about it and it gives me a lot of pleasure. At other times I've felt very tired of doing it; I've felt like I've done too much; I've wished for changes. There's a quality in me where I become alternately disaffected with either books or films, depending on what I've had the most recent difficult experiences with. I think for a long time I thought, "I don't see why I should continue writing books; I'd just rather work in movies." Then, at a certain point, I thought, "Wait a minute now. If I write a book, I don't have to talk to anybody else, I don't have to get anybody to say the lines, I don't have to get anybody to put up the money, I don't have to make any changes. I can have it be exactly the way I want and I only have to deal with myself. Why is it that I'm not doing so? What was so wrong with that again?" So I really reconceived the advantages of that work.

**Swaim:** Almost every writer I've talked to who's written for the movies, from Sidney Sheldon on, have said they prefer to write novels. It's easier, for the reasons you've outlined, and, ultimately, it's their work without the changes. It's usually the director's vision that alters books. Sometimes they destroy what the book is supposed to be.

**Crichton:** Yes.

**Swaim:** That really hasn't happened to you so much, has it?

**Crichton:** It happened one time in a book called *Dealing*, which was intended to be an anti-drug book and by the time the movie came out it was a pro-drug movie. [Laughs] But no, I've actually had, in most cases, pretty good success with the movies—but it's an inherently hazardous undertaking. Movies are a large collaborative enterprise and there are many, many pressures on it.

**Swaim:** You're living in Los Angeles?

**Crichton:** Living in Los Angeles.

**Swaim:** Why don't you move out of Los Angeles? That helps to avoid the temptation a little bit.

**Crichton:** You mean the temptation to work in films?

**Swaim:** Yes, doesn't it?

**Crichton:** I like to work in films. I find that it's a good counter-balance in some way. In other words, for pretty much the last two years I've been very much in isolation. I get up at four or five in the morning. I go to my office and make a cup of instant coffee and sit in front of the Macintosh and write. Around ten o'clock people come into the office. Eventually, I'll go to lunch; then I'll come back and work some more. About three o'clock I'll quit for the day, take an exercise class and go home. I'll do that five or six days a week for months. It takes a lot of energy so I don't really want to go out very much at night; I don't want to go to dinner with people—I'm really focusing on my work. After a couple years of that, I think it's probably healthy for me to be on a movie set and have a hundred people and a lot of talk and not to be by myself so much. I feel that I could easily become hermit-like if I'm not careful.

**Swaim:** The movies pay well, too—so I understand. That's also an inducement that has helped in many instances. I was talking to John Gregory Dunne, for example, who writes screenplays with his wife Joan Didion, who says that movies have effectively helped to finance the writing habit.

**Crichton:** I think that's true of John. My experience is: yes, they do pay well; and yes, you earn it. [Laughs]

**Swaim:** Well, Michael Crichton, after four years it's great seeing you again. *Sphere* is a really fascinating book; a page-turner that—unless you drop off to sleep in the middle of a line, and that's very hard to do—is almost impossible to put down. For my small listenership, I'm certainly going to recommend it highly. I appreciate your coming in. I know you have a coast-to-coast schedule and it's probably a pain to have to come in and talk to another radio guy, but I appreciate it, and sharing your thoughts about the Macintosh as well. Thank you, very much.

**Crichton:** Thank you, Don.

# Rising Sun

## Don Swaim/1992

Recorded on February 6, 1992, for *Book Beat*. Reprinted by permission of CBS Radio News.

**Swaim:** With *Rising Sun*, your latest book, did you have something against the Japanese?
**Crichton:** No, not at all. I like the Japanese.

**Swaim:** Personally, you like the Japanese?
**Crichton:** Yes. One of the interesting things about this has been to hear responses from other people. A number of people have said to me, in effect, "How could you attack so strongly?" In a way, I feel able to criticize because I like Japan. I'm very attracted to it and drawn to many aspects of it. From my point of view, I'm merely criticizing what I think ought to be criticized. I don't have another agenda. It's not racist, it's not anything else.

**Swaim:** I imagine, since I heard your broadcast last night on *The Larry King Show*, much of your interviews will focus around the political and economic aspects of the book. Of course, that's very important to the book. In fact, something unusual for a novel is that you have a postscript and a bibliography. In fiction, that's not really heard of, is it?
**Crichton:** Yes, I've done it before.

**Swaim:** In *Jurassic Park* I believe you did.
**Crichton:** Yes. I did it in *The Terminal Man* and I'm not sure whether I did it in another book. But it's certainly an unusual thing to do.

**Swaim:** It's unusual because it makes people think the book is less fiction than it is nonfiction. That's what nonfiction writers do—they have footnotes and bibliographies and this sort of thing.
**Crichton:** I've always felt very uneasy about the distinction between fiction

**43**

and nonfiction in the sense that it seems to me that a lot of nonfiction, or what passes for nonfiction, is contrived; and a lot of fiction is in many ways more real than not. At one point I wanted to write a history book. I started reading the history of the American Revolution in some breadth and I was continuously shocked at the speculations that historians make, which as a novelist I would never dare to make. I thought, "There's no basis for these ideas. Why are they saying these things?" So I guess the rules of the game are slightly different but they overlap.

**Swaim:** It is said that nonfiction tells you what happened, but fiction tells you what people really think and what really happened. Nonfiction is almost like a chronology of events, but with fiction you can get into characters and get into thoughts and lives in a way you can't do with nonfiction.
**Crichton:** That's right, and I think there's some advantage to that.

**Swaim:** You could have written a nonfiction book called *Rising Sun* and it may have been read by some people. But you can also get a message across in a fictionalized way that says much the same thing, only it will carry an audience in a way that a nonfiction book often cannot do. Would you agree to that?
**Crichton:** Yes, absolutely. Certainly the subject area in this case, which is economic relations between the United States and Japan, is not something that seems to be of tremendous immediate interest to the American population, although lately that seems to have changed.

**Swaim:** Yes. I saw a photograph; I believe it was of a car dealership in California. People could go up to a Toyota and, if they made a donation, slam the Japanese-built car with a sledgehammer—which sounds like a childish thing to do. It doesn't really address the problem of Japanese-American relations, does it?
**Crichton:** No, it doesn't. That's the kind of symbolic event that is, in the end, very empty. In a way, the symbology of Bush's most recent trip to Japan was his vomiting on the Prime Minister's trouser. I had a sense that was about all that was really accomplished on that trip. One of the things I feel very strongly about and try to convey in the book is that if the United States is to have a better relationship, from our standpoint, with Japan, we're really going to have to change our attitudes. It's pointless, as in a marriage, to ask the other person to change. If you want a change, you better change yourself and see the relationship change on that basis.

**Swaim:** Let's go back to the beginning. Let me ask you how *Rising Sun* came about and why you have decided in this form to address this problem which has been growing for some time?

**Crichton:** My interest must go back to the late '80s. I have notes for a book in '87–'88 and I'm not exactly sure now what the initial provocation was. I think I became disturbed about the sale of American high-tech companies to Japan. Starting in the late '80s we began to sell one American company every ten days or so, and we've done that for the last five years. To look at a list of a couple hundred American companies that have been sold is a very disturbing thing. It really raises questions about how long we can continue to sell our technological future to our chief competitor and expect to have anything left, in terms of our own future.

**Swaim:** You say a lot about American society as well in this book. Somewhere in the book you write that the Japanese consider us barbarians. Look at our crime rate—no civilized country on earth has the crime rate the American people have. You said something to that effect; it really stuck out because there are a lot of things wrong with our society and I think you pinpointed it very well in *Rising Sun.* Maybe you could elaborate on that?

**Crichton:** There's absolutely no question we have made decisions in our society that no other industrial state has made. We have, for some reason, elected to tolerate the highest crime rate in the world. Last year we had twenty-five thousand murders in this country. The rate is twenty times higher than in England, one hundred times higher than in Japan. The difference is so striking that when you're in a Japanese city it takes a little while for you to realize you don't always have to be looking over your shoulder at night; you can go anywhere you want to go; you can be alone or in a group and you're safe in any case. We are so accustomed to maintaining a constant level of tension and alertness and fear that we're going to be assaulted, that we're going to be shot, that we're going to be mugged, raped—and that's starting to become a part of the fabric of our society. It's crazy when you think about it. When you start to talk about what there is about America that's different, the thing that immediately leaps out is gun control. Ours is the only nation I'm aware of that has elected to say there are no limitations on ownership of guns. Every other nation makes another decision and in return gets safe citizenry, gets safe streets. We are the only nation left that has no healthcare policy. We are the only major industrial nation without an industrial policy. Look at Japan, look at Germany—those countries have decided on the proper way for industry and government to work together.

The United States once had a clear idea about how government and the defense industry would work together for the defense of America, and there was no foolishness about that in the United States. People wanted a strong defense; they were willing to pay for it; they didn't care what administration was in power. The belief in a strong American defense cut across party lines, cut across presidential positions. That's what we wanted and that's what we continuously had. That sort of across the board national policy is how the Japanese feel about their industry and their exports. It isn't really surprising that when you see a country in which the people, the industries, the government are in agreement about what ought to happen in economic competition with a nation like the United States—which is in disarray, which has no agreement about how it ought to proceed, which has totally open markets, which has no assistance from government of business, often interference— that the organized country just wipes us out. And that's what's happened.

**Swaim:** Back to the crime problem we have in this country. Are you saying gun control is the key to it?
**Crichton:** I don't know what the key to it is. Don, when you compare any two countries—whether you're talking about crime, whether you're talking about education, whether you're talking about drugs—you can see differences between how one country does and how another country does. Then you can ask, "What are the differences related to that?" There's certainly a strong element in this country that says gun control and crime are not related. But, as far as I know, we're the only country without gun control—strict gun control—and we have the highest murder rate. So, if they're not related, it seems to me the burden of proof to demonstrate the lack of relation is on the people who feel it's necessary that everyone should have a gun.

**Swaim:** There's another problem, too. It's our horrendous rate of drug addiction. These are often the people who have come into possession of guns because these junkies are absolutely desperate for fixes and it doesn't matter to them who they kill as long as they get the high from the drugs. They obviously can't earn the money for drugs, so they have to take it.
**Crichton:** Right. I don't know the statistics offhand, but it seems to me that even if you place the drug-related murders at the highest percentage—I'm just sort of guessing at statistics—you would still have about half the murders; you would still lead the world with non-drug-related murders.

**Swaim:** Another phenomenon, too—most of these mass killings have happened within the last ten years. Every time there's a mass killing, the *New York Times* runs a list of mass killings in recent memory and you see that they have increased over the years in numbers. It's frightening that someone gets an assault weapon and mows down ten, twelve, fourteen people at one time. It's frightening. It's the kind of thing that might happen in a war.

**Crichton:** Yes. I don't know how to talk about this except in very vague terms, but one of the things that struck me most about my last trip to Japan was that Japanese schoolchildren cross the street without a crossing guard. At each side of the street there's a little metal cup attached to a stand or to a telephone pole, and inside the cup are flags—yellow flags on little sticks. What the children do is, as they come to school in the morning they each take a flag and wave the flag and cross the street. The cars all stop. When they get to the other side of the street they put the flags in the other cup so they'll be ready when they come home going the other way. No one steals the flags, no one defaces the cup, no one trashes it, or tears it, or messes it up. It's perfectly safe. The society has coherence and an agreement. In some way that we're not really acknowledging, the crime rate is a function of social controls that are instilled in all of us as a group agreement. There are, of course, in every society people who break out or who become crazy or who, for one or another reason, break free from the social order. But there is a social order most places. America seems to have lost the sense that that even ought to be. You can watch Americans step over a homeless person in the street as if that person isn't in the same environment, as if they are not also a part of this country, as if we don't all share something together. The Japanese understand very clearly that they have a country and they share something together. Americans, even though we are a melting pot, used to have some coherent feeling, some sense of community and some sense of national identity that seems to have dissipated.

**Swaim:** You went to Japan how many times?

**Crichton:** I've been there many times, but for extended periods only twice. I was meant to go back this past November to attend a conference in Kyoto and I broke my arm at the Christo Umbrellas in California. I was a casualty of the Christo Umbrellas.

**Swaim:** A survivor.

**Crichton:** I was a survivor, yes. Exactly. [Laughs]

**Swaim:** What was it like? I've never been to Japan. I've talked to some people who have enjoyed it and other people who didn't like the Japanese at all. Tell me about your experience. What has it been like for you?

**Crichton:** I like it very much. I think one's experience is, in part, a function of small things. For example, I have a much easier time there than my wife because I like the food. I'm perfectly happy to eat raw fish all the time and she has a lot of trouble with that. So on a daily, ongoing basis, I have an easier time—even though, because I'm so tall, I'm continuously the subject of interest in Japan. I clearly don't fit in a physical sense.

**Swaim:** How do they treat you?

**Crichton:** The ordinary reaction is to giggle. It produces laughter. It's a nervous or uncomfortable feeling, particularly with women—they laugh. That laughter doesn't mean to them what it means to a western person, but there are times when I really can't help having a western reaction to seeing a couple of dozen people in a department store laughing at me.

**Swaim:** But they are unfailingly polite, as you indicate in *Rising Sun*.

**Crichton:** They are polite, yes. They don't mean [to laugh], but I still have my own reaction to it. Ordinarily, I don't have that sort of experience and in some ways I feel more comfortable in Japan. I like the way everyone really takes pride in their job and everyone really does it as well as they can do. It's clean; it's safe; in a funny way you have more personal freedom because of that.

**Swaim:** In *Rising Sun*, the older detective, I believe his name is Connor?

**Crichton:** Yes.

**Swaim:** He educates the younger detective, Smith, I believe, Peter Smith, as to how the Japanese are socialized and how their body movements convey certain messages. Maybe you can elaborate on that for me?

**Crichton:** There's a feature that's most difficult for Americans to comprehend because it's so alien to us, because we assume that we are whatever we are—white, black, Hispanic—that we are a segment of the society and that there are other segments that are different from us. The Japanese do not have that conception of the nation. They imagine that everyone shares certain kinds of perceptions and beliefs. As a result, they are able to communicate heavily in nonverbal ways. The analogy for us would be the kind of communication that can occur in a family between a father and a son or a mother and a child—that kind of unspoken understanding of what's going on, what the other person is feeling. Even Japanese who don't know each other well have some sense of that between them in a way that Americans don't. Americans always want things spelled out. Americans always want to know what the deal is—"What do you mean by that?" Americans have a wish for a certain explicitness that the Japanese find mystifying and unnecessary.

**Swaim:** At the heart of *Rising Sun* there's an old-fashioned murder mystery.
**Crichton:** That's right.

**Swaim:** While it's assumed that the Japanese, or a Japanese, has committed the murder—we won't give away how it ends, because there is a twist—one of the interesting things about it is the technology involved because part of solving the crime is based on analyzing a security videotape. It's interesting—you note that the Japanese are actually three years ahead of us technologically, electronically. Is that really correct?
**Crichton:** Certainly, in some of these areas they're now moving well ahead. I think it was the defense department which, a year or so ago, identified ten or twelve significant technologies for the '90s and into the twenty-first century and made an assessment of which of these technologies America was doing well in comparison to Japan—where we were slipping and where we were leading. We were, in fact, moving ahead in only one; we were holding our own in three or four; we were slipping in all the rest. The Japanese, which in American fantasy have been copycats, people who have taken things that were invented here—and many things that they are famous for like the fax machine and the VCR and the digital watch were all invented here—the Japanese are moving ahead and they are developing strategies for innovation. Certainly in areas such as video technology they are the world leaders.

**Swaim:** Sometimes we shoot ourselves in the foot. Look at the digital audiotape machines—the DAT machines—supposed to be clearly superior to anything we have now, including the CD. We have them, just barely, but because of competition or because of something, these machines have been kept artificially high in terms of price and are not universally acceptable. Is that the result of our doing something wrong? What's going on here? I'm sure the Japanese are using them to great advantage.

**Crichton:** I wasn't aware there are any American manufacturers of DAT machines. Is that true?

**Swaim:** No, I don't believe there are. We're importing these machines but are not using them to the degree we probably should.

**Crichton:** The understanding I have is that there are about to be competing formats and it's not clear right now that DAT cassette technology, as it presently exists, is the one that's going to emerge as the final one. Philips has a competing technology; Sony has one. I'm not sure exactly what's going to happen but that's the sense I have about the price structure of those machines. It's a little bit undecided still.

**Swaim:** Tell me a little bit about the research you did with regard to *Rising Sun*, because you have an awful lot of information about Japanese customs and habits and how they do business.

**Crichton:** I'm not easily able to answer that question because when I start to work on a book and work in an area, I am aware of reading and clipping and making notes over a period of years, so that at the time I come to write I don't have much sense of doing any research at all. I just kind of write it. Then, inevitably, there arises the question of how I know something. The lawyers always go over it and say, "How do you know this?" and "Can you demonstrate that?" Often I have to go back—as if I hadn't written the book—to the library and look it up and say, "How do I know this?" It's a funny problem.

**Swaim:** Did you have some Japanese friends who analyzed the customs in the book for you?

**Crichton:** I certainly had some expert readers who went over it and one Japanese translator who brought the language into line. But yes, a number of people who have what I would consider expert knowledge checked the manuscript for me at various points—corrected me when they felt I was going astray.

**Swaim:** The publisher, Knopf, made a rather unusual decision about this book. Can you tell me about that?

**Crichton:** Are you talking about the decision to advance the publication?

**Swaim:** Yes.

**Crichton:** I finished the book in August of last year—August of '91—and it was scheduled for the end of February, and then for March, and it came out in early February. So I'm not really sure what the factors were in why it moved around.

**Swaim:** You turned in the manuscript in August of last year, so what the publisher decided to do in terms of its publishing timetable really didn't have much impact on you—except in terms of publicizing the book. Is that correct?

**Crichton:** Right. It's enough work for me to just write the books and I feel that I have a really good publisher. They must know more about publishing books than I do, so I just take their recommendation. They said, "It ought to be published at this time." I said, "Fine." Then they said, "It ought to be published earlier." And I said, "Fine."

**Swaim:** It's such an odd, staggered timetable with regard to publishing. By the time you finish a book, months, years sometimes go by before it gets into print. What is this like for an author? Do you ever lose feeling contact with the book because of this gap?

**Crichton:** I don't know what other writers feel, but the sense I have always is: First of all, by the time I've finished a book I'm usually very thoroughly sick of the subject and never want to think about it again, or talk about it again. [Laughs] I suppose if I were to finish the book and then immediately do publicity I would be quite cranky. On the other hand, several months later—in this case it's six or seven months later—there is a certain feeling of distance, as if that's an old marriage we're now reviving and talking about. So I get back a new feeling of interest because the time has gone by. I also have a sort of distant sense about it.

**Swaim:** What's it like picking up one of your older books like *The Androm-eda Strain* and looking at it? You see your name on the dust jacket and everything, but do you really feel it's yours with all the time having gone by?

**Crichton:** I don't. It's funny—it's odd you mention that. For about ten years the books seem to be something that is recognizably mine, but further back I look at them and I sometimes literally think, "Who wrote this?" It has no sense of relating to me at all. First of all, I don't really remember much about the writing—the activity of the writing—whereas a more recent book I can turn pages and I can come to some sections and remember this was a hard thing, I had to do this many times, or something happened to my daughter at the time I was working on this and I was interrupted. I have all these memories that are related to parts of the text, but as time goes by that fades and eventually I don't have any sense of association to the text—it is literally as if someone else wrote it.

**Swaim:** Kind of like life itself—which is why we keep photographs.
**Crichton:** Yes.

**Swaim:** You remember that happy day on the beach or that terrific birthday party for your daughter or the great meal you whipped up one night for a bunch of people and you had so much fun—but they're just little glimpses into the past as though they were lived by someone else. It's really eerie, isn't it? Well, I know you have another appointment and I'm sorry we had to be kind of rushed—[I] always like to talk to you and [it's] certainly a pleasure. *Rising Sun* is a terrific thriller with a socio-economic message. I hope it catches on and I'm sure it will. I'll be anxious to see it at the movies because I heard you last night saying that was going to be the case—so I'll be looking forward to that. Michael Crichton, thank you very, very much.
**Crichton:** Thank you, Don.

# *Rising Sun* Author Taps
# Darkest Fears of America's Psyche

## T. Jefferson Parker/1992

From the *Los Angeles Times*, July 5, 1992. Reprinted by permission of T. Jefferson Parker, author of *Iron River*.

Michael Crichton's new novel, *Rising Sun*, rose to the bestseller list and stayed there nineteen weeks—buoyed largely by the controversy and heated opinions the book has aroused. Crichton's premise—that Japan's rise to economic power is a serious danger to our own economy—has left people predictably polarized.

*Rising Sun* is a cautionary tale couched as a mystery. In it, Crichton argues that the United States is a second-rate economic power and is going to have to make some profound changes if it wishes to compete with vigor in the changing world economy.

Crichton, of course, has already proved himself a master at tapping into the near-atavistic fears of American readers. In his movie *Westworld* and novel *Jurassic Park*, technology runs amok and attacks its handlers with a serious vengeance. In *Rising Sun*, the Japanese pose a similarly dramatic threat by which our darkest intimations of a collapsed U.S. economy dominated by Japanese interests are encouraged to flourish. Crichton is fluent in the language of America's popular nightmares.

Crichton himself is a well-spoken and deliberate man, apparently used to bringing all of his considerable attention to bear on whatever situation is before him. Though just forty-nine, he has written eight novels, four works of nonfiction (ranging in subject from Jasper Johns to "electronic life") and has directed the movies *Westworld*, *Coma*, and *The Great Train Robbery*. On top of all that, he graduated Harvard Medical School and, in 1969, was a postdoctoral fellow at the Salk Institute in La Jolla. For the record, Crichton stands six feet nine inches tall, and weighs a slender 235 pounds. He was not prone, in this situation at least, to jocularity. He is married, has one child, and lives in Los Angeles. He sat talking amid books ranging from *Strategic Use of Scientific Evidence* to Gary Larson's *The PreHistory of the Far Side*. A bevy of toy dinosaurs sat atop one end table—presumably they were his, not his child's.

**Question:** *Rising Sun* makes a strong argument that Japanese business is unfairly aggressive and Americans are foolish to have tolerated this unfairness for so long. Is that a decent synopsis?
**Answer:** Not exactly. Let me just restate it. In the immortal words of my hero, Ross Perot: "It's not a two-way street. It never has been a two-way street. It's not their fault." It's our fault.

**Q:** That stated, then, I'd like to talk to you about two things—Japanese-American economics and race. Let's get to the dangerous stuff first. Are you a racist?
**A:** No.

**Q:** Do you consider the Japanese racist?
**A:** Yes. Well, first of all, let's track. There's an extended discussion of race in the book. Different characters represent different views on perceptions of race. The central character, John Connor, who is the voice the reader is asked to believe, says, "Japan is the most racist country in the world."

Now, how people respond to this comment is, in my experience, a function of how much they know about Japan and how much experience they've had there.

Many people who have worked extensively in Japan will point to that statement and say, "That's true." When I did the Dick Cavett show—and Dick Cavett has a good knowledge of Japan—he made a joke. He said, "Yes, that's true. In fact, I invented racism. Ha, ha."

But what are we talking about here?

We're talking about a historically inward-looking nation, an island nation, largely monoracial. That's a good structure in which to have the rise of feelings of superiority about your own people as opposed to other people in the world. Of course, these broad statements can't be applied to the individual Japanese person. One of the things that Americans, as a multiracial society, feel is a tremendous sensitivity to racial comments of all kinds.

In the book, one of the things I tried to say to Americans was: Hey, while you're tiptoeing around the race issue, your competitors are a monoracial country, very much aligned, and tend to hold in common beliefs that would astound you.

**Q:** Have you been accused of Japan-bashing in *Rising Sun*?
**A:** Yeah, sure. People who read the book tend to see one of two attitudes. Either they see this is a book about Japan, or a book about America. This is a book about America. My interest is America, and my whole focus is on how America is responding and behaving in the contemporary world. I'm not interested so much in how Japan is behaving because we have no control over that.

Unfortunately, our postwar policy has been to ask Japan to change so that our economic policies will dovetail. I think that is completely wrong. The solution is for America to change.

Anyway, you asked bashing. If Japan-bashing means an unreasoned and intemperate attack based on some irrational motive, then *Rising Sun* is not Japan-bashing.

**Q:** If we loosely define racism as an inherent desire in a person to promote and advance the interests of his or her race, I would contend, for the sake of discussion, that most people are racist. And that racism, as defined, can be a good and healthy thing. Would you agree?
**A:** No. No, I think we live in an increasingly small world, and to make divisions based on race is not to anyone's benefit.

**Q:** How about nationality?
**A:** I think nationality is inevitable and necessary. The reason is that, although we may be moving toward a world economy, many aspects of economic behavior are still determined by nationality—they just are. In other words, I can buy a car that comes from many parts of the world now. But I will drive it on an American road; if I get in an accident, I will be in the American legal system; if I get injured, I'll be in the American healthcare system.

So, it's not unreasonable to imagine that, at least as we're in a transition to a world economy, it's still necessary now to pay attention to how our country is doing economically in comparison with other countries. To become poor, to move in the direction of decline, to have the good-paying jobs disappear, to abandon our manufacturing sector, to not have a national economic policy as do our competitors—these are all bad ideas.

**Q:** Has the continued decline in the Japanese stock market, their falling real-estate value and shrinking foreign investment caused you to rethink your views of Japanese-American business dealings?
**A:** No, not at all. I've not seen figures on what the growth of the Japanese GNP will be this year. You hear stories about economic distress in Japan, but you see that the growth rate is going down to four percent from five percent. If this country had a four percent growth rate, we'd all feel like we were pumped full of testosterone.

**Q:** How did you feel when Matsushita bought Universal Studios?
**A:** Fine. It didn't bother me a bit, because that sale doesn't have large economic consequences for the nation. Did it bother you?

**Q:** Yes. My reaction was best put by Akio Morita, whom you quoted at the end of *Rising Sun*, saying, "If you don't want Japan to buy it, don't sell it." I was more aggravated by the owners of Universal than I was by Matsushita. In the book, you seem as ready to blame the U.S. for its own decline as you are to blame Japan. True?
**A:** There's no question it's an American problem.

**Q:** What allowed us to contribute so willingly to our own weakening? Greed? Altruism? Shortsightedness? Arrogance?
**A:** (Following a large sigh) You have to look back at broad time periods. It's possible now to argue that Americans have had no increase in real earnings power since 1962. Some economists would dispute that and set the date at 1973.

Either way, the country is in a steady, consistent, and ongoing decline. Why? That's an extended conversation. I'll just mention three things I think are of equal importance.

First, American business emerged from the postwar period in a position of tremendous superiority. Principal competitors of pre–World War II—Germany and Japan—are devastated. So American business is pumped up from wartime production, and everyone is feeling really good. We are on top of the world. That inevitably breeds complacency, and Americans had a long period of complacency.

Secondly, in the postwar period, Americans turned away from quality as the principal goal of manufacturing and made cost the principal goal. Japanese, restructuring their companies, made exactly the opposite decision. American quality-control experts who worked in America during the

Second World War became very nearly living treasures in Japan. So Japan and Germany have had decades of structuring business in the direction of quality, whereas Americans have had decades structuring business according to . . . other principles.

Thirdly, the cost of capital. The decline of the individual investor and rise of the institutional investor as the primary player in the stock market, and the change in tax laws so there's no advantage in long-term as opposed to short-term investment, have meant that the American stock market is now entirely speculative.

No one invests in a company anymore, in the way it was done in the '50s, say, because they believe the company is good. They buy because they think the price of the stock will rise or fall. What this means is that American managers are obliged to manage in the short term. There's no incentive for an investor to hang on with a company for the long term. In Japan, savings—up to a certain point—are tax free. Why is that not also true in America? You want savings? Then don't tax it as ordinary income.

**Q:** OK, a shift of focus. As you probably know, your statement in *Rising Sun,* that two floors of the Hitachi Chemical Research building at the University of California, Irvine, are accessible only with Japanese passports, caused quite a ripple at UCI. But the university says your statement isn't true. What do you say?

**A:** My understanding is there is a building on that campus, part of which is private and closed. How closed is the subject of this debate. My answer would be that the sentence I have in the book is not technically accurate. But the feeling is not wrong. Is the sentence wrong? It's not wrong enough. There's a problem of Japanese investment in American universities. We are not being careful about where the money is coming from. More than ten percent of the endowed chairs at MIT are paid for by Japanese corporations. Is anybody worried about that?

**Q:** Your critics say that you're exploiting an irrational fear of Japan, making Japan a kind of economic great white shark. Was *Rising Sun* written with an eye for the U.S. book market, or from your heart?

**A:** Absolutely from my heart.

**Q:** Do you have Japanese friends?

**A:** (Laughs) Yes, I still do.

**Q:** Without talking specifics, would you describe the advance from your Japanese publisher as large, small, or in-between?
**A:** I would say the advance is a lot.

**Q:** Any tugging at your soul there?
**A:** For a Japanese translation? No. I think it's very important it be translated in Japan. I'm not xenophobic. I believe we should be in business with Japan. What would I do, say "no" to a translation? I wrote the book to be read.

# *Jurassic Park*: Michael Crichton on Adapting His Novel to the Screen

## Steve Biodrowski/1993

From *Cinefantastique*, August 1993. Reprinted by permission of Steve Biodrowski.

In his novel *Jurassic Park*, Michael Crichton comes close—or so it would seem to a careless reader—to reworking the standard science fiction plot of portraying the havoc that erupts when scientists meddle in things they were not meant to experiment with. However, instead of telling us that there are some things man was not meant to know, *Jurassic Park* tells us there are things we cannot know. The plot of the disaster which engulfs the park is an illustration of the book's theme: that there are limits to our ability to understand and control the world and that science, whose premise is that we can understand and control everything, is an outdated system that needs to be replaced by a new paradigm.

Of course, that's not what's going to draw audiences to theatres this summer. People will come because they want to see dinosaurs roaring and rampaging across the big screen. And as a matter of fact, Crichton originally conceived his dinosaur-cloning story as a screenplay, minus the thematic subtext. "I had become interested in the notion of obtaining dinosaur DNA and cloning a dinosaur in 1983," he recalled of his initial effort. "The script didn't work, and I just waited to see if I could ever figure out how to make it work. It took quite a few years.

"It was a very different story," said Crichton of the original script. "It was about the person who did the cloning, operating alone and in secret. It just wasn't satisfactory. The real conclusion for me was that what you really wanted in a story like this was to have a sort of natural environment in which people and dinosaurs could be together. You wanted the thing that never happened in history: people in the forest and swamps at the same time as dinosaurs. Once that notion began to dictate how the story would proceed, then everything else fell into place, because there are certain things that I wanted to avoid, like the dinosaurs in New York City—that's been done."

Working with his new slant on the story, Crichton opted to write a novel. "I didn't revise the script," he said. "By the time I got around to doing it, there were other considerations. The most important is that it wasn't clear that anyone would ever make this story into a movie, because it would be very expensive. So one way to get the story done was to write a book. I could do that."

Despite the story's origins as a screenplay, the novel expounds on its thematic material in depth, mostly through the character of Ian Malcolm, played by Jeff Goldblum in the film, a mathematician whose eponymous theory "The Malcolm Effect" predicts the failure of the park. Of course, this material had to be condensed or deleted when the story came full circle to being a script again. "I feel very strongly that books should be the best books they can be, and you should not worry about what the movie will do," Crichton said of his uncinematic approach, which makes the novel stand up as a work in its own right rather than a stepping stone to a film deal. "In movies, a little bit of that kind of dialogue goes a long way. A movie like *Jurassic Park* is not the format to have extended discussions on the scientific paradigm."

Crichton did several initial screenplay drafts for Spielberg, retaining the basics of his novel in condensed form. "I think everyone's feeling was they liked the book in its overall shape and structure, and they wanted to keep that. So the question was how to get it on film since there are some parts—but not a tremendous number of parts—where it's clear that you can just lift it out and the structure remains. It was a question of paring down and trying to keep things from the original, simplifying."

Further describing the adaptation process, Crichton went on to note that, "It's a fairly long book, and the script can only have somewhere between ten and twenty percent of the content. So what you're really trying to do is make a sort of short story that reproduces the quality of the novel and has all the big scenes retained and has the logical flow that appears in the much longer and more extended argument.

"A similar issue has to do with what you call 'visceral things,'" said the author-adapter. "You can have gory descriptions in a book, because everyone is their own projectionist. I've always found it unwise to do that in a movie, because it throws you out of the movie. As soon as you see guts, you immediately think, 'Where did they get them? How did they do it?' You do not believe for a moment that that's actually happening. Since I see it as an insoluble problem to present viscera, the movie wisely doesn't do that. I also think the explicitness of the violence serves a different purpose [in the book]. You don't have certain advantages a movie has, so in a way the violence is a way to say, 'These are real dinosaurs, and take them seriously, O Reader.' In the movie, if they look wonderful, then you take them seriously; you don't have to see them tear people open. Your decision about taking them seriously is based on other things, so [graphic violence is] unnecessary.

In the adapting process, Crichton was forced to drop several scenes he would like to have retained, but his previous experience as a screenwriter taught him to be philosophical about the process. Noted Crichton, "Scenes went for all kinds of reasons: budget reasons, practical reasons, in the sense that they were difficult to do; they went out of the belief that they were repetitive in some way. But I think the primary thing that drives something like this is budget. You have to stop somewhere and where you stop, people will say, 'Oh, that was my favorite scene and it's not in.'"

Although authors sometimes adapt their own novels to the screen in order to try to protect their work from hampering filmmakers, this was not Crichton's intention; in fact, he did not initially intend to do the adaptation himself. "I didn't have it in my mind to do the script, but Steven said, 'We really need somebody to pare this thing down into some kind of manageable shape so we know what to build and it has to happen fast.' I said, 'I do have the advantage of having tried many versions of this, so I know what works; I'll whack it down. Then when you want to do your character polishes, get somebody else.' I really wasn't able to stay with the project for three years; I had other things to do. I really didn't want to do the script; I had a lot of confidence in Spielberg.

"There are disadvantages to having the original writer," continued Crichton. "People think writers fall in love with their own words. I don't have any sense of that at all. What's difficult for me is that in doing a story like this, you do several drafts which change the story dramatically from one to another—at least that was what happened in this book. So you've rethought it several times; now you have to rethink it again for a movie, and it's just hard to rethink it too many times. It's hard to take the same elements, toss them up in the air and rearrange them again and again and again."

Crichton is confident that those elements have been rearranged into a satisfactory order. "I think it's going to be a pretty amazing movie," he suggested enthusiastically. "I think it's going to have stuff in it that people will be floored by—they are not going to believe what they see. That's always nice."

# The Admirable Crichton

## Zoe Heller/1994

From *Vanity Fair*, January 1994. Reprinted by permission of Zoe Heller.

When Michael Crichton, author of *Jurassic Park* and *Rising Sun*, turned fifty last year, one of his friends gave him a hand-drawn birthday card depicting fifty of his favorite things. In the Santa Monica bungalow where Crichton writes his bestselling books and where I have come to meet him, the birthday card, now framed, hangs amid a selection of Jasper Johns prints on the living-room wall.

Many of the items on its list are unremarkable. It is nice to know that Crichton likes Theater, Blondes, his wife (the actress Anne-Marie Martin), his daughter (four-year-old Taylor), Aspen, Film, Computers, Harvard, and Good Wine—but not, in the end, particularly surprising. More interesting are the abstract nouns that have been included: Balance, Clarity, Brevity, Vision, Global Thinking, Strategy, Direction, Elegance, Excellence, Beauty.

I am wondering if there isn't something a little icy and Nietzschean about a man who counts brevity and global thinking among his fifty favorite things when Crichton, who was taking a phone call when his secretary let me in, arrives in the living room to greet me. He is vertiginously tall—six feet nine, to be exact—and has to stoop to make it through the doorway.

"So, you like blondes?" I ask chattily as we settle down in our chairs and he crosses his great spaghetti legs.

He pauses for a long time before answering—so long, in fact, that I have started to say something else by the time he finally speaks. "Three of my four wives have been blonde," he says. "Make of that what you will." He digs into a bowl of cereal—something grainy and healthful-looking—and offers me a cool smile.

Crichton has the super-calm, detached manner and the propensity to curt, slightly gnomic utterance that you often find in shrinks. He observes you like a shrink, too—quietly nodding as you start babbling to fill in his silences. Even his editor at Knopf, Sonny Mehta—a man with quite a reputation of his own for formidable taciturnity—admits to finding Crichton's self-containment a little awesome. "Michael doesn't talk much," he says. "He just acts."

This can be daunting—especially at eight in the morning. Santa Monica is only beginning to wake up: it will be another three hours, at least, before the girls with Rollerblades and bored expressions begin whizzing up and down the beach walkways. The cabdrivers waiting outside the hotels are still slumped over their wheels. The roads are dead calm. But here, on a pretty residential street just north of Wilshire Boulevard, the laconic super-author has been up for hours.

Today, he explains, since he's not working on a novel, he is taking things pretty easy. In the first stages of a book, he drives here, from his rather grander residence two miles away, at six in the morning. As the book proceeds, he will get up earlier and earlier. "It's five, then it's four, then it's three," he says. "Eventually, I'm going to bed at ten and getting up at two."

He knows, because he has a computer program that keeps track of it, exactly what his work rate is. "I am not in any way a natural writer. I find writing difficult and I am always looking for ways to do it quicker. I write in very short bursts—ten or fifteen minutes. Sometimes, I can write a page an hour. On a good day I can write five pages. The average is four pages. I can do a first draft in forty days."

For the duration of that draft, he lives the life of an eremite. He works seven days a week and cuts out all leisure activity apart from jogging and some time spent with his wife and daughter. In an effort to reduce unfocused variety, he contrives to eat exactly the same thing for lunch every day.

"When Michael is working," his wife, Anne-Marie, says, "he works hard. Toward the end of a book, it's like I'm living with a body and Michael is somewhere else. Then, when the book's finished, Michael comes back."

Lesser mortals can find Crichton's rigor hard to take. Mike Backes, his co-writer on the screenplay for *Rising Sun*, describes the minimalist environment that Crichton has developed to enhance his writing efficiency. "External distractions are practically nonexistent," he says. "Every paper clip is organized." Adapting to such working methods was, he adds, like "trying to leap onto the wing of a passing Concorde." Despite the steely discipline, Crichton's friend writer Joan Didion says she is amazed at the idea of Crichton's being considered aloof or Howard Hughesian. "He's just in another place," she says. "He is shy and there is a great natural reserve about Michael, but it is not actual weirdness. He is one of the smartest people I know."

Using this intelligence, Crichton has produced some of the most lucrative prose in literary history. *Jurassic Park*, first published in 1991 and currently in its sixty-sixth edition, has now sold more than nine million copies. *Rising Sun* has sold more than six million. Since June 1992, sales of Michael Crichton books have reached thirty million in the United States alone. Worldwide we're talking McDonald's figures. The number of Crichton books in print has now passed the 100 million mark.

Lynn Nesbit, Crichton's agent for some twenty-five years, refuses to reveal how these sales translate as royalty statements, or what kind of advance her client will command now that he is about to negotiate a new book contract with Knopf. Doubleday's David Gernert, who edits John Grisham, Crichton's biggest rival on the bestseller lists, says the advance will certainly be seven figures, "possibly eight, depending on how many books it's for. Crichton has yet to go over the million mark in sales of hardbacks, but *Disclosure* may be the one to do it."

You can also get a sense of Crichton's earning power from the movie deals he has made in recent years. Together, the film versions of *Jurassic Park* and *Rising Sun* earned Crichton around $3 million. The deal he made with Warner Bros. in June, for his latest novel, *Disclosure*, a novel about sexual harassment to be published in January, is worth $3.5 million. Long before he had completed the manuscript, the rumor that Crichton was writing a novel about gender politics was sufficient to make Hollywood's studio executives mad with desire. Bob Bookman of CAA, who conducted the auction for the film rights, said he had never received so many calls about a book. The $3.5 million figure was, at the time Crichton signed the deal, the highest that had ever been paid for film rights on a book. (A couple of weeks later, not wishing to be outdone in extravagant gestures, Universal paid John Grisham $3.75 million for a book he hadn't yet written.)

Crichton shrugs and shifts uncomfortably in his chair when the subject of money is raised. He truly isn't much interested, he says. "I think it's true what John Kenneth Galbraith says—that there's a very great difference between not enough money and enough. And very little difference between enough money and more than enough. When I was a student, I was always on a tight budget. I wanted to be able to go to a restaurant and order without looking at the prices on the menu. That was what signified 'enough.' But

I also saw how people developed a very expensive existence and then had to work to maintain their lifestyle. I made a sort pact to myself that I could always go back to a one-bedroom apartment. I always wanted to work because the work interested me and not because I needed the money."

He admits that he may have welshed on this pact with himself. He says that despite his phenomenal earnings in recent years he would only be able to go at most eighteen months without working before his standard of living began to suffer. "And I'm concerned that I'm getting used to having money!" Nonetheless, he is adamant that *Disclosure* was not written with an eye to what would make the bestseller list.

His story of a female boss who sexually harasses her male employee advances a generally skeptical view of attempts to render corporate life an offense-free zone. It also argues against any "special protection" for women. Like *Jurassic Park* and *Rising Sun*, it seems destined to spark a national furor. "To say anything on this subject," Crichton comments a little wearily, "is to be controversial. To say anything." But the lure of Mammon, he says, did not motivate his choice of subject. "I don't have any sense of the commercial marketplace. I feel that when you start to think, 'Will this sell?,' that's death. As soon as you allow those considerations into your thought, then you're lost, you know?"

I glance at him to check whether he is saying this for real or just being cute. But he looks perfectly earnest. Cuteness doesn't figure large in Crichton's conversation.

"People do imagine cynicism in me," he observes. "I don't know why. I'm the least cynical person I know. I'm clearly often culpable of the charge of naiveté. But I'm not cynical. Cynicism is cheap."

There are several reasons people might want to impute cynicism to Michael Crichton—not least of all envy. The gods are famously unfair in allocating gifts among mortals, but we like to believe that their decisions follow some system, however crude. Great beauties, we observe, are rarely blessed with great brains. And, conversely, towering intellects don't often come in gorgeous packages. By such generalizations are we reassured that a sort of rough justice does, after all, prevail. But Crichton messes everything up.

The knowledge that a man with an uncanny knack for writing bestsellers is also handsome (he was recently voted by *People* magazine one of "The 50 Most Beautiful People in the World"), tall enough to be a basketball champion, and ludicrously fit (he looks twenty years younger than his age) is enough to make some people feel a little queasy. That he is also academically brilliant represents what is generally known as the last straw. Just how many good fairies were in attendance at Crichton's birth, people ask. And what were they on—amphetamines?

Crichton's curriculum vitae makes for wide-eyed reading. After graduating summa cum laude from Harvard (with a thesis on ancient Egyptian racial history) he was a visiting lecturer in anthropology at Cambridge University at the age of twenty-three. He trained as a doctor at Harvard Medical School and paid his way by writing thrillers—at first under a pseudonym and then under his real name. By the time he qualified to practice medicine, he had already written a bestseller—*The Andromeda Strain*—and sold it to Hollywood. He then pursued postgraduate studies at the Salk Institute in California for a year, before he decided that he was "too imaginative" for medicine, and took up writing full-time instead.

It gets worse. Aside from having written thirteen novels, each of which displays an intimate knowledge of a different, specialist subject—Viking warriors, primatology, neurobiology, biophysics, international economics, genetics—Crichton has directed seven movies (including *Coma, The Great Train Robbery,* and *Westworld*). He is a computer expert who wrote one of the first books about information technology. He has designed a computer game called Amazon. He is a committed collector of modern art and the author of a learned study of Jasper Johns. He is a fine cook—his preferred cuisines are Italian and Indian. He has also built his own rocket and flown it to the moon . . . no—just kidding.

"I feel very blessed, very lucky," he says of his polymathic achievements. "But if you push me, I don't know what luck is." He massages his face thoughtfully, leaving large white fingerprints on his pink-brown skin. "I think . . . my perception still is that accomplishment is a consequence of effort." (Crichton often talks this way—picking up his interlocutor's ragged sentences, tidying up the ideas a little, and then submitting a careful, superrational response.)

Insofar as he will acknowledge the concept of luck, good or otherwise, he thinks he is probably lucky to have had parents who encouraged his intellectual development. He grew up in Roslyn on Long Island in New York State, the eldest of four children. His relationship with his father, an executive editor of *Advertising Age*, was not a happy one. (In *Travels*, his book of autobiographical essays, Crichton describes his father as "a first-rate son of a bitch." His immediate response to his father's sudden death at the age of fifty-seven was, he writes, "'Yea? Fuck him.' . . . That pretty much summed up my feelings.") Nonetheless, he credits both his father and mother with giving him a very useful belief in his own abilities.

"My parents," he explains, "were very inclined not to set limits on the exploration of their children. They were always saying, 'You can do that.' So I never had the feeling there was some area that I was incompetent in. I mean, computer programming—why not? If it's something to learn, I can learn it. I didn't have that sense of 'I'm not good at that' or 'I can't do that.'" He pauses for a moment to consider. "Well, there were a few areas where I did feel that, rightly or wrongly."

"Oh? What were they?" I ask. (The question comes a little too eagerly.)

"Well, I think I have bad balance, so all things that require balance—like skiing—I feel I'm not good at." Not much of an Achilles' heel, but, hey, it will have to do.

Crichton's continual mastery of new subjects and ideas can boggle even those who know him well. "A while back, I heard he'd given a lecture on hotel design," Sonny Mehta says. "I was somewhat surprised, so I asked him about it. He said, sure, he'd become interested in the subject while he was doing research into controlled environments for one of his books."

And it is this autodidactic impulse, rather than any longing for the big time, that has really shaped and driven Crichton's career, his friends say. "His books all emerge organically from his own interests," Bob Gottlieb, his former editor at Knopf, says. "That's what makes them different from everybody else's. They stem from his intellectual curiosity, from Michael becoming interested in a certain subject and wanting to figure it out."

To the extent that his intellectual curiosity has often interrupted the steady production of novels, it has probably impeded his commercial success, Gottlieb goes on to say.

"Michael's books have been successful for a very long time, but one of the reasons why he had to wait for the kind of success he's having now is that he's moved in so many directions. Most bestselling careers have a rhythm to them—a book a year, say—but Michael has always pursued whatever he's interested in and been ready to leave writing to do other things."

In the Hollywood context, all of this helps to make Crichton a little bit of an oddball. "We prefer crappy, dive restaurants to expensive French places," his wife says. "We're both homebodies. We don't feel good going to Hollywood parties—we find it's just anxiety-provoking, so we stay away."

Crichton's retiring ways have sometimes been interpreted not just as eccentric but as cold or standoffish. "There is this idea about Michael—that he is just locked within his mind as far as emotions go," Mike Backes says. "It's really not true. He can be a little buttoned-down with people he doesn't know very well . . . but he has a lot of emotional accessibility." Henry Aronson, an old friend of Crichton's from Harvard, believes that Crichton, for all his wunderkind credentials, is a profoundly shy man. "Shy people are often perceived as being clipped or arrogant," he says, "and certainly you would never employ Michael to work a crowd for you. He's not good at that stuff at all. But the idea that he is cold or whatever is completely wrong. He is a wondrous gem of a resource as a friend. He's just very private."

The point is driven home on my second stopover at his bungalow office. We had agreed that today we would visit his house, but overnight he had second thoughts and decided that he doesn't feel comfortable letting me into his home. Instead, he takes me over there in his Land Rover and allows me to look at its exterior. The house, which appears to have two stories (Crichton's office will not confirm this), was built in the 1920s and is now painted a pretty, cornflower blue. It seems a rather modest place for a megaselling writer to shack up. It has no pool. The front drive is filled with Mexican workmen who are in the midst of an elaborate project to shore up the house's foundations and keep the hillside in back from sliding down. "That's where all the dinosaur money has gone," Crichton sighs. "It's been spent on holding back the hills."

The workmen begin to stare at us with curiosity. They are wondering, no doubt, why their boss is lurking in a car outside his own house, with a strange female. Crichton is perfectly friendly about this rather bizarre outing and clearly doesn't want to be obstructive. ("Do you want to drive by one more time?" he asks.) But he is firm. He isn't going to relent and let me inside. I feel vaguely foolish driving up and down the road, rubbernecking at a housefront, so I put him out of his misery and we leave.

"Michael has to guard his privacy very carefully," Anne-Marie tells me later when I comment on her husband's reticence. "All the publicity and attention has made it much more difficult for him to just be a mole in his room, and that's what Michael likes to do best." Even when the attention takes the form of extravagant approbation, Crichton is apparently unmoved. Appearing in the *People*-magazine list of "The 50 Most Beautiful" struck him as ludicrous, and he aims for a similar indifference to the critical attention he receives. "I am reminded," he says, "of that famous comment made by Tommy Lasorda, the manager of the Dodgers. 'Opinions are like assholes. Everyone's got one.'" But some opinions clearly have the power to get him riled. "I don't like being attacked," he admits. Thus, while he claims he is resigned to being placed at the bottom end of the literary caste system—to having his books dismissed as airport reading—he is clearly maddened by what he sees as a critical bias in favor of highfalutin obfuscation.

"Listen, I have absolutely no difficulty being obscure. I don't think it's difficult to write prose where you have to read it ten times and by the end you're still saying, 'What the hell is he talking about?' But I think there is some obligation to keep your audience awake and interested. Even as a student, I hated Henry James. I hated it. Every time I read one, it was like, Why? No! What is this? No! I mean, Jane Austen—of course, please. But it was absolutely obvious to me that a lot of Henry James was incredibly badly written. It looks like a first draft! I have always been drawn to people whose reputation is less secure. I like Poe and Conan Doyle and Louis Stevenson."

Even his biggest fans are inclined to admit that Crichton is not a great stylist. "He's not interested in literary style," Lynn Nesbit says. "That's not what he's after. He's interested in educating people." But Crichton contends that he is actually rather interested in matters of style. "It seems to me that I spend a tremendous amount of time working on the prose and engaged in some intricate juggling act about what I'm going to say in a way that's comprehensible to someone else."

The commonplace complaint that his novels are entirely "plot-driven"— that his characters are mere ciphers—also bugs him. It springs, he says, from a misunderstanding of what he is trying to do. The first epigraph to his 1972 novel, *The Terminal Man*, is a quotation from the English scientist J. B. S. Haldane: "I have come to the conclusion that my subjective account of my own motivation is largely mythical on almost all occasions. I don't know why I do things."

Crichton believes that none of us really knows why we do things. (After years of being in therapy, he has concluded that it is mostly tosh: "The superego," he says, "does not have the validity of Newton's law of gravitation. Bring me someone's superego—cut a brain open and hand it to me. It's not there! It's all baloney, all late-nineteenth-century Viennese wank.") And if we don't know why we do things, it is not, he believes, the novelist's job to make guesses.

"So all you can plausibly point to as an author is your characters' behavior?"

"Yes. That's absolutely right. Because everything is supposition. . . . I think the people of the twenty-first century will look back at us the way we look back at people who believed in the four humors. They'll laugh and say, 'Those were the days when human beings thought you could explain why people did something. They thought they knew why people acted as they did.'"

Crichton's real interest as a novelist is in Big Ideas. Increasingly, his novels have come to function as the mere wrapping paper for political or philosophical arguments. Lynn Nesbit calls them "issue books." The reviews they receive treat them accordingly—dissecting their theories in much the same way that a treatise or textbook might be dissected. This was particularly true of *Rising Sun*, a book which was widely taken to task for advancing racist ideas about the Japanese and which has served to establish Crichton, in some quarters, as a dyed-in-the-wool reactionary. Crichton insists that his political opinions are not so easy to categorize. He has great admiration for Ross Perot. ("There's no market research with Perot," he says. "He's just saying what he thinks is right. Everybody else is a manipulator of opinion polls or whatever the political context is that they can manipulate. . . . I feel that the country needs a person of conviction.") But he is, he claims, a "liberal" on most social issues.

"I guess I'm a social liberal and a fiscal conservative—a combination that tends to produce some areas of conflict!" he says. "I mean, I was at a thing for Al Gore the other night and a very well-known Hollywood person came up to me. He said, 'What are you doing here? You're not a liberal!'"

"What did you say?"

"I said what is true—I said, 'I don't vote the straight ticket on anything.' He says, 'Well, you're contrary.' I said, 'I'm not contrary!' If you notice, the people who really look at the world and draw their own conclusions, they tend to adopt positions which don't follow any easily defined alignment."

But Crichton knows very well that in the publishing niche he occupies nonaligned political positions tend to get traduced. When the first reviews of *Rising Sun* appeared, he had already begun to work on *Disclosure*, but he was so discouraged by the reactions that he temporarily ground to a halt. "I couldn't proceed for several months. I thought there was a possibility of such a strong response to this book that, emotionally, I wasn't sure I'd be able to do it." He now seems pretty much steeled for the inevitable onslaught.

As one reads *Disclosure*, it is quite easy to anticipate the form the onslaught will take. As with *Rising Sun*, the book's plot and dramatis personae, particularly when conveyed in broad strokes, are easily seen as serving a reactionary viewpoint: an extremely unsympathetic female protagonist makes a lurid sexual advance toward her male deputy (who is also a former boyfriend). When she is rebuffed, she claims that he has sexually harassed her. The male in question is given the option of leaving his job with a handsome payoff, but instead of going quietly he decides to fight back. His honorable struggle to preserve his career and good name sheds light on the double standards and knee-jerk hypocrisies that have come to characterize the feminist cause.

However much complicating nuance Crichton adds to this basic scheme, one might argue that the fundamental opposition of good man versus bitch-woman is what really takes root in the reader's consciousness. Crichton's fury that his "subtle" arguments about Japanese trade policy in *Rising Sun* were interpreted as "Yellow Peril"–style racism did not take into account the way in which mass entertainment tends to be consumed—the way it registers in the popular imagination. He is perhaps guilty of a similar naiveté concerning *Disclosure.* The book contains a far more complicated argument than any simple "anti-feminist" label would suggest, he says. It is an attempt to explore some of the problems, both ideological and practical, that often get overlooked in the debate about sexual harassment. "All these areas, it seems to me, are characterized by extremes that are black and white. Whether we're talking about rape or about sexual harassment, there is some category of behavior that everyone agrees is illegal and inappropriate. And there are some categories of behavior that everyone would agree are not illegal, but simply part of the wear and tear of daily life. And then, in the middle, there is a gray area where people differ. What's happened is we're attempting to find our way in this gray area."

By making the book's exemplary harasser a woman, Crichton says, he aimed to illustrate that abuse of power is not a male monopoly. The view of sexual harassment as an exclusively women's issue is predicated, he says, on a belief in special treatment for women which is profoundly anti-egalitarian. The feminist movement has, he claims, developed an unhealthy attachment to the cult of victimhood.

"People in this country now perceive great power in the strategy of terming themselves victims. I think it's a very bad deal to define yourself as a victim—a very bad strategy for women. I'm not in any way opposed to feminism as it was initially defined in this country. My view is that feminism has been phenomenally important and, in broad strokes, a very successful movement. But every movement enters a crisis when its initial goals start to be attained, and it is at that point that the pedants enter—that you begin to get foolish elaborations. It's like the politicians who lived through the Cold War. The Berlin Wall comes down, Russia collapses—but they can't give up the Cold War. They're still talking in exactly the same old terms, and you can see them becoming fixed in some anachronistic posture."

His view of feminism, as having achieved pretty much everything it set out to achieve, is perhaps a little premature, I suggest. Most of its triumphs have, after all, not been felt outside the ranks of the white upper-middle class.

"Absolutely," Crichton says. "No question about it—but that's the group I'm talking about. If you want to talk about blacks and Hispanics, then you're talking about something that, I'm sorry to say, feminism in this country has never addressed. And nobody knows it better than black women. They often say to the feminists, 'I'm not with you—my mother worked for your mother.'"

But even if you define feminism as an exclusively white, middle-class movement, it still seems a little hasty to assume that its most important work has been done. There are lots of women even among the privileged group that Crichton describes who still encounter problems in combining family and career. There are lots of men who still have problems dealing with powerful women. I remind Crichton of an essay in *Travels* in which he describes the unpleasant experience of being "treated as a sex object" by a twenty-eight-year-old Los Angeleno career girl called "Andrea."

"I lay there in bed, feeling worse and worse, while she got dressed," he writes of the postcoital scene, "and pretty soon she waved goodbye and then I heard the door slam . . . and I thought, I feel used."

Crichton says he doesn't have a particular problem with aggressive women. "I don't find aggressive behavior more unattractive in women. I just don't like it, whoever is being pushy." And there are plenty of men, he says, who feel very happy playing second fiddle to a female. "I know plenty of men who are, in essence, kept by their wives," he says. "Plenty! And they're quite content to be more home-focused, to earn less. It's just a question of picking the right mate!"

Crichton knows a lot about picking a mate. Although the problems he has experienced have not been those that average guys encounter in their search for a partner. Many of the women he has dated in the past proved to be too beautiful and too famous for comfort, he says. "You were always dealing with the attention that followed them at all times and it was just very hard to have a normal relationship."

At other times, his girlfriends found him too beautiful and famous for comfort.

"Even though you keep out of the spotlight for most of the time?"

"Yes, I was aware that they would go off into whatever their world was and people would say to them, 'Oh, you're going out with Michael Crichton. Blah, blah, blah,' and it would be made into something in their minds and I couldn't control that. Everyone has their stories—what they've heard, their points of view. This is a town that just parboils itself in gossip. I got very irritable about it, and there was a period when I decided that if I was seeing a woman and she came back to me and said, I've been talking to so-and-so-and-so and they say you're hostile to women or you live only in your head, I would stop seeing her."

That was a bit harsh.

"It was harsh, but I got annoyed about it. It's very important for me in an intimate relationship to be seen . . . seen for what I am. There is a fantasy about me—there is speculation about who and what I am—but there's an actual person, and I want the relationship to be about the actual person."

Even applying this vetting rule, Crichton has still managed to make a lot of mistakes. ("Haven't you ever heard of premarital sex?" Steve Martin once asked him.) But Crichton says getting married so often was surprisingly easy to do. "I'd fall in love and my notion of love relates to family and making a unit. I always thought it was better to do that married—that's what made me comfortable. I surely didn't marry everybody I met or even everybody I lived with. But as a general statement, what happened to the marriages was that we found ourselves in disagreement about goals. In one case, she wanted to start a family and I didn't. In another, I wanted to start a family and she didn't. These are very major gulfs. It's very difficult to bridge it when you really start to have diversions of that kind."

Throughout his first three marriages, he believes, he was an unhappy, confused person, "fumbling around" for a way to handle life. Occasionally, he would sense a sort of contentment in older friends like Jasper Johns or Sean Connery, but he had no notion of how to acquire it for himself. In particular, Connery, whom he directed in *The Great Train Robbery* in the late '70s and for whom he subsequently created the role of John Connor in *Rising Sun*, provided a puzzling source of inspiration. "Sean would sit there, and I would think, 'He has figured something out. What has he figured out?' I didn't know—I just knew he had his hands on something. . . . It took me a long time to understand the general shape of the issue, which is that at some point in your life you say, 'O.K., now what? Why? What for? Write another book? Why? How about another marriage? What for?' You know, you want to know, what are you doing?"

In search of answers, Crichton spent several years in the '80s traveling in remote areas of the world and trying out some of the more unconventional routes to enlightenment. He visited psychics, he had his aura "fluffed," he bent spoons, he traveled back to his past life as a gladiator in ancient Rome, he went to the desert and enjoyed very moving conversations with a cactus.

And, strangely enough, all of this nonsense seems to have proved helpful. Crichton came out the other end of the decade feeling a lot better. What made the crucial difference? What was the epiphany?

"Everything was helpful," he says.

"But not one thing in particular? Like talking to the cactus, say?"

"No, it isn't a one-thing thing. I mean, if you could get this into a store, if you could bottle it, there would be a run on it."

Pressed to divulge a little more, Crichton eventually elaborates. What has provided him with fulfillment turns out to be a suspiciously conventional-sounding set of precepts. "It's paradoxical, but diminished expectations seem to make for more happiness," he says. "You don't expect to eat birthday cake every night. And, actually, in the periods of your life when you did eat birthday cake every night, you were sick. It's not actually very rewarding to eat birthday cake like that."

Diminished expectations! It sounds like one of those T-shirt slogans: "I traveled back to a past life as a Roman gladiator and all I came back with were these lousy reduced expectations." Crichton waxes stern.

"Sean [Connery] once said something to me that I've never forgotten. He said, 'Discipline is always worthwhile.' That's absolutely right. But this is a society that thinks discipline is for drones or for people who don't know any better."

Crichton's journeys of discovery have earned him the intense admiration of his agent. "Michael," Lynn Nesbit says, "has gone through real periods of depression in his life—we're not talking about Mr. Narcissist here. But he's one of the few men I know who've really devoted time to thinking about their interior life. He has really tried to make changes."

And this readiness to make changes is what has finally enabled the success of his fourth marriage, Crichton believes. "In the past, I really did have the belief that if something was wrong in my relationships it was because the woman was wrong. Because how could I be wrong? I was perfect! And at some point it became clear to me that that simply couldn't be true. And I was having one of my on-again, off-again relationships with Anne-Marie and I just decided, you know, I really want this relationship and I'm going to do whatever it takes to make it work. What's it going to take to make it work? Well, you've got to change. O.K., I'll change."

In Anne-Marie he has found, he says, his perfect mate. "Sometimes when I talk to my wife, I'm aware of what a rare person she is. She's very beautiful, very athletic, very funny, and very smart. That combination is rare. I can really talk to her in a way that is natural to me and she understands it. She isn't always saying, 'What are you talking about? Why did you say that?' She sort of gets it." She is also tough, he says. "I mean, I know I'm no day at the beach, but she's tough. She's tough in all ways. She's physically tough, she's mentally tough, she's a pain in the neck, and she's great, you know?" Crucially, she never came home and reported rumors about him during their courtship. "She heard all the stories," Crichton says, referring to the usual remarks about his aloofness and emotional coldness, "but she never ever mentioned them. It was years later when she looked at me and said, 'Oh, God, you have no idea what people used to say about you.'"

Not only has Crichton now found the right relationship but, like so many men of his generation, he has also discovered the joys of late fatherhood. Driving me back to my hotel, he points to a miniature tiara lying on the floor of his Land Rover. "That," he says adoringly, "is part of Taylor's Princess Jasmine outfit." I look blank. "You know," he says, "from *Aladdin*." Family life has now superseded professional ambition in his priorities, he says, and at last, after many years of confusion, he has entered a "happy time."

"You know, the first therapist I ever saw," he says, "was a very distinguished senior person. I was young and my life was in disarray. He said to me, 'I look forward to every day. I get up eager to see what the day will bring.' And I thought, 'I don't. How do you get to do that? I get up bored. Or fearful. Or angry. Or hungover. But I don't get up excited. I'm just sort of dragging myself through it all.'" Crichton smiles a knowing, Zen smile. Things change. "Now," he says, "when I get up in the morning, I feel excited, too."

# An Interview with Michael Crichton

## Charlie Rose/1994

From *The Charlie Rose Show*, January 14, 1994. Reprinted by permission of Charlie Rose Inc.

**Rose:** Welcome to our broadcast. Tonight we'll have an hour-long conversation with bestselling author Michael Crichton. Depending on who you talk to he is either a renaissance man or, in terms of some, simply a commercial success. Few would disagree that he is one of the most prescient authors in America today. Michael Crichton is a trained physician, a film director, a cook, an art collector, a computer hack, and, of course, one of the most commercially successful novelists of our time. The author of *Jurassic Park*, *The Andromeda Strain*, *Rising Sun*, and others has more than one hundred million books in print. In his latest novel, *Disclosure*, he turns sexual harassment on its head—making the harasser a woman. The publisher has already printed 950,000 copies. I'm pleased to have him. Welcome.
**Crichton:** Thank you, Charlie.

**Rose:** It's great to have you here. I can also say this: Sunday week it will be number one on the *New York Times* bestseller list and it will knock Robert Waller—who's been on there forever, it seems—as the number one fiction in America; and probably for the first time, I assume, will give you a bestseller that sells more than a million copies in hardback. Right?
**Crichton:** Yes, that might happen.

**Rose:** So what do you think of all that?
**Crichton:** Pretty amazing. [Laughs]

**Rose:** [Laughs] All that work, all that energy. What does it mean to you?
**Crichton:** It's gratifying in one sense, and in another sense doing the work is where my primary interest is. I've always been very aware and I think it's necessary to feel this way: you write the book, you do it as well as you can,

and it comes out. What happens to it—if it sells a million copies or if it sells ten thousand copies—that's not to do with you.

**Rose:** I understand, but it says something—that you have touched a nerve; that this is good writing; that people want to read your story—that's basically what it says, right?
**Crichton:** I hope so. I'm not sure what it says.

**Rose:** What it says is somebody wants to read what you're writing. It's not about hype. It's about a book that people are reading. What do you think the nerve is you've touched? Why this book?
**Crichton:** There are two answers. One answer is that in the last few books the audience has been increasing.

**Rose:** That's right.
**Crichton:** That you do start to have an audience.

**Rose:** Crichton is a name brand.
**Crichton:** Yes, something like that. Or so many of the people liked the last book, so they'll read the next one; they found it interesting. That's part of it. The other thing is that there's a tremendous interest in society on the relations between the sexes, and harassment as an issue is a sort of distillation of that.

**Rose:** How did you come to write this story? First, just the notion of a plot dealing with a question of sexual politics; a question of sexual harassment; a question of the relationship between men and women?
**Crichton:** Somebody told me a story.

**Rose:** What story?
**Crichton:** A story about a man who was harassed by a woman who was his former lover.

**Rose:** And she was his superior in a company?
**Crichton:** She'd gotten the job he wanted. They had had a meeting behind closed doors. No one else was there. They both came out and accused the other of improper conduct. This was in 1988, before some of these issues, and it was told to me as an example of the kinds of difficulties that corporations can have in trying to assess how to deal with their employees. These

were two very highly placed, very valuable employees who had had a prior relationship and who were now at each other's throats.

**Rose:** Did a light bulb go off in your head?
**Crichton:** Yes. Immediately. [Laughs] And it wasn't somebody saying, "This is a good story for you to write." It was just talk.

**Rose:** Now what happens to you—are you out looking for ideas or are you just out, in a sense, and they come to you? In other words, you didn't say, "I've got to find another idea for my next novel after *Jurassic Park*. What's it going to be? Something's happening on the sexual landscape; I'm looking for the right peg."
**Crichton:** No.

**Rose:** All of a sudden you hear a good story and you say, "Wow."
**Crichton:** Yes. I thought, "That's a good story. That's interesting." What interested me was the reversal of roles because I thought that made a new opportunity to look at the assumptions society makes about who's responsible, who's at fault, who's the aggressor, who's the victim. I thought, "that's a very interesting thing," and then it sat there for several years.

**Rose:** Sat in the back of your head?
**Crichton:** Right.

**Rose:** You didn't touch it, you didn't do anything, you didn't do any research, you weren't reading about this stuff, you didn't go out and say, "I've got to understand feminism. I've got to understand what's been happening in this society."
**Crichton:** I did in a sort of informal way because it was an interest anyway. My way of working is to have an idea like that and then see if it continues to push at me. At some point I think, "Well, I guess I have to write this."

**Rose:** At what point is that?
**Crichton:** I had finished *Rising Sun* and I had decided to start working on this. *Rising Sun* had this odd thing for me—it was finished quite a long time before it was published. So I was well into the next book when it came out. Then there was this great controversy about *Rising Sun* and here I am writing about sexual harassment and I just stopped.

**Rose:** Because you thought you were heading for another controversy and you'd had it with *Rising Sun*?
**Crichton:** Worse.

**Rose:** It was distasteful for you?
**Crichton:** Yes.

**Rose:** Because they perceived it as Japanese-bashing on your part?
**Crichton:** Racism.

**Rose:** Racism; that was not what you intended.
**Crichton:** Not what I intended and it's a very, very tough criticism.

**Rose:** What's the risk here? [Touches copy of *Disclosure*] The risk here is that you're saying . . . Well, you tell me. What do you think the risk is—that the controversy might attend this book?
**Crichton:** I hesitate to guess. I think in any discussion about gender relations the feelings are so strong that people kind of lift off. I've watched a lot of discussions on television with people who're discussing these issues in the last six or seven months because I'm trying to see how it goes. The most striking characteristic is how confused it is; how people will talk about three or four different ideas at the same moment. They'll talk about legal issues and social relations issues and feelings issues—they're all mixed together.

**Rose:** In fact, you don't believe there has been a real genuine dialogue about the question of harassment in America, do you?
**Crichton:** No. I think men have been silent.

**Rose:** Men have been silent?
**Crichton:** Yes.

**Rose:** What is it men should be saying? That we should not be characterized or stereotyped because of our chromosomes?
**Crichton:** That's certainly part of it, yes; this notion that we are the testosterone-poisoned sex.

**Rose:** Always the aggressor and never the victim.
**Crichton:** Yes—always on the sexual lookout; always predatory; always violent; always insensitive; always withdrawn—I think is a remarkable stereo-

type. You cannot make a similar stereotype about women, although women will make it about themselves. They'll say they're nurturing and cooperative and so on, and that's part of the current ideology in some feminist groups.

**Rose:** Alright, let me draw you out on this, come on. [Laughs]
**Crichton:** [Laughs] Let's commit suicide.

**Rose:** Well, let's do it together here. Here's what you believe: You believe sexual harassment is about power, it's not about gender; and that the more women who climb into the power chair, the more sexual harassment by women we'll see.
**Crichton:** I think so. I believe this—and I should say immediately: there are not good statistics, so to debate this on the level of statistical things is a fool's game.

**Rose:** Most sexual harassment against men is men against men, isn't it?
**Crichton:** Yes.

**Rose:** Twenty percent. About five percent is women against men.
**Crichton:** Yes, so eighty percent of male claims are against other men. The overwhelming majority are women against men. The reason why I have this feeling is that it is my perception in life and my reading of the literature that there are essentially no differences in behavior between men and women—adult men and women. So I would not expect as women move into positions of power that they would behave in substantially different ways from men, which suggests as far as I can tell that a certain number of people in supervisory positions will abuse, in various ways, their subordinates.

**Rose:** But women step forward, as you know, to say—some say, "It's not that way because women are different. They are more different than you think they are between the sexes—as adults. It's not going to happen as you think it's going to happen because they are just different about power." Now, how do we prove one point or the other?
**Crichton:** I think this will all come clear. I'm interested in the kinds of informal things. For example, *Working Woman* did a survey of women about women bosses. There was a tremendous dissatisfaction among working women about their bosses because they had the expectation that they would behave in a way that was more nurturing; that they would be supportive, mentoring women; that they would have a kind of cooperative thing. It

turned out that they were doing the bottom line and being just as tough and just as aggressive as the man who had previously held the job. When the women themselves were confronted, they would say, "Hey! I have a career; I have a corporate position; my job is to make money; get out of my face." The reality of hierarchical structures is that the hierarchy strongly determines the behavior of an individual within the hierarchy. None of us in a hierarchy have a tremendous amount of flexibility. I think there certainly may be some changes in tone and attitude, but the notion that major changes will occur because someone of a different sex sits behind the seat is going to prove to be a fantasy.

**Rose:** If you are looking for confirmation of your point, I suspect you could look at the exercise of power by women in politics. It has not been noticeably different because of their gender.
**Crichton:** No, and everyone agrees that that's the case.

**Rose:** Exactly, and you're saying the same thing will happen in terms of sexual relationships.
**Crichton:** Absolutely.

**Rose:** Power will control. Dominion will control.
**Crichton:** Yes.

**Rose:** You quote Katherine Graham saying, "Power is neither male nor female."
**Crichton:** That's right. She said it—she believes it.

**Rose:** And Henry Kissinger's "it's the ultimate aphrodisiac."
**Crichton:** [Laughs] Yes.

**Rose:** What do you think we will understand more because you flipped the characters over? This is Meredith "man-cruncher" Johnson as the harasser. What will we understand more about the issue because you did that?
**Crichton:** We're already starting to have some women in positions of power who are starting to feel and complain about what the harassment threat can mean, and how it can—sometimes at least—be unfairly applied. There is absolutely an unacknowledged vulnerability of the superior person, whether male or female; and there is an unacknowledged power of the subordinate or "victim"—which is equally unacknowledged.

**Rose:** There's power in the potential to claim, "I've been harassed."
**Crichton:** Absolutely.

**Rose:** There's no presumption of innocence.
**Crichton:** No, there's an assumption of guilt. It'll freeze your career. It'll freeze your position in the corporation. It may ruin your career. By the time the thing gets settled—thirty, sixty days down the line; if it goes to litigation its several years—your life may be over.

**Rose:** Do you know men and women who are paranoid about this? Who've changed their behavior?
**Crichton:** I know attorneys, which is interesting. The attorneys who handle these cases are the most cautious people I know in the workplace. A lot of them are what many people would consider very extreme or paranoid. They will not take any kind of a business trip with a female colleague; will not get on an airplane with a female colleague.

**Rose:** Will not have drinks in a hotel somewhere out of town.
**Crichton:** Absolutely not. Will not. Will not under any circumstances. Will be fired before they do it; say, "If you want to send me on a trip, send a woman and another woman, or another man who is willing to take the risk, or send me with a man. I will not travel with a woman. I will not risk it."

**Rose:** How did you prepare for this? There's a lot of thinking now going on about feminism. We did a thing the other day, here on this broadcast the other night, about gender. It was billed as a gender war but it became much more an examination of the changing attitude towards women's sexuality by feminists. Naomi Wolf was here, and some other people. Tell me what you found about feminism when you began to read and to rummage around in these ideas. I'll give you one example: I suspect you didn't find a lot of conflict among feminists at that time.
**Crichton:** No. Very striking, very striking. My initial impulse was to read the literature because that's how I'd begun with *Rising Sun*—another business story. In U.S.-Japan relations there's tremendous open conflict, vigorously expressed. So I was accustomed to that. When I started to read feminist writing, I found it at first oddly bland because there didn't seem to be this conflict at all, apparently. It took me a long time to realize, reading a certain woman, that she was actually disagreeing with another trend of thought; it was very subtly expressed, very much in line with the notion that we are cooperative and we are not going to openly attack one another. It makes

tedious reading and it's, of course, not true. Feminism is seriously, deeply divided. There are many people who speak of the feminisms. There are camps that absolutely disagree. So my initial experience was to read this literature that was not surprisingly uncontentious. Then when I went to look at corporations and talk to people who worked in high-tech companies of the sort that I was going to write about, the first thing I discovered was that none of this literature was known, none of the major figures were known—no one knew who Katherine McKinnon was; she's a major figure.

**Rose:** University of Michigan; wrote a new book.
**Crichton:** Nobody knew who she was. As soon as they heard the word professor they turned away. "Nope, not interested in anything academic." I was absolutely stopped in my tracks because I thought, "Here's this set of ideas, but it turns out in the workplace no one knows it, no one cares about it." On the contrary, there's a kind of rough-and-ready, very fast-paced way of addressing harassment and it's very much different, very much more pragmatic; different from the ideological way that the discussions are carried out.

**Rose:** Where do you think it's going? Do you think in the workplace in ten years we'll have a sort of sex-free zone; that somehow this'll work itself out so that people understand the rules and understand what's proper? Right now what you have is: everybody agrees on the extremes; everyone agrees that certain things are blatant. On the other hand, there're certain things that people agree are not, that are clearly not. But there's a grey area in there—that's what scares everybody; produces the paranoia. How will we work that out?
**Crichton:** I think we'll work it out in the way that, historically, societies have always done. In human relationships there is anxiety or tension; and there is always inherently anxiety and tension in superior-inferior relationships in hierarchies. When you meet the king, you're nervous; and the king may be nervous for his own reasons.

**Rose:** It reminds me of a story I'll tell you quickly: I've heard a thousand times of people who say, "I'm going to go in there and tell the President what's on my mind. I'm going to tell him how he's screwing up as President." Then aides will say the guy walks in there—he may be a captain of industry and he may have a $150 billion company—he walks in there, "Yes, Mr. President. You're doing a very nice job. Count me on your team." The Oval Office and all that does it.

**Crichton:** Very tough to maintain that. I think there's a similar kind of anxiety between the sexes. Whenever there's the possibility that I'm attracted to you, we might have a sexual relationship, this might happen, whatever—that's tension. Sex is tension. So what the society ordinarily does, what human beings have historically done, is stereotype behavior in order to reduce anxiety. We shake hands—we touch one another in this special way—and if you don't shake hands you will immediately raise the anxiety not only of the person whose hand you won't shake but everyone else who's present; you break that convention and there's tension. We say, "How are you?" and we do not want to know. Whenever you say, "Hi. How are you?" and someone starts to tell you, you think, "Oh, no! I didn't want to know how you are. I'm saying I acknowledge you in the physical space"—stereotype. In the last thirty years the stereotypical behavior between men and women, the social role-playing—opening the doors, helping with coats, all that business—was broken by women for very good reasons. They were saying, "We're changing the power structure. We want a new deal. Don't open the door for me, don't help me with my coat, don't patronize me; and by the way, don't call me Miss or Mrs.—my name is Ms." And that's wise; that's sensible. That got a lot of attention; it woke the men up; it was great. But we cannot continue to have this lack of definition. It's too uncomfortable for everyone. I think we will settle into new forms and styles where everyone is comfortable. For example, it's really necessary in the workplace for people who work together and who know each other to make a personal comment or a comment about appearance. We have to. We see each other and we think, "Gosh you look tired," or, "Is everything okay?" or "That's nice clothing."

**Rose:** "I love your hair; obviously you've done your hair. I love it, it's terrific."
**Crichton:** Yes. That's a natural human thing and we need to be able to do that. We need to know what's going to be offensive; we have to decide what can I say where you really can't take it as offensive, and where am I overstepping. That's not clear now and it needs to be.

**Rose:** A couple of things. This is the *Rising Sun* metaphor: You're worried they're going to think you're anti-feminist. You're worried they're going to think you're sexist and that you have some message; that you are reactionary; which is sort of what they said after *Rising Sun*. That's what worries you?
**Crichton:** Right-wing paranoia.

**Rose:** You are right-wingaphobic. [Laughs] Right? That's what you're worried about?

**Crichton:** No. The interest in this particular story for me was that whatever attitude you take, whatever point of view you have coming in—this story will disturb you. I hope it will.

**Rose:** And make you ask hard questions.

**Crichton:** Yes. Say, "Now, wait a minute. How about this?" Particularly in gender relations I'm surprised. When I was talking about U.S.-Japan relations, not everyone is interested or very knowledgeable about that—many people will say I'm not knowledgeable, either—but at least that has it's arcane aspects. But we are all sexual creatures.

**Rose:** This is something everybody can touch and know; it's part of their own experience. Everybody has this as part of their experience.

**Crichton:** Yes, and I'm always surprised. We must surely know how complicated it is and how ambiguous and how we all sometimes get into a situation that we wish we weren't in; or maybe try and backpedal or do it well or badly. We all have to turn things down.

**Rose:** I want to move on—you've got a whole long life we want to talk about—but what's been the reaction to it? What kind of reaction, what kind of mail, what kind of feedback are you getting from people? What are they saying to you, author?

**Crichton:** It's interesting. What's most interesting to me is that a tremendous number of people just say, "Good book. I liked it." Particularly working women enjoyed it.

**Rose:** Working women, "Opened my eyes as to how people might feel in a different. . . ."

**Crichton:** I think they just look at it and say, "I know a woman like that. I know a corporate attorney like that." They just see that and read it and enjoy it.

**Rose:** Film; it has already been sold—$3.5 million is the figure that's been bandied about—to Warner Bros. You are going to produce this one. You were so unhappy with *Rising Sun* that you not only are going to write the screenplay here, you're going to produce this sucker. Right?

**Crichton:** Yes.

**Rose:** You've already had a conflict with the original director, Milos For-man.
**Crichton:** Yes.

**Rose:** Are these painful questions, Michael? Am I asking terrible questions?
**Crichton:** No. Actually, Milos and I had a really interesting time together and we kind of agreed to disagree.

**Rose:** Because you saw what differently?
**Crichton:** Everything.

**Rose:** Everything?
**Crichton:** Yes. We really saw what this story ought to be differently.

**Rose:** What are you going to do? Is it going to be different as a film than it is as a book? Do you have actors in mind already? John Grisham now acknowledges—different writer, fiction writer—that he thought about Julia Roberts when he was writing *The Pelican Brief*.
**Crichton:** No, I don't. In fact, when I wrote *Rising Sun* I thought about Sean Connery.

**Rose:** Because he's your friend?
**Crichton:** Yes, but that's very unusual for me. Particularly with this, because it was based on a real story with real people, I was primarily imagining those people.

**Rose:** What are the mistakes that were made with *Rising Sun* that you don't want to see happen with *Disclosure*?
**Crichton:** I don't know how to say. There's a way in which a book can be changed in many different ways. I really feel that film is a different medium. They have different values, different things work well, so major changes can occur. I really look to see if the movie works well on its own terms. From my point of view, the greatest disappointment about *Rising Sun* is not so much any modification of content, although that occurred; it's that what really should have been a bang-up police thriller wasn't very thrilling, as far as I was concerned.

**Rose:** No, it wasn't.
**Crichton:** It didn't work very well as a movie.

**Rose:** You and Kaufman had some conflict over that, did you not?

**Crichton:** Actually, I had a working difficulty with Phil and left the project very early—only a few weeks in—so there weren't actually content matters.

**Rose:** Why not direct it yourself?

**Crichton:** Each time that comes up, Charlie. Particularly with *Disclosure* I thought, "Maybe I should direct it." And then there's another book. I want to write another book.

**Rose:** What's the next book?

**Crichton:** Well, I can't say.

**Rose:** Oh, come on! [Laughs] Because you don't want to give it away? I respect that, but what is the reason people don't want to talk about it? Is it a jinx? Is it because you don't want other people going out writing your idea?

**Crichton:** No, it's none of those things. There's something about the energy of it being retained.

**Rose:** If you only know about it, it will maintain its own energy?

**Crichton:** Twenty years ago, somebody came to me and said, "Here's a good story for you to write." And it was, in that rarest of moments; it was a good story for me to write. I listened to him; I thought, "This is a fabulous story." For the next two months everywhere I went I said, "This guy told me this great story and this is the story." I told everyone, and then never wrote it.

**Rose:** I got you. So the energy was dissipated in telling the story rather than sitting at the typewriter. But you might direct this project?

**Crichton:** Yes, there's always that possibility.

**Rose:** Is it more than fifty percent?

**Crichton:** I don't know. I never know until I get there.

**Rose:** What about Steven Spielberg? *Jurassic Park, Disclosure.* He's just made a brilliant film—*Schindler's List.* Maybe he's looking for something different—a nice contemporary story.

**Crichton:** Steven, of course, saw this as soon as it came out and called me. He was very complimentary about it. I was in Japan.

**Rose:** They let you in?

**Crichton:** Oh, yes. I have a wonderful time in Japan. But what was fascinating was Steven Spielberg is just revered in Japan.

**Rose:** Because of *Close Encounters of the Third Kind,* I guess.

**Crichton:** I think it's the whole body of work; but the Japanese respond to him very much. I had been at the Imperial Hotel for several days and the word got out that I had received a call from Steven Spielberg. My status—I was suddenly a very important person.

**Rose:** "Maybe we were wrong about Mr. Crichton. He may be a good guy after all." So why not Spielberg to direct *Disclosure?*

**Crichton:** He doesn't want to do it.

**Rose:** He doesn't want to?

**Crichton:** No.

**Rose:** Who might do it, if not Spielberg? Do you have anybody, any other choices there? Whose work does Michael like?

**Crichton:** I like a lot of directors. We can't say right now, Charlie. We're in the middle.

**Rose:** You will write the screenplay?

**Crichton:** Yes.

**Rose:** Back when you were growing up, you always had this yen to write.

**Crichton:** I did.

**Rose:** What was it?

**Crichton:** I don't really understand it. I think it had to do with seeing my father do it.

**Rose:** He was a journalist turned advertising executive.

**Crichton:** Right. And he used to do some freelancing. I'd see a person at home typing and that turned into money, so I had an idea that could happen; certainly the notion that you could do writing wasn't strange—somebody in the house did it.

**Rose:** It was acceptable.

**Crichton:** Yes.

**Rose:** See, I never knew anybody who ever did television when I grew up in a small town in the South. It was an alien place to go do television.

**Crichton:** I'm sure.

**Rose:** Still is.

**Crichton:** [Laughs] It's okay now.

**Rose:** I keep practicing though—practicing, practicing, practicing. [Laughs]

**Crichton:** You're doing fine, Charlie. It's good; it's going to be fine. You're coming across very well. [Laughs]

**Rose:** Can I come and practice more often?

**Crichton:** Yes, you can. Come and practice your show. You can do whatever you like.

**Rose:** I sometimes wonder. So your parents liked books; I think about this because I think about family today because of all the problems we're having. Everybody—across the spectrum of ethnicity and racial background—is acknowledging the centrality of family. It's something that's always been there, but more and more as we search for roots. To read about you and your family, they encouraged you to believe everything was possible.

**Crichton:** Yes.

**Rose:** They took you on trips.

**Crichton:** Yes. Very encouraging.

**Rose:** What did it make you think about nurturing? You're a kid that did real well academically—what does that make you think about nurturing?

**Crichton:** Now that I'm a parent, of course, all that's important. But sometimes I'll be telling a story to my daughter, who's five, and she'll say, "No, Dad. Wait a minute. Why should the giant leave the cellar now? Keep him in the cellar and then Jack can get out." She's rewriting. And I think, "What do you know about it?"

**Rose:** She says, "Genes!"

**Crichton:** That's right. I wonder. Is there a storytelling [gene]? My father used to tell us stories when putting us to bed. What's involved in that interest in storytelling? My daughter used to talk about herself in the third person. She'd say, "Here she goes, hiding in the closet." What is that?

**Rose:** Why medical school for you?

**Crichton:** Sometime in my university training I read a statistic—I don't know where—that only two hundred people in America could make a living only writing books.

**Rose:** And Michael Crichton—who's sold a hundred million copies—didn't believe he had the goods, the right stuff, to be one of those two hundred.
**Crichton:** I have a question for you: Who counted those hundred million? How do we know?

**Rose:** And where's your take?
**Crichton:** That's right.

**Rose:** And whatever happened to it? On with the Michael Crichton story: You went to medical school, and while you were there you wrote *The Andromeda Strain*, which did pretty well; maybe five hundred thousand copies? Maybe more?
**Crichton:** Oh, no! The books didn't sell anything like that—a hundred thousand.

**Rose:** Hundred thousand copies?
**Crichton:** Yes; enormous for its day.

**Rose:** Did that tell you anything? Did it change your life? Did it make you say, "No internship for Michael?"
**Crichton:** I had, in fact, already decided not to go forward by that time. The reason was really that I had discovered—you didn't know anybody in television, I didn't know a physician, really, except my family physician; no one in my family was a physician—I had only fantasies about what it was like to be a doctor and in school I found I really wasn't suited for it; it wasn't for me.

**Rose:** Academically you did well, though?
**Crichton:** I did okay; middle of the class.

**Rose:** You had an aptitude for it; you just didn't have an interest in it?
**Crichton:** I'm not sure I can differentiate aptitude and interest anymore.

**Rose:** I'm not sure, either. So you write *The Andromeda Strain* and what happens then? What do you do? You go out to Los Angeles.
**Crichton:** Actually, at that point I was about twenty-five and I'd spent all of my life in some academic setting and now it was over. I was about to be ejected into the world and I needed a kind of halfway house, so I went to the Salk Institute in La Jolla.

**Rose:** What a great place to put down, on the banks of the Pacific.
**Crichton:** That's right, it was great.

**Rose:** Louis Kahn building and everything.
**Crichton:** It's a wonderful building.

**Rose:** Thinking what? Maybe you'd be a medical researcher?
**Crichton:** No. Salk had an idea that along with the biomedical people who were primarily staffing the place, he was going to have writers and artists in residence. So I sent him a letter and said, "I'm a writer." He said, "Come." So I went. It was great.

**Rose:** What did you think of him?
**Crichton:** I think he's wonderful.

**Rose:** What amazes me about him, even though you can never be sure all of his ideas are going to be proven right, is the passion he has even today. I was with him about three, four months ago when we were out in San Diego. It's extraordinary.
**Crichton:** Remarkable man. A wonderful person for me to know at that time because I was being hit by a tremendous amount of publicity about: He's the medical student who quit medicine, made all this money in the movies and so on. Salk knew everything there was to know about publicity and fame and knew exactly what a lot of baloney it was; he was a wonderful anchor for me.

**Rose:** You directed, and we're going to see a clip from *The Great Train Robbery*. Was that the first direction?
**Crichton:** No, that was the third.

**Rose:** That was the third. What was first?
**Crichton:** A movie called *Westworld*.

**Rose:** Why'd you want to direct?
**Crichton:** There are a couple things. One was the desire to protect material; the traditional reason to do it.

**Rose:** Protect i.e. the artist's vision.

**Crichton:** Yes. I was not very happy with the film that was made of *The Terminal Man*. The other thing was that when they were shooting *The Andromeda Strain* I went on the set. Bob Wise was very good about having young people come around. I looked at it and I thought, "This is kind of interesting. I can do this." Of course I didn't really know what I was looking at; I didn't know why I said, "I can do this." I don't understand what it is that makes you think, "I can do this," or "I can't do this."

**Rose:** But don't you say that about most things? Tell me something you just know you can't do. I don't obviously mean brain surgery; something you know you can't do that's reasonable for you to say. You've written a monograph on Jasper Johns. You are evidently a terrific cook. There are those of us more mortal people who are enormously jealous of people who have a range of skills.
**Crichton:** I think everybody has a range of skills.

**Rose:** So what's the difference then? You simply are out there willing to . . .
**Crichton:** Try. But you asked me what I can't do—my guess is you do not want to hear my opera, and you do not want to see my ballet, and probably you don't want to hear my epic poem, either.

**Rose:** No. There you go. But do you dream that you could write the great epic poem?
**Crichton:** I do, actually. I just got a cramp in my leg, what does that mean? Somebody's speaking to me.

**Rose:** It means you probably skied too much over the holidays. Now, do you have that epic poem there in your pocket?
**Crichton:** No, I don't.

**Rose:** So you start directing. Roll clip; let's take a look at one thing you've done. *The Great Train Robbery*—here it is. [Clip of *The Great Train Robbery*] Tell me about the friendship with Sean Connery. Was this the first time you two had worked together, knew each other?
**Crichton:** Yes.

**Rose:** And you came out of that as pals?
**Crichton:** Sean is an inspiration to many people who know him. He has this wonderful spirit. I don't know how to describe it differently. He's one of the

few people in the world that I would say is delightful. He's delightful. How can I explain it? Some of the things you don't see about him is that he's a remarkable mimic. Every once in a while he'd say, "Come on, let's go rehearse the next scene." We'd go into the next room while they were setting up and we'd rehearse and lay out the scene. Sean would play all the roles—women's roles, men's roles. He would very quickly, very efficiently, be mimicking Leslie Ann-Down, and then he'd be onto the next person and you'd see these glimpses of things as he'd do it. It was extraordinary and he loved to do it. He just had a wonderful time. I think of him as a complete person. He has his adult side and he has his childish side; he has his male and his female side; he has everything.

**Rose:** Do you think you're any good as a director?
**Crichton:** I don't ever think I'm any good at anything.

**Rose:** 950,000 copies later you're not sure.
**Crichton:** No, I see only faults.

**Rose:** You've had periods of writer's block, right?
**Crichton:** Yes.

**Rose:** Olivier's had his own periods where he was fearful of going on stage. How could that happen? What happens? You sit there in front of the typewriter or the computer and just nothing comes out?
**Crichton:** Here's the problem, Charlie. Since I don't know what happens when it does work, all I know is it's not working. I have this similar thing about cars because I'm not mechanical in any way, so all I can say is, "The car doesn't work."

**Rose:** Yes, but you can take the car to the service station.
**Crichton:** Yes, you can.

**Rose:** To the garage.
**Crichton:** And I took myself to the service station.

**Rose:** Okay, that's what I want to talk about. That's exactly what I want to know, because you went off on a whole thing of trying to find out who Michael was. Right?
**Crichton:** Yes.

**Rose:** And what'd you find out?

**Crichton:** I found out that I really didn't have any idea.

**Rose:** Who you were and what motivated you?

**Crichton:** Right. Most of my ideas were wrong.

**Rose:** About yourself?

**Crichton:** Yes.

**Rose:** Like what?

**Crichton:** I imagined that I was a person who was physically frail, kind of a weak person, a person who was easily shaken out of his determination. I was somebody who didn't like to get my hands dirty; literally.

**Rose:** To fight for what you believed in?

**Crichton:** Yes. In my middle thirties I climbed Kilimanjaro, by a kind of accident. I had no idea what I was in for or I never would have done it.

**Rose:** Blisters on your feet and everything else; physical pain.

**Crichton:** Yes. Tremendous pain—bleeding blisters because the shoes didn't fit and because I wasn't in shape. My idea of getting in shape to climb an 18,000 foot mountain was I quit smoking two days before.

**Rose:** You're not really as bright as I thought you were.

**Crichton:** No. People would say, "Have you ever been at altitude?" And I'd say, "Oh, sure. I've been in Denver."

**Rose:** Denver.

**Crichton:** That's right.

**Rose:** Eight thousand, nine thousand feet. How big is this mountain?

**Crichton:** What's the difference? At a certain point, around 15,000 feet, people were starting to say, "Is this worth it? Let's stop." I was not going to stop. I was going to get to the top. It was going to happen. Coming down I realized that I had a lot more strength and a lot more determination than I was acknowledging; and also that I'd really enjoyed this experience.

**Rose:** What difference did it make in your life—that you found this out?

**Crichton:** The most important thing was I realized that all these ideas I'd had about myself were wrong; and in that case, what other ideas might be wrong?

**Rose:** Stay with me, though. What else did you learn, other than the fact that you were not frail, that you did have this strength; what else did you find out?
**Crichton:** I like climbing; I didn't mind being in the cold; I liked challenges; maybe one of the problems I'd had was that I was not setting high enough goals for myself; I was actually quite energized by the thought that I couldn't do something.

**Rose:** What do you find as you grow older about setting goals and expectations? Are you still as driven? Has having a five year old—Taylor, your daughter—changed what you expect of yourself?
**Crichton:** Well, it certainly provides other pulls for me from work, and it certainly redefines in a very strong way for me this notion of a career—which is a sort of fantasy.

**Rose:** I can reassure you that you are among the two hundred now, Michael—if you need some reassurance—only two hundred writers who can make a living in America.
**Crichton:** What I really think, Charlie, is that there's this joke that on your deathbed nobody ever says, "I wish I'd spent a few more days at the office."

**Rose:** Paul Tsongas.
**Crichton:** When you get to that point you realize the only thing that matters is your experiences and your human relationships. That's all. Everything else is baloney.

**Rose:** Your experiences and your human relationships.
**Crichton:** That's right.

**Rose:** Those people that are part of your family and those people that you care about.
**Crichton:** That's right.

**Rose:** Those people who care about you. In the end, that's where it's at.
**Crichton:** That's it.

**Rose:** Everybody comes to that and it takes us all a long time to get there.
**Crichton:** Yes.

**Rose:** Especially those of us who grew up and progressed into middle age—
we're about the same age—driven to do things; a whole range of things and
a whole range of curiosities. No one has ever said, "Limits. Limits. Limits."
Right?
**Crichton:** I think at some point I at least started to say, "What are we really
trying to accomplish?" And kids have their way of stopping you. My daughter one day said she didn't want me to go into the office. I said I had to, but
now you're thinking, "What is so important?" She said, "Dad, your publisher
must be the luckiest person in the world because he gets to see you every
day." I thought, "Wait a minute. Wait a minute. How are we spending this
time? Hold on!"

**Rose:** [Laughs] "Thank you very much Taylor for helping me rearrange my
priorities real quick."
**Crichton:** Yes.

**Rose:** The marriage thing—number four.
**Crichton:** "The marriage thing" sounds like "the vision thing."

**Rose:** The marriage thing—four. Why did it take you four to get it right?
**Crichton:** I don't know. I'm only grateful it didn't take five, Charlie.

**Rose:** No, come on.
**Crichton:** What actually happened?

**Rose:** Yes.
**Crichton:** There're two things at work. One is some aspect of self-awareness.

**Rose:** On the mountain.
**Crichton:** Yes. I really did have a period in my life when I thought that if
there was something wrong with the relationship, it was her.

**Rose:** Her?
**Crichton:** Yes, had to be her.

**Rose:** Because you're perfect, aren't you?
**Crichton:** Yes, I am. What could be wrong?

**Rose:** What's there not to like about Michael?
**Crichton:** That's right. I have absolute self-awareness and I'm a swell guy.

**Rose:** "If you want a good time you've come to the right place."
**Crichton:** That's right. And if there's any problem it must be yours.

**Rose:** Exactly. "You didn't measure up, kid; thank you very much." And then you found out—not so.
**Crichton:** Can't be true, can't be true.

**Rose:** Did your fourth wife help you understand that? Or did you find that out yourself?
**Crichton:** By then I was in serious questioning. What happened with Ann-Marie is I got to the point where I said, "I really want this relationship and I will do whatever it takes to have it." I guess that's what you have to do.

**Rose:** Oh, I know. I know. It is the notion that the relationship—fighting for it and making it, keeping it—means something. You can't just say, "It means something."
**Crichton:** I think there's something else, too. Because I grew up in the period of sexual freedom, it took a long time to decide that actually that was not the valued goal we all imagined it was; and actually a committed relationship that lasted a period of time was more interesting. It was more interesting than continuously changing up.

**Rose:** I want to take a clip, because I want to talk about *Jurassic Park*. Here's what surprises me about this film. I don't want to be crass, but did you just sell them the rights to this and walk away?
**Crichton:** Is this a technical question?

**Rose:** I'm from the IRS—no. [Laughs]
**Crichton:** Are you asking about points?

**Rose:** Yes, I'm asking about points.
**Crichton:** No, I didn't just sell it and walk away.

**Rose:** So we're okay; we don't need to worry.

**Crichton:** No, no. We don't need to worry. Everything's fine. [Laughs]

**Rose:** [Laughs] *Jurassic Park*—roll tape. [Clip of *Jurassic Park*] This is the biggest grossing film ever now, right? And everybody thinks they were underpaid. You think you were underpaid; Steven thinks he was underpaid; the studio thinks they didn't get enough.

**Crichton:** They do, they do.

**Rose:** Is this what we mean by greed?

**Crichton:** No, I just think it's something about working and having things be successful or not successful. Finally, when something has this kind of enormous success there's some human thing where you immediately think, "I didn't get enough."

**Rose:** Is there a great mountain—I don't mean physically; you've done Kilimanjaro and you may want to do Everest. Do you want to do Everest?

**Crichton:** No.

**Rose:** You don't. You've done that?

**Crichton:** No, I haven't.

**Rose:** You've climbed a mountain, is my point. You've climbed a mountain so there're no more mountains on your agenda. Is there any great thing that sits in the back of your mind that you're saying to yourself, "This is something I've got to have?" You have a million-seller here in hardback, we think. What's the unattainable goal so far? What's the mountain you want to climb? You have a wonderful family, you have a happy marriage, you have a daughter that seems to be smarter than you are.

**Crichton:** Hope so. It's funny to talk about but I think at this point in my life . . .

**Rose:** The ripe old age of fifty-one or fifty-two . . .

**Crichton:** That's enough to start to think that it does not last forever. I'd like it to continue for a while, and I'd like to continue to be interested in my work. I don't think there's any way to say, "I want to work on the most successful movie in history or to write a book that sells."

**Rose:** No, it wouldn't be that. [Holds up a copy of *Travels*] This is autobiographical—*Travels*. Hard for you to write or easy for you to write?
**Crichton:** Easy, easy. Easiest book I ever worked on.

**Rose:** Was it cathartic?
**Crichton:** Yes, and also I had great admiration for the subject.

**Rose:** [Laughs] And small ego.
**Crichton:** At least I knew him well.

**Rose:** [Sorts through copies of Crichton's books] This is *Sphere*. My God, this man is prolific. *How to Think about Computers.* Do you have this notion that you pick a subject and write about it in an interesting way and make it interesting to a curious audience?
**Crichton:** I'm interested in doing that, but what it comes out of, Charlie, is this feeling that ordinarily I go into some area because there's something I want to know. In this way I feel very lucky in that I'm able to say, "What about the workplace? How is it going over there?" I can stop and do reading and then I can get on a plane and go visit companies and talk to people and form some conclusions—and I do have to write a book then, but I'm able to really explore this; then when that's done I can go do something else.

**Rose:** What's the hardest part of the process for you—the writing process?
**Crichton:** Oh, that's easy. The hardest part is starting to write.

**Rose:** How do you know when you're ready to do that? Because you do all this traveling, you talk to all these people, you do the reading, you do the research. How do you realize you're ready? I think an expression you use, "Ready to put butt to chair."
**Crichton:** Yes. I have a good answer for that—at the last possible moment when you cannot postpone it any more.

**Rose:** When your publisher's on the phone saying, "Michael!" Or Lynn Nesbitt's on the phone saying, "Michael, we have a serious problem here!"
**Crichton:** Then you wait another month and then you start.

**Rose:** Then you start. But once you start, people say to you that you take leave of your body; that you become so focused and you sit there. Then you begin to get up in the morning at six. The second week you're getting up every morning at five—always eating the same food. This is a little strange. All of a sudden you're getting up at four; and then you're going to bed at ten and getting up at two—your four hours of sleep; then you're really churning on all cylinders.
**Crichton:** Yes.

**Rose:** And it takes you about forty days to do this? Is that right?
**Crichton:** Just about.

**Rose:** Forty days. A couple of chapters a day or a couple of pages a day?
**Crichton:** Yes. The first drafts are shorter and they usually get elaborated later. I think of it as like a convulsion or a seizure or something.

**Rose:** Does it bother you that you are considered a popular writer and some say have not received the literary accolades that you probably think you deserve?
**Crichton:** Goes with the territory.

**Rose:** Goes with the territory? If the public buys you in huge numbers it's hard for the critics to climb aboard?
**Crichton:** Traditionally, that's true.

**Rose:** Is that what you believe?
**Crichton:** Yes.

**Rose:** You believe you're better than the critics think you are?
**Crichton:** Sure, doesn't everybody? [Laughs]

**Rose:** [Laughs] *Disclosure*, by Michael Crichton. It's a pleasure to have you here.
**Crichton:** Thank you.

**Rose:** It was great; an hour.
**Crichton:** You're kidding?

**Rose:** No.
**Crichton:** Wow.

**Rose:** Thank you for joining us. We look forward to seeing you next time.

# An Interview with Michael Crichton

## Charlie Rose/1995

From *The Charlie Rose Show*, September 22, 1995. Reprinted by permission of Charlie Rose Inc.

**Rose:** Michael Crichton is on the cover of this week's Time magazine as "The Hit Man with the Golden Touch." He is a trained physician—Harvard; film director and screenwriter. He recently added "television producer" to his list of achievements with the Emmy Award–winning series *ER*. But, of course, he is best known as one of the most successful novelists of our time. Spanning almost thirty years, his prolific writing career includes such blockbuster hits as *The Andromeda Strain, Rising Sun*, and *Disclosure*. His latest book is *The Lost World*. It enjoys a national release of two million copies. It is the sequel to *Jurassic Park*, whose film version grossed a record-breaking $912 million. I am pleased to have Michael Crichton back at this table. Welcome.

**Crichton:** Thank you, Charlie.

**Rose:** Why this for you now? Was it things that you wanted to say about dinosaurs? Was it simply easy for you to do? What caused you to write, one more time, a book about dinosaurs [and] the fact that there was a second site?

**Crichton:** It was really something that came from the readers. From the first publication of the book, kids began to read it and they would send letters: "What about the sequel? What about the sequel? What about the sequel?" I had not ever done a sequel before and would always say, "There won't be one." Then, as time went on, they would say, "Well, this would be a good sequel. Here's another idea for a sequel." Now you're reading them thinking, "No, that's not right. No, we wouldn't do that." Then you start thinking, "Well, why not? Well, what would be good?" Eventually there did seem to be

ld be another film and Steven seemed to have some

lot of interest in that.
o speak for him but I think there's always a mixed
ʒ back and doing it again. Would it really be inter-
ʒ different?

ι its own two legs?
ιings.

ιur—depends on the species. I'd never done a se-
do.

**Rose:** The trepidation is what?

**Crichton:** It's a very difficult structural problem because it has to be the same but different; if it's really the same, then it's the same—and if it's really different, then it's not a sequel. So it's in some funny intermediate territory.

**Rose:** What happened to cause you to say, "Alright, I'll go ahead?" Did you think about characters? Did you think, "There are things about the story I have not told?" Was there some metaphor you wanted to bring to the fore?

**Crichton:** Yes, there was some of that.

**Rose:** Which?

**Crichton:** There was the feeling that I would be able to talk to a large audience, particularly a large audience of kids, so what would you talk to them about?

**Rose:** Something they can relate to.

**Crichton:** Yes, or something they ought to be thinking about.

**Rose:** What else, in terms of ideas, did you want to massage?

**Crichton:** There's hardly anything more difficult to talk about in a popular book than evolution. It's just an innately complex subject.

**Rose:** But that's your genius, Michael. Let me suggest you go to a publisher

or you go to a movie company and you say—before the Simpson trial—"I've written a book about DNA." [Laughs] And didn't mention dinosaurs, didn't mention storytelling.
**Crichton:** They wouldn't say, "Can't wait."

**Rose:** They wouldn't say, "Can't wait." But when you wrote this, you really wanted to treat some subject matter—evolution being one, but also some sense of natural selection, and also you wanted to say some things about behavior, did you not?
**Crichton:** Yes, I had some ideas about behavior. But there's a third thing I ought to tell you. [Just before] *ER* came on the air, all the press questions had to do with whether it was going to be very controversial and very contentious; because that's the way anything I was involved with was perceived.

**Rose:** This was after *Disclosure*?
**Crichton:** This was after *Disclosure*, which was controversial enough. I thought, "*Rising Sun* was controversial enough. Maybe it's time not to be so controversial."

**Rose:** Be comfortable.
**Crichton:** Just break the pattern. Also, you can become a scold.

**Rose:** Once you made the decision, was it easy then? Once you found the peg that you wanted to hang this story on—because you had a lot of stuff to go with, you're building on something—you don't have to establish the scientific bona fides, do you? You've already explained that.
**Crichton:** My feeling was you had to address a different scientific subject. The first book for me was about micro-subjects: DNA and technology. This one is about macro-subjects. It's about populations and it's about long-term trends; it's about extinction.

**Rose:** Do you think the human species is on the road to extinction because of its behavior—because it's lost control of civility?
**Crichton:** Are we on the road to extinction? Absolutely, because all species become extinct.

**Rose:** And because we aren't treating the planet very well.
**Crichton:** Yes, although there're questions about that. But at least there's an argument to be made that we're not doing our best. In terms of civility, I

don't know. The most important thing for us as a species: Unlike other species, we evolve and adapt to our environment through our behavior. Our bodies have not significantly changed in thirty-five thousand to fifty thousand years, but our behavior has changed enormously since the time we were chipping flints in caves.

**Rose:** Because our brain has been at work.
**Crichton:** Our brain has been at work, but our brain hasn't changed. It's the same brain.

**Rose:** It's accumulative wisdom.
**Crichton:** Right; elaboration of stuff. The need we have as a species, therefore, is similar to what a population needs in terms of variability inside the population. There has to be a variation inside a species so that if something happens, like a plague or something, there's enough variation that some animals survive because they have an innate resistance or something like that. For us the equivalent of that is ideas. There has to be a variable pool of ideas; diversity of ideas, ways of thinking, notions of what to do. One of the concerns I have is that our technology now is shrinking the pool of ideas. Certainly the current tendency in this country—the lack of civility—it's really true that some people are suggesting that maybe the Congress needs a timeout the way children do. This kind of shrieking timbre . . .

**Rose:** You gave a speech in which you talked on the periphery of that particular issue, but coming back to the extinction of the species—is this something you worry about, or is this just something of interest and curiosity to you because it is fodder for a next great book?
**Crichton:** Do I worry about it personally? No. It's not around the corner. In fact, most of the things people are worrying about here—the trends in global warming or the changes in the rainforest—I'm really not persuaded; maybe they're not good, but it's not clear exactly how dire they are.

**Rose:** That the threat is as characterized?
**Crichton:** Right. On the other hand, we are in a position to recognize that certain kinds of changes, certain kinds of behavior, can produce catastrophic change and it's not always clear where those things are. This idea of civility to me is an example of that. We're in a nation that really wants to shout everybody else down at the moment. We're really shrinking the notion of available options; we're shrinking the diversity of opinion on almost every

subject so that you're either "for it" or "against it"; you're "part of the problem" or you're "part of the solution." This is not healthy.

**Rose:** I want to come back to something else you said and funnel into that. Why is technology shrinking the body of ideas? Why does it do that?
**Crichton:** I don't know.

**Rose:** I would think it would expand ideas.
**Crichton:** Yes, that's right; and that was always the promise. The promise was always five hundred television channels . . .

**Rose:** Information superhighway . . .
**Crichton:** This great diversity . . .

**Rose:** The internet, and we can speak to everybody, and we have access to everything and, "My God, the global village is upon us."
**Crichton:** We have now five hundred channels and we know what that's like.

**Rose:** Nobody wants to watch them—that's what it's like! [Laughs]
**Crichton:** Yes, and why that shrinking occurs, why there's a sort of limitation, I'm not clear at all about—but it does seem to be happening.

**Rose:** Let me come back to the book. Characters—who comes forward from *Jurassic Park*?
**Crichton:** Only one, Ian Malcolm.

**Rose:** He's the only one.
**Crichton:** Yes.

**Rose:** He's played by Jeff Goldberg in the film, right?
**Crichton:** Goldblum.

**Rose:** Goldblum, right. He goes to Costa Rica.
**Crichton:** Yes.

**Rose:** He's the only one that will make an appearance?
**Crichton:** I don't know. Steven may do something else. But in the book, my thinking really was that I desperately needed that character back because he

is the ironic commentator inside the story who talks about the action as it takes place.

**Rose:** We thought he was dead—but?
**Crichton:** That's right. It's Sherlock Holmes and the Reichenbach Falls.

**Rose:** Speaking of that, why the title *The Lost World*?
**Crichton:** It's a reference to a Conan Doyle story called *The Lost World.*

**Rose:** Why did you choose that one?
**Crichton:** It was a thing I liked as a child. It's one of the more pulpy Conan Doyle stories; it's a Professor Challenger story. It's actually not a very good story, but it's a wonderful title and it's about an expedition back to a place where there are dinosaurs.

**Rose:** Let me talk about you and satisfaction. In the creative process, when is Michael Crichton happiest? At what point in that process? Gathering the idea? The concept? The research? Beginning the first chapter? Getting to the end, as your work day begins to grow from maybe ten hours to twelve to fourteen to sixteen to eighteen?
**Crichton:** If I was charting it, there's an early dissatisfaction which has to do with, "what will I do next?"

**Rose:** You mean how do I go from chapter to chapter to chapter? How do I keep the audience?
**Crichton:** No, just choosing the next project. That early decision: Will it be this or that? And if it's that, how exactly will it be? Then at a certain point, when doing focused research and it begins to come together, I start to get quite excited. Of course, it's still just ideas, so it's quite wonderful. It has no concrete form to be disappointing yet. The first sixty pages are very exciting. It's this wonderful future ahead—I just can't wait. Eventually, it starts to be another book. [Laughs]

**Rose:** [Laughs] So, where you began to think you were going is not where you're going to end up ever?
**Crichton:** No, it isn't that. It's just that this wonderful nebulas thing starts to be concrete, starts to be this page, this way of formulating the ideas, and then its specific expression kills that beautiful idea. It's like your hopes for working on a movie. You start, "Oh, it's going to be so great." In the end,

it's just a movie. That's all it ever is. So I begin to have that sort of feeling as well—and I'm still enthusiastic. Then, as I finish, there's a part that gets kind of hard—it starts to be a grind always.

**Rose:** Now what is that part?

**Crichton:** There's a lot of cleaning up to do. "You said you went to Costa Rica for four days but it says he left on Tuesday and this is only Saturday, so isn't that just three days? And isn't he thirty-six? Because if he's only thirty-six, how can he be an assistant professor? Shouldn't he be an associate?" Endless.

**Rose:** Closing all those loopholes. Someone, I think it was Steven, called you "The high priest of high concept." What did he mean?

**Crichton:** I don't know. I wanted to ask him about that. [Laughs]

**Rose:** [Laughs] You did, too?

**Crichton:** I think I know what he meant.

**Rose:** Tell me what he meant.

**Crichton:** I think he means that I seem to be able to come up with these ideas that, in themselves, look as though they can hold a movie.

**Rose:** And they're interesting ideas. They're on the edge of what people are thinking about at the time—certainly with *Rising Sun* and certainly with *Disclosure* and *Jurassic Park* and DNA and all of that—now a question of evolution and extinction and natural selection. Is it just that you smell the air and that your instinct and your assimilation process is superb?

**Crichton:** I have no idea.

**Rose:** You don't?

**Crichton:** Charlie, I really feel if you try and hit it—you can't. All you can do is do it interesting. There's a certain way where every time I'm working on something I wish I was working on something else. I just think, "Why am I doing this?" Particularly because a lot of my research is directed toward answering some kind of question, and I've got the question answered before I start to write the book.

**Rose:** You do?

**Crichton:** Yes. So now, writing the book is just sort of . . .

**Rose:** Does the answer come from the research?
**Crichton:** Usually.

**Rose:** So you ask the question. The research gives you the answer. Then you've got to write the book.
**Crichton:** Yes.

**Rose:** What's the question here?
**Crichton:** How are we going to think about our own behavior? How much rope has evolution cut us? How much slack? Do we really have a fair amount of maneuvering room here or is it all kind of unknown? Is there a cliff somewhere where you just fall right off very rapidly and go, "Whoops!" and there's a long drop?

**Rose:** And it's over.
**Crichton:** And it's over.

**Rose:** So that's the question you're asking?
**Crichton:** Yes.

**Rose:** And you do it through dinosaurs because they were there, because it's a connection to a previous work and because it's a species that became extinct.
**Crichton:** Exactly.

**Rose:** So that provides you the fodder that you need. You're going to direct this?
**Crichton:** No.

**Rose:** You're not?
**Crichton:** No.

**Rose:** Because you don't have time? Because other people can do it better? Some other reason?
**Crichton:** No, I think Steven Spielberg is. [Laughs]

**Rose:** [Laughs] Well, okay.
**Crichton:** I hope he will.

**Rose:** You do. You're counting on it, aren't you? [Laughs]
**Crichton:** I'd like it very much.

**Rose:** I know you don't like to deal in questions like this, and I'm not that intrigued by them, but do you believe it will be bigger and better than *Jurassic Park*? Because the ideas, the characters are there; it has been a huge success; it's going to draw them into the tent and as long as they can find out that you're onto some new idea that's equally interesting, and perhaps more so.
**Crichton:** I can't imagine anything being bigger than that.

**Rose:** *Jurassic Park*.
**Crichton:** Yes. But it will be as good as it is.

**Rose:** There is this sense about you: Somewhere up there [Laughs. Gestures to his head] a series of ideas are feeding into you. I base this on the speech you made at the National Press Club, on some conversations you and I've had, on a series of interviews, that—in terms of where our society is, in terms of media, in terms of violence, in terms of behavior, in terms of popular ideas that are out there—you are percolating with some great story; and it's sort of there, filling—as you do this [Gestures to *The Lost World*], as you do other things. Am I even close?
**Crichton:** I really hope it's true. [Laughs]

**Rose:** [Laughs] Yes. I do, too.
**Crichton:** Some of these areas I'm trying to figure out how to do something. I'm concerned about them.

**Rose:** Concerned about which?
**Crichton:** All of them.

**Rose:** What's your reaction to the Simpson trial?
**Crichton:** I don't know that I have an unusual response. It's horrifying to me, you know. My inclination is to say it's something very unraveling about the American judicial system and, in that sense, probably good for people to see.

**Rose:** Great lawyers have come to this desk and said the same thing. Arthur Liman, people like that.
**Crichton:** He's a great lawyer. I like him.

**Rose:** Yes, he's a great lawyer.

**Crichton:** One of the things I'm always struck by is how many commentators are saying, "Other judicial proceedings are not like this." As far as I can tell, they all are; this tendency to trash reputations and the effort to divert everything to side issues.

**Rose:** It's all about winning and losing. How about victimization and the notion of victimization in terms of the way so many people say, "Give me a pass. I had a bad childhood. Give me a pass because I didn't have as equal playing field. Give me a pass for whatever I did." It's a little bit of the Menendez Brothers.

**Crichton:** Right. I'm very interested in this. I think there are two problems with it. One part of it I tried to do in *Disclosure* because one element of feminist thought tends in this direction. It seems to me it's a very bad strategy. It's a strategy of saying, "I have no power, and somebody has to give me some." It's just very difficult to walk down the street if that's how you feel and it would be much better to choose another strategy. I certainly didn't want my daughter thinking, "I am not able to take care of myself unless all the men in my environment behave themselves." Teach her something else and she'll take care of herself fine and she'll be able to influence those men as strongly as she needs to. So that's the first problem. The second problem, really, is that the insistence on a lack of responsibility—which is what we're talking about here—is, it seems to me, not true. As far as I can tell, the correlation between life experiences and behavioral outcomes is loose at best. There are people who've had terrible, terrible early-life formative experiences, just shocking and awful and abusive, and they turn out to be just great. And then there are—and everybody knows about them—these privileged, rich brats that go out and kill people. So those links, it seems to me, are not at all demonstrated—far from demonstrated. Therefore, when we start to say, "No one's really responsible for anything. Our behavior is simply the sum of all of our past life experiences. By the time I get to this point in life, a stack of cards behind me of events that lead up to this or that will decide whether or not I pull a gun and shoot you or not. I'm not really responsible for it—it's all predetermined in a way." That, it seems to me, is a very, very difficult thing for the society to work with, if people start to believe it.

**Rose:** Also abhorrent.

**Crichton:** Yes.

**Rose:** These themes—they're there, you think about them, you see something.

**Crichton:** Trying to get a story. *Disclosure* was a true story, so it was just dropped in my lap and I went, "Ooh." I think, "Is that a good story? Will that do it? Can I take that story? Can I pull it apart?" In a sense, *Rising Sun* was based on a true incident, so my tendency is to take real things. I'm looking for a real thing.

**Rose:** One day you'll pick up the paper or a magazine like *Time* and there it'll be: "My God. There it is."

**Crichton:** "There it is." Hope so.

**Rose:** Then what will you do? You'll just say, "This is it?" and you'll want to know everything you can possibly find out about that story.

**Crichton:** Yes.

**Rose:** Where it leads and what it says.

**Crichton:** And then change it.

**Rose:** [Laughs] And make it your own!

**Crichton:** [Laughs] Make it better.

**Rose:** I don't want to talk about this for more than a moment, but the notion of character and motivation and all those qualities—does it interest you any more as you write more books and have more life experiences?

**Crichton:** It does now; and part of what we're talking about here relates to that. In writing, I have always felt that I don't really understand why people do what they do. I really don't.

**Rose:** Or don't do what they should do.

**Crichton:** Yes. So I'm always doing an external kind of description. All I feel comfortable with is what happens. I'm very uncertain about inner life and motivation, because I think that's all . . .

**Rose:** All what?

**Crichton:** It's either fantasy or it's ex-post-facto rationalization. Certainly I've gotten into certain kinds of situations, or certain things have happened to me that have upset me, and later I think, "Why did you do that? Why did you walk into that room? Why did you say that?" I don't have a good explanation to that.

**Rose:** I don't either, and I have never bought into the idea where people say, "He wanted to get caught, and that's why he did it." I have never believed that. Somebody wanted desperately, because they took a risk and they were on the edge. What makes some of us more risk-takers than others? What makes some of us want to go on the high wire is one factor. Other people wiser than I can grasp it, but the simple explanation, "He wanted to get caught, that's why he did it," I don't understand.

**Crichton:** It's probably true of some people, or it's probably true of some kinds of repetitive behaviors.

**Rose:** Wanting to get caught; or just some uncontrollable rage or urge.
**Crichton:** Yes.

**Rose:** As a medical student, were you interested in psychology at all?
**Crichton:** Yes. My choice as a medical student was to become a surgeon or a psychiatrist.

**Rose:** A brain surgeon?
**Crichton:** No, just a surgeon; a general surgeon. When I started directing I thought, "This is really interesting. It is somewhere between being a surgeon and a psychiatrist."

**Rose:** [Laughs] How so?
**Crichton:** Surgeons and ship captains are the last bastion of "we're going to do it my way."

**Rose:** "I'm in control of the destiny of this craft."
**Crichton:** That's right.

**Rose:** "Sink or swim—blame me or credit me."
**Crichton:** And so are film directors.

**Rose:** Of course, the film directors always say, "The studio made me do it. It wasn't me. If you would've used my finish, we'd have had a winner."
**Crichton:** That's sometimes true.

**Rose:** Why haven't you directed more then?
**Crichton:** It seems to me as though there are periods in my life where sometimes I really want to direct and not write, and sometimes I really want to write and not direct.

**Rose:** Life has turned out quite well for Michael.
**Crichton:** Knock on every piece of wood I can find. Yes.

**Rose:** You've found happiness in marriage; you have a child; you're a father—you enjoy that? Find it satisfying?
**Crichton:** Yes.

**Rose:** Forget the commercial success, which I know you've been savvy about. What you have written has an appeal. You may not understand it and I may not understand it, but an audience reads it and likes it and people turn it into interesting and exciting movies. You may not like some of those movies, as you haven't. Right? You didn't like *Rising Sun* at all?
**Crichton:** No, I didn't.

**Rose:** You thought *Disclosure* was what? Because that's been out since you and I've talked.
**Crichton:** I liked it a lot.

**Rose:** A lot?
**Crichton:** A lot, yes.

**Rose:** *Jurassic Park*?
**Crichton:** Liked it.

**Rose:** Couldn't have been better, probably. So what's the drive, in a sense? What's the mountaintop for you?
**Crichton:** I'm not clear. There was a time a few years ago when it was to pay the house payments. That's clear, that's easy. At some other point I think, "Maybe what I do really is compulsive behavior. Maybe I'm just compelled to do it." I also think there's something that happens to me a lot where the conventional wisdom frequently irritates me so much. I'll hear somebody talking or I'll read something and I'll think, "That is so . . ." I. I. Rabi, the physicist, used to listen to certain presentations and he would say, "He's not even wrong."

**Rose:** That's a great line. [Laughs]
**Crichton:** Not even in the ballpark.

**Rose:** Exactly what I was going to say. Not even wrong!
**Crichton:** I get so annoyed and a lot of that drives the writing.

**Rose:** That compulsion?
**Crichton:** Yes.

**Rose:** Anger; and saying, "They don't have any clue as to what's really going on."
**Crichton:** Right.

**Rose:** Frequently the ideas you attack, though, or you address or you engage, are ideas that there's so much conventional wisdom out there about. Right?
**Crichton:** Yes.

**Rose:** Nature/nurture, selection, DNA, all this stuff. Could you imagine yourself as a lawyer?
**Crichton:** Yes.

**Rose:** You could?
**Crichton:** Yes. I could easily see myself doing it. I think my mind works that way.

**Rose:** How is that?
**Crichton:** I'm not sure.

**Rose:** Powers of deductive reasoning?
**Crichton:** Yes, and a kind of disputatious turn of mind. [Laughs]

**Rose:** [Laughs] Like what?
**Crichton:** A tendency to niggle over details.

**Rose:** Really? We thought Michael sits there at home with a computer and there's no haggling over small points.
**Crichton:** That's all there is.

**Rose:** A little bit anal?
**Crichton:** Yes, I think so.

**Rose:** Do you ask yourself where it comes from; like going into that door? Where does all this come from?
**Crichton:** Often, and I haven't a clue.

**Rose:** What is interesting about you is you have thought about these things. You ask yourself introspective questions, but I'm not sure how many answers you come up with—just from your response.

**Crichton:** Charlie, I think there is very little real understanding of human behavior. I was interested, of course—here's my child . . .

**Rose:** She's six or seven or eight?

**Crichton:** She's six now, but as she's developing, one of the things I'm really interested in is some sense of causality and motivation. She'd say, "Daddy, I want this." I'd say, "Why?" She'd say, at a certain age, "Because." I'd say, "Because what?" "Because." There was nothing; it was "because." I want it because I want it. It was quite a long time later, two or three years later, that there began to be a narrative: "Well, I want it because I have to take this to do that, or I want it because I need this for school." But that's baloney; she wants it "because."

**Rose:** Some "because."

**Crichton:** I think that's true of all of us.

**Rose:** I'm an only child. My parents would say, "You can't do that." I'd say, "Why?" "Because." That's different though, because hers is just a perfectly natural want, desire, interest, curiosity.

**Crichton:** I think also if a kid says he wants something, you say "Why?" At a certain age they start searching around for the answer that will satisfy you so they can get what they want. That's all it is, and I'm not sure it's any more complicated when you get to the Menendez Brothers.

**Rose:** Just that they thought they wanted it. They wanted the family fortune and to get it they had to kill their parents.

**Crichton:** I don't know.

**Rose:** You don't know that that's plausible?

**Crichton:** I think so.

**Rose:** That's conventional wisdom. You're really interested in that trial, aren't you, because of the gruesomeness of standing behind . . .

**Crichton:** I'm interested in the notion that whatever happens in upbringing could be sufficient reason to allow you to shoot your parents and pause to reload. That's not an act of passion.

**Rose:** Or rage.

**Crichton:** It's not. It's very clear, by the way, that people can have brief psychotic episodes—they really can. They can go crazy, they can have drug-induced psychoses or they can have simple psychotic breaks. During that time they can not be in control and they can do terrible things. Later they're okay again, and they really don't know what happened—but that's not what we're talking about.

**Rose:** Have you thought about the notion of Bosnia and the kind of brutality that takes place still. Rwanda. It's just extraordinary to me. To hear stories of a soldier bringing a family together and, in front of the children, raping the mother, slitting the throat of the father—it's just, for us, a concept about the mind that just is another level than you can conceive of.

**Crichton:** I think we live in a rarified world.

**Rose:** You and I.

**Crichton:** I think that's the world.

**Rose:** I do, too. That's probably true.

**Crichton:** One third of the population of Cambodia killed; two million people out of six. For what? For what? Mass graves. There's been a lot of that in this century and at some point it gets harder and harder to say, "Oh, that's a special case or that's a special case or that's because of Stalin or because of Hitler." It keeps happening. It's us.

**Rose:** What's next for you?

**Crichton:** I haven't a clue.

**Rose:** Does that feel good, or anxious-producing?

**Crichton:** It really fills me with anxiety and dread. I'd much rather have things planned out, but I think it's not an accident that sometimes I get to this point and think, "I don't know what I'll do next." It's opening its wings.

**Rose:** We've talked about motivation, understanding. Do you understand your talent?

**Crichton:** No.

**Rose:** You don't?

**Crichton:** No. My experience is of not being—and there are a lot of people who'd agree with this—not being very gifted at writing and of having to try really hard, to work very hard at what I do, to put in long hours and to concentrate on it. I don't feel in any way that I have natural abilities in this. I just work hard—that's my experience.

**Rose:** Working hard.
**Crichton:** Yes.

**Rose:** Keeping your eye on the goal.
**Crichton:** This is something I wanted to do—I wanted to be a writer and I'm very happy to be doing it.

**Rose:** Is it easier?
**Crichton:** No, it's harder.

**Rose:** It's harder?
**Crichton:** Sure.

**Rose:** Why? Why do you say, "Sure?"
**Crichton:** I think that's a common experience for people who do some activity repeatedly.

**Rose:** The better you do it, the more difficult it is because you understand the levels of proficiency. Second, the more you do it, the more you understand about something, the more you appreciate the complexity of it.
**Crichton:** Yes. And pretty soon you've done all the easy things.

**Rose:** It's a pleasure to have you here. It's always a great conversation. I wanted to go longer, but I made a promise to your people that I would get out of here within a reasonable time.
**Crichton:** Thank you.

**Rose:** Thank you, very much. Michael Crichton. *The Lost World.*

# An Interview with Michael Crichton

## Charlie Rose/1996

From *The Charlie Rose Show*, December 26, 1996. Reprinted by permission of Charlie Rose Inc.

**Rose:** Michael Crichton is here—he is one of my favorite guests. His new book is called *Airframe*; it is about an airline accident. He is also one of Barbara Walters's "10 Most Fascinating People," which aired on ABC on Friday night. You know all about *The Lost World*—his other book; you know all about *Twister*—he wrote the screenplay for that; you know about *Jurassic Park*. Michael Crichton is an industry; he is also a good writer; he is also a friend of mine, and I am pleased to have him back on this program. Welcome.
**Crichton:** Thank you, Charlie.

**Rose:** I'm going to tell you something. What's that song they used in the Michael Jordan ad? It's called "Be like Mike, be like Mike, be like Mike." I always thought that was about Michael Jordan but now I know—having read about you—it's about you.
**Crichton:** [Laughs]

**Rose:** What I was going to do, knowing how you normally dress, I was going to wear this tie because I know you have a tie just like this; but you smartly and savvily decided this was the day not to wear the tie.
**Crichton:** It was a narrow escape. It would have been very odd.

**Rose:** It would have been mirror images. I want to talk about this [Holds up *Airframe*] and a lot of other things. First, tell me why you decided to write about this, because one thing you're becoming noted for is this uncanny instinct to produce a book about a subject that is timely and on the minds of people, at least in this country.

**Crichton:** I'm interested that has happened, because my real impulse in starting this was to do something about media. For a long time I'd been looking for a story that would enable me to talk about tabloidization.

**Rose:** Let me just note: I read a speech you gave at the National Press Club in Washington in which you took media to task for cynicism; for a lot of other qualities.

**Crichton:** That was 1993, so it was since then, at least. What I could never find was: What's the subject? In other words, there's a media dealing with some topic—what topic? What is the topic that everyone cares about? You think something about the government or the budget or entitlements—it's too complicated and too abstract. Eventually, a person who worked in aerospace called and said, "You're not going to believe what I just heard about this flight." Out of that discussion—this very unusual event that happened on this airplane—I began to think, "Everyone's interested in airplanes. If the media isn't telling us what we need to know about that, then that's something every reader can immediately identify with—are we getting the story or not?"

**Rose:** I think media is interested in three things. Number one: scandal—they love scandal. Number two: they are compelled forward by tragedy; airline crashes are tragedy. Thirdly: they are fascinated by horseraces; whatever kind of up and down—who's up and who's down. It's a version of gossip—who's in and out; it's the political horserace; it's who's going to get this and who's going to get that; it's the list of the top ten; all of that kind of thing is the third subject of fascination. You wanted to write about news covering something and the guy telling you about the airline gave you the peg to write your story?

**Crichton:** It did. He told me this very odd event, which is roughly the event that's in the book, somewhat changed. Then I said, "Okay, that's interesting, but obviously it's going to be widely reported." He said, "No, it's not." I said, "Well, why not?" He told me why not. I said, "We do know about airplane crashes and we know about . . ." The conversation drifted and pretty soon we were talking about the DC-10 crash in Chicago in '79 that gave that airplane such a bad name. He said, "There's nothing wrong with that airplane." I started to think, "Maybe I don't know anything about this subject."

**Rose:** And you did what then?

**Crichton:** I started talking to people, and since it's about accidents, I read a lot of NTSB documents.

**Rose:** You once told me that when you write, you begin to do research in search for an answer to a question. What was the question here? What causes planes to go down?
**Crichton:** In part; or how common is it? What are the reasons? But also, the question that I had I do not yet have an answer to—the original question.

**Rose:** Which was?
**Crichton:** What are we going to do about the media? It's not okay the way it is. In other words, this book I think of as a kind of case history to demonstrate that there's a very complicated event that's taken place—an accident involving an airplane. The media team that's portrayed has its own pressures. They have to fill twelve minutes of airtime in forty-eight hours; they have to put the story together; it has to work; it has to appear on primetime; it has to be snappy and interesting; it has to beat what's already been reported. They're going to do something that isn't accurate—that isn't, in a certain sense, honest.

**Rose:** To hype their story.
**Crichton:** Yes, and they're not really going to have any choice about it. If they're going to do this story, there's only one way to do it, and they don't really have a way to postpone it.

**Rose:** There's a great line that comes from the managing editor or the executive producer: "Don't make this a part story!"
**Crichton:** That's right.

**Rose:** Because a part story's boring.
**Crichton:** Yes, and it's been done.

**Rose:** And it's been done.
**Crichton:** But it turns out it was a part story.

**Rose:** Let me come back to this in a second and tell the story to bring all this to focus. This is a story of a plane that leaves from Hong Kong; a plane made by Norton—Flight 545. That plane has to make an emergency landing in Los Angeles. In the process of coming there to ask for forty-some ambulances on the ground, several people are killed because the plane goes into a giant up-and-down. They don't quite know why—we suspect why. There is, at the same time, your media. Newsline has a magazine show emanating from New York and Al Pacino, in your book, walks off the set because he doesn't like the tone of the interview. So they have a news hole; they have to find a story. All of a sudden they see a report off the wire about what happened. They all of a sudden end up with some videotape; and now—questions of judgment, questions of time, questions of compromise. With the airline there's also a question of what caused this crash. There's corruption, there's commercial pressure, all of this is here. I just say that so the audience at home, which wants to read this but may not, knows what we're talking about. Let me go back.

**Crichton:** That's really good.

**Rose:** Is it alright?

**Crichton:** Yes, that's good. I can never summarize it! I like that! [Laughs]

**Rose:** [Laughs] I could never write a book that Disney would want to buy for $12 million, either. Let me stay with the notion of: What do you want to say through this magazine show? What happens within a news organization that is less than the truth?

**Crichton:** There are several things. The first thing is, the story is decided before anybody goes out. This is what the story's going to be. Once the reporter's in the field, her boss doesn't want to hear it; a very common experience for reporters—again and again they say that. In some senses a lot of what was happening in Vietnam—the early reports: unacceptable.

**Rose:** "We don't want to hear that this is an unwinnable war. We don't want to hear that American troops are misbehaving. We don't want to hear anything." Later, they didn't want to hear about the heroism, didn't want to hear about the courage and didn't want to hear about the quality of the people that were there.

**Crichton:** Exactly. Second thing is that the format they are going to follow, in order to build a twelve-minute segment to talk about an airplane, is going to not let anyone speak for probably more than ten seconds, at most maybe twenty seconds at a shot. Then they're going to cut away, they're going to show some visual, they're going to do something else. This means there isn't any possibility to make an extended argument. There's not any possibility to talk about anything of any complexity. It does seem to me that, more and more, complex issues get shrunk until they're only one word. What will we do about entitlements? Mediscare. It's one word. It's not an answer. It's just a collapse of the whole issue. Filegate. These things could be pointers to something else, but they're not.

**Rose:** It is necessary to make this caveat—an important one: There are a lot of very good reporters writing for a lot of very good newspapers and producing and reporting on television stories that are as good as they know how to be; not always marching to the notion of get the sensational; a lot of economic stories—I see it every day on television. You may say, "Not enough." You may say, "Too frequently they can't do the job they could have—because I recognize their talent—because of the time pressures, because of the commercial pressures." I would agree with you that, especially with magazine shows in primetime, they do what they do because they read those ratings every day and they know, minute by minute, what draws the most audience.
**Crichton:** Right, and they do have to live by them.

**Rose:** Otherwise they're off the air.
**Crichton:** They're off. So they're going to do what they have to do within the system. My ultimate question is: We have airplanes, we have questions about safety and we have this information processing system. But if you look at the requirements of the information processing system, it is never going to be able to address the complexity of the airplane—you're never going to find out. There isn't any possibility that it can happen. In fact, all the trends in broadcast journalism, particularly in the news magazine, are going the wrong way: the sound bites are getting shorter; everything is getting more chopped up. What's the outcome? We live in a very, very complicated society. How are we going to deal with questions, not only about our own governance, but also technical questions like air safety, like nuclear waste, all this kind of thing—pollution? How are we going to do it if there's no way to talk about it?

**Rose:** What brought you to this subject and led to that speech and this continued interest? Was it what was written about you, or something else?
**Crichton:** No, no. It's just watching. It's being a consumer of information more than a source or a target. I think I've actually been very well treated.

**Rose:** I do, too. But you have a deep interest in this and you made that speech in 1993; it's now 1996. This book comes out and it's a theme of this book.
**Crichton:** I have this odd life, which is that I alternate between being the subject and the interviewer. It has certainly been my experience that each time I go out there is more caution, there is more skepticism, there is more hostility. In trying to find a subject area I also looked, for example, at biotechnology and I tried to go see some biotech facilities. They just said, "No."

**Rose:** "Don't even want to be bothered, because we don't think any writer, any reporter, will give a fair story."
**Crichton:** Or, "We don't know what you're going to do but we're not interested."

**Rose:** Akin to that is that there are a lot of very good people—I share some of your frustration—a lot of very good people do not hold themselves up for public office for some of the same reasons.
**Crichton:** Yes, exactly.

**Rose:** Not that there shouldn't be a high standard if you run for public office, not that reporters ought not be finding out who you are and what makes you tick and what recommends you to the public's trust, but at the same time, good people don't do it because: "It is not worth it for my family."
**Crichton:** Or myself.

**Rose:** It is not worth taking one little thing I might have done and blow it way out of proportion so it projects to full screen.
**Crichton:** Right.

**Rose:** Do you think it will change, or get worse?
**Crichton:** It looks to me like it's getting worse.

**Rose:** Some will argue that the answer will be the multiplicity of channels.
**Crichton:** I doubt that very much.

**Rose:** Okay, but let me make this argument—you may be right. Take NBC News: It's still a thirty-minute news broadcast with Tom Brokaw; but on MSNBC they now have plenty of time to sit around and talk and investigate—I don't know how much investigation they do, they seem to be primarily talk, but they have an hour interview show at 8:00; Brokaw and others do it—Katie Couric and Gumbel. Brian Williams does the news for an hour at 9:00. So they are giving you more. Whether it's being recycled and whether they're taking time to do longer stories, I haven't watched enough to know. But some suggest that's at least one possibility to see more. You can see more documentaries on television today, including about the airline industry, because there's a Discovery Channel; you can see more history because there's a History Channel. There is access. Whether it's on the cutting edge of what this society needs to know about the pressing problems is another issue.

**Crichton:** Yes. Everything you say is true.

**Rose:** But?

**Crichton:** The other side of that is: I'm old enough to remember when television was first sold as this wonderful educational medium that was going to transform all of our lives. I think we have an understanding about the limits of television, but simply in terms of increasing the number of channels—I have four movie channels and frequently, it seems to me, that literally the same movie is running so I can flick from one channel to the next if the phone rings and pick it up five minutes earlier.

**Rose:** Wait until you get digital satellite. You're going to go nuts when you move east and get this new house in the country—you're going to love it; except you probably don't watch much television.

**Crichton:** I don't watch too much, no.

**Rose:** Do you watch *ER*?

**Crichton:** Absolutely. Everybody watches *ER*!

**Rose:** Of course they do! That's another reason people want to be Mike. [Laughs]

**Crichton:** [laughs]

**Rose:** It's true! I want to shift to the airline business for a while and then talk about you, because we have an hour. The airline business—did you find out that more things than you expected are pilot error than mechanical failure?

**Crichton:** I don't know what I expected.

**Rose:** I know the theme of your book, but . . .

**Crichton:** Sixty percent of all accidents are human error.

**Rose:** Human error.

**Crichton:** Yes. I don't know how that compares to nuclear power plant accidents, or other kinds of accidents. My suspicion is that's probably an irreducible number. In other words, whatever the system, sixty percent of things that go wrong are going to be attributable to people. The two discoveries I made that were really interesting to me were: One was the way the airplane manufacturers treat their products. For a person who walks into the system as I did, in a certain way cynical, it was really eye-opening. They really pay attention to how they're built. They're built extraordinarily well; they're designed extraordinarily well; they're made to withstand phenomenal stresses—to last twice as long as they're supposed to last. If anything goes wrong with them, these guys are on the phone all around the world, everyday, talking to the carriers about cargo doors that won't close, pilot lights that don't go out. They track the problems, they fix the problems, they watch the planes afterwards to make sure the problems really are indeed fixed. If there is a systemic problem, they get the bulletins out and notify everybody—it's really impressive how they do it, and I was very pleasantly surprised and in a way permanently changed. Now I step on an airplane—I have a very confident feeling.

**Rose:** More confident than you did before?
**Crichton:** Yes.

**Rose:** What did you find out about the black box? One out of six times it succeeds, or something like that?
**Crichton:** Yes. They're not required to be checked before every flight.

**Rose:** Why not?
**Crichton:** FAA doesn't require it.

**Rose:** Do you think deregulation is a bad idea or a good idea?
**Crichton:** My suspicion is that there's a pulse in all this. In other words, there comes a time when very strict government controls . . .

**Rose:** The pendulum swings too far over this way, then swings back.
**Crichton:** Overly high prices—people realize it can be cheaper. There's pressure to get the government out and then eventually we're going to see some pressure for some degree of oversight, however that occurs.

**Rose:** How about private planes? Do you feel as comfortable about private as you do about commercial?
**Crichton:** They are statistically, of course, much less safe. The big commercial airplanes are stupefyingly safe—that was the other discovery.

**Rose:** What does old man Norton say in your book? He says they take these big things and fly them around—they go around the world. He makes this amazing, almost hymn to what happens to get a plane that big in the air—to do what it does.

**Crichton:** Right. Something that's more than half a million pounds, that will fly seven, eight thousands miles at a time carrying people in the kind of comfort where their greatest irritation is they don't like the quality of the air.

**Rose:** Let me come back to reporting, though. There have been a lot of reports about pilot fatigue and things like that, which were well researched, well documented, not intended to scare people—but because they knew there was great curiosity about airline safety. They're curious about it, and when something happens as it happened to ValuJet, or when something happens that happened to TWA Flight 800, the interest rises.

**Crichton:** The interest rises.

**Rose:** You and I are complaining about the fact that a news organization would do a fifteen-minute piece about pilot fatigue.

**Crichton:** No, no. But I am complaining that if a ValuJet plane goes down— and this is a very inexpensive operation that's put itself together in an innovative new way, let's put it like that—it's not exactly the same as other airlines; it doesn't handle its liabilities and its responsibilities exactly like other airlines and it can offer very cheap fares. Down goes such a plane. In this new deregulated environment, in a situation where fleets are aging, is the pressing question that we all want to know: How quickly are the bodies decomposing? I don't think so. But that's primarily what's reported—what's in the muck. The more abstract question that is nevertheless the more important question isn't addressed very much—gore pushes it out; and if the time is devoted to that, to the sensational, then the time will not be available to be devoted to the core issues. I'm not going to die on that ValuJet plane— it's already down. I'm going to die, you're going to die, if the system that we have put in place is moving toward the edge of the table and is going to fall off; maybe not this week, but next week. The real question about ValuJet is: Is it a harbinger of things to come, or not?

**Rose:** Was there something wrong with that plane that is likely to happen again and again and again? If so, let's figure out what it was and stop it.

**Crichton:** Yes. Or is it, in fact, simply too risky to assemble an airline in that fashion—subcontracting the maintenance and all the things they do?

**Rose:** Did you have any reluctance to move to this, because *Jurassic Park* and *Twister* were not controversial works on your part? *Rising Sun* was. Now you're back in the midst of controversy. Did you have any resistance to going into those turbulent waters again?
**Crichton:** I kind of like it.

**Rose:** [Laughs] You do, don't you?
**Crichton:** Yes.

**Rose:** Because it sells.
**Crichton:** No, because sometimes I sit there and feel no one will talk about this. From time to time I'd look at some show on why planes go down or something like that, and there'd be this phenomenal dramatic footage—it was all completely irrelevant! The relevant fact is that planes, to an astonishing degree, don't go down.

**Rose:** Come on, that's silly; the notion that we know that planes don't go down—we know that. The news is about the plane that goes down, that's the nature of news; not that in America today five million planes landed safely.
**Crichton:** No. Don't misunderstand me. I'm not saying the news ought not report the murder, the disaster, the rape, and the fire. Of course, it's going to. I'm saying—is that all it does? Particularly I'm saying, if I'm going to watch a show called *Why Planes Go Down*—is the essential feature of the content only going to be "Oh my God we're all going to die!" It's not good enough.

**Rose:** You and I share some sense of an indictment of the cynicism that exists within my profession, and some sense of the exploitation and some sense of how news becomes entertainment and slides deeper into that place. On the other hand, I suspect there are more inquiries of a legitimate nature than you give the profession credit for. Let me move now to the question of TWA Flight 800—they don't know what caused that crash. There has been all kinds of speculation, and it's all been reported. But there has been a very judicious effort to examine everything, including the fact that we will never know, including the fact that it may have been mechanical failure, and not all this speculation that somebody with a missile shot up there or somebody put a bomb on the plane—which is a sexier story, in terms of the way we think of violence and conflict in our society. What are your thoughts about TWA Flight 800?

**Crichton:** From the very outset, it seemed to me to be anomalous. In other words, that's a very successful, safe airplane that's been in service for almost thirty years.

**Rose:** 747.

**Crichton:** Yes. It explodes midair, also quite an uncommon event. It seems to me, from the very beginning, whatever happened to it is pretty unusual. I think it's quite reasonable to say: "Is it terrorism? Is it a missile? Is it some kind of very weird exploding spark or something?"

**Rose:** Was your first instinct, as a consumer of information, when you heard the news of that explosion—it must have been a bomb? First instinct.

**Crichton:** Sure.

**Rose:** Mine, too; and that's a reasonable expectation. Do you believe now, knowing what you do about airlines and airplanes and safety and what causes planes to go down, it was more likely to be mechanical failure?

**Crichton:** No. I don't think there's any way to make that assessment.

**Rose:** We just don't know.

**Crichton:** Yes.

**Rose:** But the body of evidence seems to be pulling away from some kind of terrorist attack, some kind of bomb, or some kind of missile to something else because they haven't found any piece of evidence that would give an indication of that.

**Crichton:** Sure. But we're dragging the stuff up from the bottom of the ocean and putting the thing together in little pieces. So what you're watching is a trend analysis as negative pieces come into play. It would only take something the size of my thumbnail that has the right residue on it and the whole things moves in another direction.

**Rose:** Let me talk about the phenomenon, if I may, of Michael Crichton. The phenomenon of Michael Crichton. You have a golden touch. You work like mad, I know you do, but everything you do turns, for the most part, to gold. *Congo*, an old novel, makes money as a new movie. They're going back doing other things you have written as they have done with John Grisham—a very

different kind of writer. *ER*—television show. This [Holds up *Airframe*] has already been sold; speculated $8–12 million by Disney—none of our business. You have *Jurassic Park*—made a ton of money. You and your wife are the screenwriters for *Twister*—made a ton of money. This book is two and a half million copies.
**Crichton:** I think it's only two.

**Rose:** Okay, let's not exaggerate. [Laughs] But it's all true. What is it?
**Crichton:** I have no idea, really. There was a time, I guess around the time of *Jurassic Park*, when I thought, "Gee, things are going pretty well." Then there was a time when I thought, "I am the luckiest person alive." Then, as things went on, I just thought, "I don't know what's happening, but this is pretty amazing." I guess I don't think about it anymore. I have no explanation for any of this. Do you?

**Rose:** No, I don't. I'm interested in what you thought. Obviously we know you have a first-class brain—that's clear. It's clear you know how to write. It's clear you have a touch and that you hit it and therefore people pay attention when you do it.
**Crichton:** I'll tell you what I think is probably true. Statistically, things do run in streaks. I had a pretty good streak in the late '60s and early '70s. I had what everyone has now forgotten—a pretty long streak of unsuccessful things from the middle '70s to the late '80s. Now I have another positive streak; but probably if you added up all the books and all the movies—it'd probably look like chance.

**Rose:** Chance?
**Crichton:** Well, I mean fifty percent, or something like that; flip of a coin, whether they're a success or not.

**Rose:** Do you think you're especially smart or that it is some other quality you have that enables you to be as productive as you are?
**Crichton:** I don't know.

**Rose:** Is it energy? Is it something else? Is it some x-factor?
**Crichton:** I don't feel smart.

**Rose:** You don't?
**Crichton:** No.

**Rose:** Smart, based on what you and I would recognize as somebody really bright.
**Crichton:** Yes.

**Rose:** Some molecular scientist somewhere.
**Crichton:** Yes. Richard Feynman wrote . . .

**Rose:** Speaking of smart.
**Crichton:** Yes. Speaking of smart—that's smart. He's smart.

**Rose:** Exactly.
**Crichton:** He wrote in one of his autobiographical books that he was listening to some philosophers and he decided to ask them a question, so his question was: "Does a brick have an inside?" I read that and I thought, "That's a really interesting question." Feynman's view was that if you could answer that question then you would know what you were talking about. I thought, "That's really interesting," and I never understood what it meant. Does a brick have an inside?

**Rose:** I don't know. [Laughs]
**Crichton:** Why would we be asking that?

**Rose:** That's a more interesting question to me.
**Crichton:** I don't feel real smart. I feel like I have to struggle.

**Rose:** You feel like it works because you work harder than most?
**Crichton:** Yes.

**Rose:** You dig harder, stay up later, get up earlier, care more, look under every rock.
**Crichton:** Yes. That's my assumption. I assume that's what's true for most people who are successful.

**Rose:** I do, too. I have never had anyone come on this program who had extraordinary achievement—and I'm talking about twenty-five Nobel laureates as well, and writers, and artists—who've ever said to me, "I can tell you the answer: I'm just smart." It's always, in their self-perception, to do with commitment, to do with discipline, to do with appropriate training, and focus.
**Crichton:** Focus is a big one.

**Rose:** Focus. You have that.
**Crichton:** Yes, I do. Concentration.

**Rose:** What does that mean?
**Crichton:** I think of it like long-distance running or something like that. I think of it as having built up a tolerance for trying to figure something out—over a period of years, even; and being patient. Like this press thing—I have notes for a novel called *Frame* in '89. I had some idea about the media in '89. I'm waiting and waiting; maybe I'll get it and maybe I won't; maybe it'll come to me and maybe it won't. That's a sort of endurance; then to just sit at the word processor; good days and bad days . . . plenty of bad days.

**Rose:** If I ask this question: "What do you want?" Is there an answer? Do you know? What does success mean to you?
**Crichton:** Success means opportunity in the area I work, because the great difficulty people have who want to write books or do movies or have TV shows is they don't feel they have access. They can't get their book published or their movie made or their TV show on the air. I can now. That's what it means—it means I have the opportunity; so, better have something to say.

**Rose:** Someone said in a different way: "Half the battle is getting in the park; getting in the ballpark so you can play." Half the battle is getting there. There are a lot of people with good ideas who can't raise money to see them through, there are a lot of people who may have a good idea who don't have access and a lot of people with access can't deliver.
**Crichton:** Yes.

**Rose:** Does any of this make sense?
**Crichton:** Yes, or it gets so that they don't want to work as hard.

**Rose:** I met the other day in California, when I saw you last—Clint Eastwood. I have enormous admiration for Clint Eastwood.
**Crichton:** Me, too.

**Rose:** Because of longevity and integrity, and he's his own master.
**Crichton:** Yes. I completely agree. And there's something else that I, at least, think about when I think about Clint Eastwood—which is all those years when people said, "Oh, yeah. Clint Eastwood—spaghetti westerns." And he was continuing to work.

**Rose:** He doesn't say anything; it's all right.

**Crichton:** He was working well and improving his craft. He was going forward and going forward and going forward. Now, he has this other kind of respect.

**Rose:** He makes *Unforgiven* and everybody is saying he's the great auteur we always thought he was.

**Crichton:** But I think of that whenever I'm feeling that I'm not getting enough respect.

**Rose:** You do?

**Crichton:** Yes. I think, "Well, so what. Keep working."

**Rose:** You got up this morning and there weren't all great reviews. Some of them were great, and all of them talk about the phenomenon of Michael— "want to be Mike." But they were mixed in some cases, in terms of picking at certain points, saying character development is not his strong suit; saying one thing or the other. It doesn't bother you?

**Crichton:** I thought they were much better than I expected.

**Rose:** You did?

**Crichton:** Yes.

**Rose:** You expected to get hit because it's a commercial topic, or what?

**Crichton:** No, I expect to get hit because at a certain point what you do won't get reviewed anymore—you get reviewed.

**Rose:** You're there. Cover of *Time* magazine '95.

**Crichton:** Those are all very distorting things for the reviewing process.

**Rose:** They review you and at some point, after everybody's talking about how successful you are, somebody comes along and says, "Prove it to me."

**Crichton:** Yes.

**Rose:** You wrote a book about Jasper Johns. The time I saw you in New York you were there at the opening of his exhibition. What do you think of the exhibition?

**Crichton:** It's beautiful.

**Rose:** Is he the greatest living artist in America?

**Crichton:** I think if someone asked Jasper that he would say, "I don't think in that way."

**Rose:** I know he doesn't, but do you?

**Crichton:** I don't think in that way either.

**Rose:** You don't?

**Crichton:** No.

**Rose:** You know what your favorite television show is, don't you?

**Crichton:** Yes, I do—and I'm there. I'm there. But what are the three best movies you ever saw? It makes my mind go blank.

**Rose:** Why do you like Jasper Johns? Why did you care enough about him to write a book about him?

**Crichton:** He does very beautiful work. He's an extremely interesting person to be around and his work I find challenging on many levels—it's intellectually challenging, it's visually challenging, and it rewards continued looking. You can have a piece of his work up for years and look at it and keep seeing new things and having new feelings about it. Not all artists are like that—in terms of their work.

**Rose:** Do you think the work today is as good as the work fifteen years ago?

**Crichton:** I think an artist's new work is always seen as less agreeable than the old work. Rauschenberg once said to me, "I have to keep doing new work so they'll like the old work."

**Rose:** [Laughs] Have you seen *The English Patient*, the movie?

**Crichton:** No, I haven't.

**Rose:** Because you've been on the tour? Because you don't watch movies that much?

**Crichton:** No, I'm looking forward to seeing it.

**Rose:** It's a good film. Do you want to direct again?

**Crichton:** I think so.

**Rose:** What are you looking for?

**Crichton:** Time. [Laughs] At every moment when I think, "Maybe it would be good to direct," I think, "If I'm going to direct something or I'm going to write something, then I choose to write something."

**Rose:** You don't want to direct somebody else's work?
**Crichton:** Not very much.

**Rose:** Not unless it really knocks your socks off?
**Crichton:** No, I think I would like to direct something I wrote.

**Rose:** You produce them now; you have the title "Producer."
**Crichton:** Yes.

**Rose:** Why do you do that?
**Crichton:** It's a way to have some involvement or some advisory function, something to say on the movie. In other words, Charlie, for someone in my position there are two ways to do this: You can either try to have your project be done by a very accomplished, very established director, or you can look for a younger person who is less established, less assured, then dominate that person and get them to do more of what you want to do. My choice is always to take it to a very good director—but then the outcome is that the director will make the movie he wants to make; that's the reality. I'm not going to be telling Barry Levinson or Steven Spielberg how to make the movie. They're going to do it in the way they think best. My best hope is that they'll do it well.

**Rose:** Except they feel the same way about you and they're going to listen to what you say.
**Crichton:** Some.

**Rose:** Not your experience, is it?
**Crichton:** Well, sometimes.

**Rose:** *Jurassic Park* is not the movie you would have made?
**Crichton:** I can't think what movie I would have made. I like that movie very well.

**Rose:** You should.
**Crichton:** And I like *Disclosure* very well—what Barry did. But I see them as distinctly their work. In being a producer I'm trying to do two things: to

head-off what I would see as a disaster, in terms of giving advice; and to have some degree of input, that's all. It's certainly not to control that process.

**Rose:** Was directing satisfying for you? You directed *Coma*, you directed what else?
**Crichton:** *The Great Train Robbery, Westworld.*

**Rose:** I can't wait to see *The Great Train Robbery*—it's now on laserdisc and it has director's notes; I can't wait. It's a fascinating film. You made it for $6 million.
**Crichton:** That's right.

**Rose:** Sean Connery, Donald Sutherland . . .
**Crichton:** Leslie-Anne Down.

**Rose:** It's the story of this great train robbery and you made it for $6 million back when?
**Crichton:** 1978.

**Rose:** It's now being released in laser and 35 mm using all the advances in technological sound reproduction. Yes?
**Crichton:** Yes, and with the audio track.

**Rose:** With the audio track.
**Crichton:** From the director.

**Rose:** In which you talk about what?
**Crichton:** The decisions that were made, how characterizations and scenes were put together, how things were moved and changed. It's fun.

**Rose:** What interested you about bio-medics and biotech before you had the door shut in your face?
**Crichton:** Why was I thinking of going there?

**Rose:** Yes.
**Crichton:** Because it's another area in which there's likely to be a very complicated story—too complicated for a news magazine to report, to be bothered with, but involving a development that we might all care about—might affect us all.

**Rose:** And it's beginning already.

**Crichton:** Yes. We're making very, very dramatic changes.

**Rose:** In the front page of the *New York Times* this week, they have discovered an anxiety gene. Did you see that?

**Crichton:** I saw it, yes, but I didn't read it. [Laughs] I'm sorry!

**Rose:** Why wouldn't you read that, Michael? I just loved that story. What in the world are they talking about? All of a sudden it explained tons of people I know. I read science stories—I can't read enough of them. It fascinated me. But you were bored.

**Crichton:** No. I think some of it is lack of patience from being on tour.

**Rose:** The focus thing.

**Crichton:** I see that as a permanently conflicted issue; the same thing as an alcoholism gene.

**Rose:** Because if you know you're going to have it, it's terrible news for you.

**Crichton:** There does not seem to be, in most of these genes, that they're behaving as an on-off switch; that it's a yes or a no. There's a predisposition, there's a tendency . . . so you're left with some amount of responsibility, aren't you? Therefore, aren't you given the choice between seeing yourself as a victim who is ensnared by their genetic heritage or are you just a person who can't stop the behavior?

**Rose:** There goes the ethical dilemma.

**Crichton:** Right.

**Rose:** But, at the same time, there's this other extraordinary parallel development which is called gene replacement therapy, and where does that leave us? If you know early you have a diabetic gene, can they do something about it?

**Crichton:** I think we're going to see more and more of that. I think that is absolutely the future—for better or worse. Probably, in many cases, it's for the better. I guess my response to the anxiety headline is, I thought, "Okay, alcoholism, now anxiety." Somebody who's nervous, they go, "Oh, my goodness, it's my genes."

**Rose:** What does lots of money do for you? Enable you to buy more Jasper Johns? Or something else?

**Crichton:** It gives you freedom. It gives you a release from certain kinds of anxieties. It gives you a surprising number of responsibilities. What is that proverb? "He who has cow has care of cow." It gives you an opportunity to affect things, to make contributions to things, to move certain things in a direction you want to go. It's very nice.

**Rose:** Any downside here?

**Crichton:** I think it's the responsibility; it's stuff; it's possessions; some sources of concern; security issues. It's not the same as it was, and it does change a lot of things. But I don't know anybody who said, "I want to go back."

**Rose:** [Laughs] Nobody said, "I've been rich and I've been poor . . . "

**Crichton:** "And poor is better"; that's right. [Laughs] Exactly.

**Rose:** Nobody said, "Mister, you had it all wrong. It wasn't like that at all. A life of service and dedication is better. Rich made me bad." What are you writing next?

**Crichton:** I'm starting a new book.

**Rose:** Already?

**Crichton:** No, in January.

**Rose:** You actually need a break between. You have all those notes you keep constantly, whether it's on biotech or whether it's on airlines. I don't feel you're satisfied yet with respect to the news thing.

**Crichton:** No, and I'll tell you why: Because these long-term trends have to do with the increasing commercialization of speech, and the assumption that is always the way it ought to be. I'm always delighted to see you, but the fact is that when we're talking it's because I have something to sell—and it's in that context.

**Rose:** That's your fault. I invite you to this program when you don't have things to sell and you don't want to come because you realize there is some value in only coming when you have something to sell.

**Crichton:** Now, wait a minute, this is unfair. I don't come for a lot of rea- sons—one of which is I'm not always so enthusiastic about talking about myself, although you seem to have gotten me to do a great deal of it right now. Let's put it this way, a lot of the people who are on your show have something to be publicized. A lot of television in general has that character; has the character of inter-mixing the information with some commercial message; and more and more, it seems to me, we expect that. We don't imagine a kind of disinterested speech.

**Rose:** It's not quite fair about me. You're absolutely right that, in fact, a lot of people come to this broadcast who have something to sell. [Holds up *Airframe*]—You're now on a big tour to sell this book because you have two million in print and we want [you] to sell as many of those as you possibly can. You have spent how many years of your life on this?
**Crichton:** About two.

**Rose:** Two years of your life. You've looked into this. You've thought about related subjects that are of interest and we spent the first thirty minutes of this broadcast only talking about that, and about news—a subject you have thought about; two particular areas of interest—in terms of the content of books and the content of news. You come having thought about these things. You're here to sell a book, and I'm happy the book sells because I enjoyed the book. But at the same time, when somebody spends a considerable portion of their life doing something—whether it is *The Wasteland* with Fiona Shaw, or whether it is Angelica Houston making a film based on a book that I admired by Dorothy Allison, *Bastard Out of Carolina*—and care about their craft—or Jasper Johns, who doesn't do any interviews, as far as I know, and I'd love for him to do one here—I'm happy to do it, because I bring to this table an opportunity for an audience out there to get to know someone in a different way.
**Crichton:** I agree with all that, and I really didn't want you to take it in any way personally.

**Rose:** I didn't take it personally, Michael! [Laughs]
**Crichton:** [Laughs]

**Rose:** Go ahead!
**Crichton:** In the way that you can be flipping from channel to channel and you would see an inordinate number of guns.

**Rose:** You're more likely to go to the guns than me, probably.

**Crichton:** No, no, no, but we all know you're going to see a lot of images of violence because that's our culture. In that same way, there are going to be a tremendous number of images of selling—both overt and covert. It's a selling medium.

**Rose:** Television delivers product.
**Crichton:** Putting you aside.

**Rose:** Sure.
**Crichton:** When you said I'm not satisfied about the media—there was a time when speech was essentially always intended for a single listener, or a group of people who could hear it without any amplification. That was communication. Print was something else. Print is very, in a certain way, limited in its ability to do many things. It's a kind of communication, but its bandwidth isn't very great. Now we have communication primarily to large groups of people. Individuality is gone and, increasingly, communication is commercial communication. I think it's odd, and I don't think we're quite acknowledging how pervasive it is, how strongly it influences everything, and what, if anything, we ought to do about it. It's a kind of pollution.

**Rose:** One last question before we say goodbye: The internet offers you access to information, all kinds of dialogue that's not based on promotion. Are you logging in? Are you doing that very much? Is there a Michael Crichton website?
**Crichton:** There is, actually, but I don't run it. It's another commercial medium. It's the new television. The claims being made for it are exactly the claims that—you can go back to the '40s and '50s and see what people said was going to be wonderful about television—that's what's being said [about] the internet. Each day, it seems to me, there's more advertising. I'm not persuaded. Yes, I'm on it some, but I'm not persuaded.

**Rose:** It's another medium; but there's nothing wrong with delivering advertising, either.
**Crichton:** No, but there are two kinds of advertising.
**Rose:** In other words, you're a capitalist. [Laughs]
**Crichton:** Yes, I'm a capitalist. There's the advertising that gives you information about the availability of a product, the qualities of the product, why you ought to buy it as opposed to others. Then there is what is now the most common kind of advertising which is advertising by association—if

you drive this car you'll be sexy and attractive and have an exciting time; it's completely untrue—it's an associational thing.

**Rose:** I was going to hold this book up and recommend you read it, but Michael has shamed me into not doing that so—Michael Crichton has written a book, I can't remember the . . . [Laughs]
**Crichton:** I've done this to myself! I can see it's my own fault. [Laughs]

**Rose:** [Holds up *Airframe*] *Airframe*. Michael Crichton. It's a pleasure as always. Thank you.
**Crichton:** Thank you, Charlie.

**Rose:** Thank you for joining us for the hour. We'll see you next time.

# Playboy Interview: Michael Crichton

## John Rezek and David Sheff/1999

*Playboy* magazine, January 1999. Copyright © by Playboy. Reprinted with permission. All rights reserved.

If you had met Michael Crichton three decades ago, you could easily have imagined a traditional future for him. A stellar student at the Harvard Medical School and armed with an impressive intellect, Crichton seemed headed for a life as a researcher or hospital administrator, the type of overachiever who would make his mark in science or public health. You never would have predicted the intense young med student would give up medicine and emerge as a dominant talent in fields of popular culture—a man who simultaneously topped all three key indicators of current American thought: the bestseller list, the box office tallies and the Nielsen ratings.

What's even more unlikely is that Crichton has done so not by pandering to mass tastes but by catering to uncounted multitudes who don't mind stretching their minds while being entertained.

Consider what Crichton has accomplished in publishing. Instead of writing cheesy, sex-filled potboilers that fill the bestseller racks, Crichton invented a genre aimed at smart readers. He elevated the basic thriller by setting it against a backdrop of important current issues—the Japanese juggernaut in *Rising Sun*, sexual harassment in *Disclosure*—and creating books that were as informative as they were fun to read.

He's been no ordinary success in Hollywood, either. Some of the movies based on his books and screenplays, such as *Jurassic Park* and *Twister*, have been tremendous box office successes. And the one TV show he created— *ER*—is arguably the smartest hour on TV ever to top the ratings.

Bouncing among books, movies, and TV has worked well for Crichton. More than 100 million of his books have been printed, and his movies have grossed more than a billion dollars. In its 1999 survey of the wealthiest entertainers, Forbes put Crichton at number seven and mused that "he could probably sell the concepts in his head for a few hundred million dollars."

Part of Crichton's success stems from his knack for predicting trends and events and for honing in on hot issues with uncanny timing. "If you ever find in a publisher's catalog the announcement of an impending Crichton novel called *Armageddon*, gather your loved ones and head for the hills," advised one journalist.

Crichton is best known for his *Jurassic Park*, a work he began in 1984 and didn't complete until 1990. The book, about the re-creation of dinosaurs from DNA culled from mosquitoes preserved in amber, popularized the cloning controversy. After it was made into a movie by Steven Spielberg, it became one of the highest-grossing films of all time, earning $912 million.

Then came the sequel, *The Lost World*, which Spielberg also made into a movie. Crichton's most recent novel, 1996's *Airframe*, is in part an indictment of airline deregulation and the resulting deterioration of maintenance and safety. In it, Crichton takes on the media—a subplot has journalists who cover a plane accident being less concerned about the veracity of their reporting than they are about the tidiness of their stories.

Crichton's eagerness to tackle controversial issues makes headlines, but it also generates criticism. *Jurassic Park* earned the ire of academics who claimed it was anti-science. Literary critics chide Crichton for his simplistic or two-dimensional characters, who get short shrift in favor of complicated plots and detailed situations.

Critics have been kinder to some of Crichton's other works, including his masterful study of Jasper Johns and a collection of autobiographical essays, *Travels*. In the latter, Crichton describes his thrill-seeking past—he used to scuba dive, climb mountains (including a memorable hike up Mount Kilimanjaro), and swim with sharks. He was born in January 1942 in Chicago, half a mile from the hospital now used as the setting for *ER*. He was the oldest of four children, and his relationship with his father, an executive editor at *Advertising Age*, was often tense. As he writes in *Travels*, "My father and I had not had an easy time together. We had never been the classic boy and his dad. As far as I was concerned, he was a first-rate son of a bitch."

When Crichton was in third grade, he wrote a nine-page play for a puppet show, which his father dismissed as the most cliché-ridden piece he had ever read. Undaunted, Crichton went on to publish his first article at the age of fourteen. In the *New York Times*.

Crichton attended Roslyn High School in New York, where he was a

Latin scholar, a student journalist, and, already 6'7", a basketball star. He still holds several records there.

He went to Harvard, where he planned to become a writer, but he says the English department was more interested in producing professors than cultivating writers. He switched to anthropology and took premed courses.

After graduating, Crichton spent a year lecturing in anthropology at Cambridge University before enrolling at Harvard Medical School. Until then he had been supported by his family, but he paid his way through medical school by writing thrillers under the pseudonyms Jeffery Hudson and John Lange. (The first was a pun on his height—which was now 6'9"; Hudson was a dwarf courtier in the service of Charles I.) *A Case of Need* by Jeffery Hudson won the 1968 Edgar Award and was the first time Crichton addressed real-life events with what was to become his signature timeliness. The book is about abortion.

In 1969 Crichton published *The Andromeda Strain* under his own name while still in med school. He was paid $250,000 for the film rights. When he visited the movie set on the Universal Studios lot, a young director working there gave Crichton a tour: He was Steven Spielberg.

Two more thrillers followed in 1972 and 1973: the novel *The Terminal Man*, in which an experimental surgical procedure goes awry, and the movie *Westworld*, a science fiction story about a theme park of the future where tourists enact their fantasies. Crichton also later wrote and directed *The Great Train Robbery*, which starred Sean Connery, who became a good friend.

Crichton has been married four times and has a ten-year-old daughter. In 1988 he married his current wife, Anne-Marie Martin, an actor and screenwriter who was his collaborator on the screenplay for *Twister*. Crichton confesses that two of his previous wives made him see a psychotherapist, and he remains committed to therapy. It hasn't cured his workaholism, however; when Crichton is working, his wife has said, "It's like living with a body and Michael is somewhere else."

His work habits have paid off—Crichton is probably the highest-paid writer in America. A *Time* magazine cover story in 1995 touted him as "The Hit Man with the Golden Touch." He reportedly earned $10 million for the film rights to *Airframe* alone.

Despite his hectic schedule, Crichton found time to meet with Assistant Managing Editor John Rezek and Contributing Editor David Sheff for a rare interview. Here's their report:

"Crichton was concentrating on one of several current projects when we arrived at his Santa Monica office. (He has homes in Los Angeles, New York, and Hawaii.) He was in postproduction for *The 13th Warrior*—a movie due out this year that's based on his book *Eaters of the Dead*—and he was getting ready to launch his own website.

"Though Crichton is famously tall, no one is quite prepared for just how tall he is. He greeted us looking freshly tanned from Hawaii, dressed in black trousers and a polo shirt, and led us through a labyrinth of small hallways that had the effect of making him seem even taller. You get the sense he seldom permits himself the luxury of straightening up.

"We talked in a bare office and, once settled in a desk chair, Crichton adopted an impressive physical concentration: He didn't fidget, he rarely moved though his face was always animated and expressive. He has a steady no-nonsense gaze and was once described as being 'affably diffident.' There were often long silences between our questions and his answers. Far from attempting to evade the questions, he was seeking the most difficult of responses: those that are simple and responsible and honest."

**Playboy:** Your books often seem eerily prescient. How does it feel when they turn out to anticipate real-life events or trends?
**Michael Crichton:** It depends. People said *Airframe* was prescient when a United Airlines flight dropped 1000 feet over the Pacific. But there are a certain number of turbulence-related injuries every year, and that book was based on a couple of real incidents. The lesson: Wear your seat belt. When *Twister* came out in May of whatever year it was, all these tornadoes hit. Everyone said, "Isn't it amazing? He predicted it!" No, it's May—there are always hundreds of tornadoes. It's tornado season. On the other hand, certain things have surprised me. When I was working on *The Great Train Robbery*, I went into Victorian England, then an eccentric and obscure period to write about. At the time the book was published, the period had a revival. When I was writing *Rising Sun*, the Berlin Wall was coming down. Everyone was looking west; no one was looking east. People would ask what I was working on and I'd say, "Japan," and they'd ask, "Japan?" as if I had said "Sanskrit." But when the book came out it coincided with George Bush's trip to Japan and enormous interest in U.S.-Japanese relations because of the trade imbalance. I was as surprised as anybody else.

**Playboy:** How do you decide which political or social problems to tackle?
**Michael Crichton:** Certain issues just stay with me while others work themselves out. In the past, certain stories were fueled by my outrage, but

then I would lose the outrage and wouldn't have the motor to do that project anymore. I'd outgrown it. Sometimes events bypass it. And sometimes somebody else does a project that makes the issues go away. Or at least I think, "Well, that's been done, at least for now." I've been interested in doing something about political correctness, for instance. It gives me the creeps. But my sense is it's started to give a lot of people the creeps. I don't think I'll have to write about it. It will defeat itself because of its basic anti-American quality.

**Playboy:** In *Disclosure*, you took on sexual harassment. Some people feel it's a central issue in the Lewinsky-Clinton scandal. Do you agree?

**Michael Crichton:** Lewinsky certainly shows one thing I tried to address in *Disclosure*: the power of the victim. Feminists still don't acknowledge that the person who is sexually harassed has an enormous amount of power. Monica Lewinsky has shown she has quite a bit of power, hasn't she? Whether she ultimately brings down a president or not, this woman has proved that the so-called victim can be very powerful.

**Playboy:** Feminists would disagree.

**Michael Crichton:** The Clinton scandal has put the final nail in the coffin of feminism, which has been in drastic decline for several years. People aren't stupid. They see the inconsistency and hypocrisy: Brock Adams? Out! Robert Packwood? Out! Teddy Kennedy? In! Bill Clinton? In! It's what I have always thought: If you like me, I can do whatever I want. If you don't, you're going to trash me for trivialities. That's the way guys always thought it was, and feminists said, "No, it's not, there's a set of rules that apply to everyone." Guess what? It's not true.

**Playboy:** It sounds as if you'd be delighted at the fall of feminism.

**Michael Crichton:** In the same way there are fashion victims in terms of clothing, there are fashion victims in terms of ideas, and there are still victims of feminism. A lot of children are victims of an era when women declared their independence from men, saying they no longer needed them: "A woman without a man is like a fish without a bicycle." Women could do it by themselves. Well, the idea dovetailed rather nicely for a lot of young men who didn't want to be needed in the first place. They didn't want to be committed to a family just because they got a girl pregnant, for instance, so it was convenient when women were saying men weren't needed. The idea that men didn't want responsibility wasn't new, but suddenly women were saying, "Yeah, we don't need you!" and men were responding, "Great, goodbye," and they were on to the next conquest. But the kids who were left behind were victims of that fashion. There are many children raised without fathers and they have suffered.

**Playboy:** Should women return home and take care of the kids?
**Michael Crichton:** I'm not saying we should go back to the Fifties—as if we could. All I'm saying is that it's frivolous to pretend kids don't need to be raised. They do.

**Playboy:** Feminists attacked *Disclosure,* saying you trivialized sexual harassment by making the aggressor a woman and the victim a man, which is unlikely to be the case in real life.
**Michael Crichton:** I didn't know that it's a writer's obligation to do a typical story. The word is "novel." My reason for inverting this story was that inversion allows you to see the issue freshly. What inspired the book was the polarization occurring in this country. I'm always interested in what's not being talked about, and at the time everyone seemed to agree that the aggressor had all the power. I know things aren't so simple and aren't so clear. It's sex. And what's ever clear about sex?

**Playboy:** Is the country less concerned with sexual harassment than it was when you wrote *Disclosure*?
**Michael Crichton:** There will be a new wave because of Clinton. I expect that we'll see formal legislative changes and changes in social standards. But much of the hysteria has calmed down. I think it's because people see how absurd some of this is. I maintain that a lot of this play between people is human nature. You cannot keep people from telling dirty jokes, for example. It's just how we are. Fart jokes, ejaculation jokes—we're animals and we think they're funny. People are realizing that it's ridiculous to try to change the stuff that is in our genes. Men and women are different. People are starting to understand that all those gender-free toys and raising kids in a nonviolent, neutral way are a lot of baloney. When my daughter was three, she went to a birthday party held in an indoor gym. The parents drew a line down the middle of the room and divided the kids up and had what was, in effect, a snowball fight with Styrofoam balls. It provided the most persuasive evidence of gender difference I've seen. All the boys were throwing the balls, trying to kill each other, while the girls were running around and picking the balls up and putting them in baskets—cleaning up. These all were children

of doctors and lawyers, all educated and aware and up-to-the-minute. You can try to change things, but parents find out that if you take away a boy's plastic gun, he'll use a stick. If you take away the stick, he'll use his finger.

**Playboy:** Are you concerned about Clinton's affair and his apparent lies?
**Michael Crichton:** Everybody has a sex life, a private life. But the time for Clinton to have handled it was back in January, when it came out. To let it go as long as he did is inexplicable. The statement he made when he finally admitted it was also inexplicable. An apology is not the time for an attack if the goal is to put the mess behind you. You say, "When I said I never had sex with that woman I wasn't telling the truth. When I let my wife go on NBC and say it was a right-wing conspiracy, that wasn't correct, either. I allowed her to make a fool of herself." You go right down the list. "When I had my advisors go out to defend me, it was wrong." That's how you end it. The guy can't do it. But what's most disturbing is the consistent pattern of incompetence in the day-to-day management of the office of the President of the U.S.—appointments don't get made, schedules aren't kept to, staff is either not getting good advice or not being held in line. The country doesn't look well run to me.

**Playboy:** You knew *Rising Sun* and *Disclosure* would get you into trouble. Do you enjoy controversy?
**Michael Crichton:** I knew that they were risky. I couldn't have written them earlier in my career. I couldn't afford to take the risk then. But the truth is that I never know what the response will be. I was surprised by the response to *Rising Sun*. I didn't expect to be called a racist.

**Playboy:** You were accused of perpetuating the stereotype that Japanese people are devious and inscrutable.
**Michael Crichton:** Yet I thought it was an economic book about the behavior of two nations; race wasn't relevant. I expected criticism, but about the economics. I expected to hear, "This guy doesn't know what he's talking about." Part of the controversy was simply that I addressed the issue. In the U.S. it was agreed there would be no criticism of Japan no matter what. That a popular novel made criticisms was seen as shocking, partly because there hadn't been anything like that for forty years. My response was, "Wait a minute! In the world I come from, disagreement is a good thing. The American way is, 'Battle it out in the marketplace of ideas.'"

**Playboy:** Were you disappointed by the reaction?

**Michael Crichton:** At the deepest level, I trust the readers. They're perfectly able to understand what I'm talking about. I have less respect for the media. The first thing I read about the book was in *Publishers Weekly*, which said I had "reawakened the fears of the Yellow Peril." I thought, "What?" It said something about Fu Manchu, who, of course, was Chinese.

**Playboy:** How did the attacks affect you?

**Michael Crichton:** They were quite alarming and made me hesitant to do *Disclosure*. I thought, "If there's anything that can bring me more flak than U.S.-Japanese relations, it's gender relations."

**Playboy:** And you weren't disappointed, presumably.

**Michael Crichton:** Definitely not. One thing I noticed when *Disclosure* came out was the tendency among certain types of guys to trash the book. I figured out exactly what they were doing. I thought, "You're going to trash me because you want to get laid tonight." Many male reviewers attacked me, thinking their girlfriends were going to read their reviews. But I was talking about something that many people responded to. I was talking about the power of the victim and the vulnerability of the boss. I was trying to talk about the other side of the equation. I'm always trying to talk about the things that aren't being discussed.

**Playboy:** How happy are you with the movie versions of *Disclosure* and *Rising Sun*?

**Michael Crichton:** What I hope for is a good movie on its own terms—one that's interesting and exciting and works as a movie. Whether or not it's faithful to what I wrote is irrelevant—impossible. There is an inherent difference in the forms. If you take a screenplay, which is 120 pages on average, and convert it into prose, it would be about forty pages. What happens in reverse is that a 400-page novel is condensed to a forty-page story. The overwhelming majority of what's in the book is gone. The only hope is that distillation, or abridgement, retains the essence of the book.

**Playboy:** Has that happened with yours?

**Michael Crichton:** I've had more luck than most people. I've often been pleased with the movies. Not always, but often.

**Playboy:** Some critics claim you write your novels with eventual movies too much in mind.

**Michael Crichton:** I've been accused of that all my life. I was accused of writing books with movies in mind even before any of my books were made into movies. But I see pictures in my head and I describe them; my way of writing is cinematic. It's just the way I work. Robert Louis Stevenson is phenomenally cinematic, and there weren't any movies at the time he was writing. If he wrote *Treasure Island* today, people would say, "He's writing with a movie in mind." *The Lost World*, in particular, was written with a movie in mind. That's why I wrote it.

**Playboy:** You once described people in Hollywood as "fabulously stupid," and the entertainment industry as "a business of idiots." Care to name names?

**Michael Crichton:** One of the stupidest people is the one who made that comment. The truth is, this is frequently a frustrating business. When I made that remark, I was thinking of a couple of people I had run up against. As I think of those people, I will stand by that comment. They are idiots beyond belief. They're famous to some degree, but I'm here to tell you they are truly idiots in the Molière sense: self-deluded, pompous nincompoops. The movie business in general is what you would expect in a high-visibility, high-paying, high-stakes industry. It tends to attract people who are smart, savvy, aggressive, and ambitious. And while there are incredibly stupid people, there are brilliant ones, too, including the people I've worked with in recent years. I would happily work again with Steven Spielberg and Barry Levinson.

**Playboy:** What do you see as the most striking change in how Hollywood does business?

**Michael Crichton:** The change that everyone used to talk about was the arrival of television and the migration out of movies of certain kinds of stories that went to TV. That's true, but by far the more powerful change has been the rise of VHS and now DVD. These are now the primary market, theatrical release is not. And so everything to do with theatrical release is actually intended to position yourself for the real market, which used to be the aftermarket. That's where most of the money comes from. Nobody knows what percentage, but at least seventy-five percent. The industry is trying to make products that will have international appeal because of foreign support. Movies are no longer locally oriented, they're not locked to a particular time and place. They tend to be action-oriented because that's an international vocabulary in a sense. They tend to be big and splashy and full of special effects because that's easily and telegraphically marketable. And they tend to be sequels and remakes. In the last ten years, something like a quarter or a fifth of all movies are sequels and remakes, because the product is so expensive that anything that gives you an edge on penetration is worth it.

**Playboy:** Your real introduction to Hollywood came in the early Seventies, right after you sold *The Andromeda Strain* to Universal Pictures. Is it true you were given a tour of Universal Studios by Steven Spielberg?
**Michael Crichton:** Yes. He was charming then as now. I was fascinated by him. He had already embarked on a course of directing at a time when I was deciding whether I would be interested in doing so. He had a quality that he still has: a naive enthusiasm, a simple excitement. He is in no way naive or simple—he's an extremely sophisticated guy and very, very subtle—but a kind of youthful excitement often bubbles up out of him. It's contagious and attractive. It's hard not to be drawn to it.

**Playboy:** Spielberg says that you have the richest imagination of anybody he knows. Is there anything an imagination-challenged person can do to enhance his creativity?
**Michael Crichton:** I'm always thinking about how to use things. Even in the middle of a fight with your loved one, when she makes some terrible, lashing remark that cuts you to the quick, some part of me is going, "Not bad, you know, I can use that one." That sort of constant, partial detachment means you are almost never fully absorbed in anything—some part of you is always watching, always noticing, always thinking, "How can I use this? Does this fit with anything I'm thinking about?"

**Playboy:** The movies you made with Spielberg, *Jurassic Park* and *The Lost World*, were based on successful but controversial books. You were accused of being anti-science. What do you say to that?
**Michael Crichton:** I've always been called anti-whatever; anti-feminist, anti-Japan, anti-science. There's a long list. The science thing was said to me directly. People said that by expressing concerns about the negative impact of science and technology, I was fueling people's fears and diminishing the ability of science to progress. But that's baloney. If it were true that *Jurassic Park* is anti-science and impeding progress and people's interest in science, why are so many natural history museums in the U.S. now running shows

called "Jurassic Park" or "The Real Jurassic Park"? They perceive that the effect of these stories is to arouse tremendous interest and enthusiasm—more than scientists are generally able to. Besides, we live in a society that in many respects is a gigantic cheerleader for science and technology. None of these advances have been as good as they originally claimed to be. I'm old enough to remember a world without television. And I remember all the claims for television—about how it was going to produce universal education and there was going to be so much exposure to the world. Some of those claims have come true, but the overwhelming majority of the claims were just baloney. It's difficult now to make the claim that television is an educational medium. It's an advertising medium.

**Playboy:** In *Jurassic Park*, you looked at the potential hazards of DNA research. What's your view of cloning?

**Michael Crichton:** I think we're a long way from cloning people. But I am worried about scientific advances without consideration of their consequences. The history of medicine in my lifetime is one of technological advances that outstrip our ethical systems. We've never caught up. When I was in medical school—thirty-odd years ago—people were struggling to deal with mechanical-respiration systems. They were keeping alive people who a few years earlier would have died of natural causes. Suddenly people weren't going to die of natural causes. They were either going to get on these machines and never get off or—or what? Were we going to turn the machines off? We had the machines well before we started the debate. Doctors were speaking quietly among themselves with a kind of resentment toward these machines. On the one hand, if somebody had a temporary disability, the machines could help get them over the hump. For accident victims—some of whom were very young—who could be saved if they pulled through the initial crisis, the technology saved lives. You could get them over the hump and then they would recover, and that was terrific.

But on the other hand, there was a category of people who were on their way out but could be kept alive. Before the machine, "pulling the plug" actually meant opening the window too wide one night, and the patient would get pneumonia and die. That wasn't going to happen now. We were being forced by technology to make decisions about the right to die—whether it's a legal or religious issue—and many related matters. Some of them contradict longstanding ideas in an ethically protected world; we weren't being forced to make hard decisions, because those decisions were being made for us—in this case, by the pneumococcus.

This is just one example of an ethical issue raised by technology. Cloning is another. If you're knowledgeable about biotechnology, it's possible to think of some terrifying scenarios. I don't even like to discuss them. I know people doing biotechnology research who have decided not to pursue avenues of research because they think they're too dangerous. But we go forward without sorting out the issues. I don't believe that everything new is necessarily better. We go forward with the technology while the ethical issues are still up in the air, whether it's the genetic variability of crop streams, which is a resource in times of plant plagues, to the assumption that we all have to be connected all the time. The technology is here so you must use it. Do you? Do you have to have your cell phone and your e-mail address and your internet hookup? I was just on holiday in Scotland without e-mail. I had to notify people that I wouldn't be checking my e-mail, because there's an assumption that if I send you an e-mail, you'll get it. Well, I won't get it. I'm not plugged in, guys. Some people are horrified: "You've gone offline?" People feel so enslaved by technology that they will stop having sex to answer the telephone. What could be so important? Who's calling, and who cares?

**Playboy:** Did your interest in medical issues such as the right to die inspire you to create *ER*?

**Michael Crichton:** Sure it did. And I wanted to do a different kind of doctor show. When I was in school, everybody watched *Dr. Kildare*. Then came *Marcus Welby, M.D.* There was a conventional wisdom about how doctor shows were done, and I wanted to change that. Part of it was the style. Television had fallen into an artificially slow pace for financial reasons. If people talked slower, if you had long shots of somebody parking a car and then walking up to a house, it was less expensive; fewer script pages was cheaper. Television audiences slipped into this languor, this assumption that whatever they saw was going to be slower than their daily life. I wanted *ER* to go at a regular or faster speed than real life. We also broke other TV conventions, such as ending scenes on the thoughtful look of a person walking away, or whatever. Instead, we just cut. It was very effective. But another essential difference is that *ER* tells real stories. The most memorable episodes are based on real stories, and that was intended. The other thing is the level of quality in the show. Executive producer John Wells has been the person on the firing line since the early years of the show, and he has been phenomenally good at maintaining a level of quality that's breathtaking.

**Playboy:** How involved are you?

**Michael Crichton:** Not at all anymore. I was very involved in the first couple of years when they needed me. I talked to John about what I wanted to happen on the show generally, rather than episode by episode. But TV is demanding and time-consuming. It was taking too much time. The most painful moment for me was at the end of the second year. Every June they lay out the major story arcs for the coming year. I tried to go to as many of those sessions as I could. When I went that year, I felt like the writers were looking at me, going, "Who are you? What are you doing here?" I was hurt and offended and my ideas didn't really fit the group's anymore. But at some point I thought, "They're right. It's their show now. They're the ones doing it minute to minute. They're in charge. My child has grown up and gone away." So I said, "God bless you" and I left.

**Playboy:** Why did you want to become a doctor?

**Michael Crichton:** When I was in college, I wanted to be a writer. But then I read that only two hundred writers in America support themselves writing. I thought, "That's an awfully small group." I didn't want to be a part-time writer with a day job—that didn't interest me. I either had to be one of those two hundred people or forget it. So I decided to become a doctor. I was attracted to medicine partly because I thought I would be doing useful work, helping people—I would never have to wonder if the work was worthwhile. But many working physicians are not convinced at all. They have all kinds of doubts, which troubled me. I also found that I was at odds with the thrust of the profession at that time, which was highly scientific medicine: the physician as technician and the patient as a biological machine that was broken. I didn't find it appealing to work in that kind of setting.

**Playboy:** Is that when you went back to writing?

**Michael Crichton:** I had been writing to pay my way through medical school. I wrote paperback thrillers on vacations and weekends at a furious pace because the bills were due. I wrote under pseudonyms. In retrospect, it was wonderful training. Most of the problems beginning writers have dealing with their egos, deciding if what they're writing is good enough for them, didn't affect me at all. No one knew I was doing it. It wasn't under my own name. It was purely to make money to pay for my education. I wasn't trying to be innovative. I was trying to do something that would sell and not require rewrites or discussions, because I didn't have time. I mean I just had to write it, it had to be bought and published, and I had to get the money and go back to my classes.

**Playboy:** One pseudonym you used was Jeffery Hudson, the name of a dwarf courtier to Charles I. Were you being ironic about your size?
**Michael Crichton:** I was. I thought it was funny. It seemed like an entertaining name.

**Playboy:** How much has being tall affected your life?
**Michael Crichton:** It's kind of startling to people and provokes comments. They used to say, "How's the weather up there?" or "Do you play basketball?" and "Gosh, you're tall!" They don't say it now. First of all, my height is no longer remarkable in a world with Magic Johnson and all those guys. And in addition, I'm somewhat recognized. People see me in an airport and you can tell that their brain is clicking: Wait a minute, who is that big guy? White guy, plays basketball, no, he's too old, hmmm, I know him from somewhere. Oh, yeah, he's the writer. But my height was a factor when I was younger. I was very tall very young. I was almost this height when I was thirteen, and so that was all mixed up with what was a difficult age anyway. Talk about an awkward time. I was really awkward.

**Playboy:** Your father was a journalist. Did you want to grow up to be a writer like your dad?
**Michael Crichton:** The fact that my father was a writer made being a writer seem normal, though I certainly didn't have a particular sense of following in his footsteps. The truth is, the origin of lifework is mysterious to me. I think it's in part accidental. But I'm also interested in the idea that there's a kind of destiny for the soul. In some ways it does seem like I'm genetically a writer, though I don't know how strongly to hold that view. I don't really believe most psychological explanations for why people are the way they are or why things turn out as they do. I think there's a lot more randomness in life. I disbelieve almost all Freudian ideas and most psychological theses. So all I can tell you is: yes, my father was a journalist, and, yes, it turned out I'm a writer, too.

**Playboy:** You don't like Freud and yet you've spent time in therapy. Do you care to explain?
**Michael Crichton:** There are a lot of therapies besides Freudian therapies.

There has long been skepticism about Freudian concepts; I've never done therapy that was much influenced by Freud. Freudian thought now isn't much more than an academic function. It sits alongside Marxist thought, which resides only in the academy and no longer exists in the real world. I've been through many kinds of therapeutic interaction—partly because it's an interest of mine, partly because I've needed help. I think of it now as a useful resource. The therapist I have now tends to talk to me about things in an interesting way: "Do you really think you can finish the book in that period of time? Aren't you once again overestimating your capabilities?" For me, it's helpful to have a therapist who knows you a little and who can look at your behavior and make you stop and think. I also believe there are certain kinds of personal transformations or transitions you cannot make by yourself. It's like trying to bite your own teeth. You just can't see certain things about yourself without another person as a mirror. Some people say, "I have introspective capabilities and can see what's going on, and I don't need any help to change," but I think they are kidding themselves.

**Playboy:** How has therapy changed you?

**Michael Crichton:** The swell, open, wonderfully easygoing person I am now is a product of therapy [Laughs]. I have changed in many ways. When I was young, I was emotionally cautious and constrained. I was pretty happy in an Ivy League environment where emotional signals were things like the kind of tie you wore. A guy who wore a yellow shirt was feeling daring. That was about as much emotional expression as I could tolerate. When I arrived in Hollywood, people were screaming and throwing things and shrieking. It was an eye-opener. We sure didn't do that where I came from in Boston. I realized it was going to be good for me to be here because I'd have to learn to yell and scream, too. I did, and therapy helped me do that. But the biggest change may have been getting over the idea that whatever interpersonal problems I had were another person's fault. For years, I thought such a swell person as I am wouldn't have any problems. If I was having problems, it was her fault. A lot of people feel that way. It's tough to recognize that you're contributing to your own difficulties, sometimes even causing them. What a shock. It was a shock to me.

**Playboy:** What about the trend toward quick pharmaceutical fixes such as Prozac and Viagra?

**Michael Crichton:** I think they are good for certain behavioral stuff. For some problems there is an underlying chemical problem. You can't treat diabetes with psychotherapy. A lot of depression is that way. The proliferation of increasingly subtle substances that work on the brain will put talk therapy in its place. We'll get better at knowing what can be treated by medication and what requires talk therapy.

**Playboy:** But Viagra is being used by men and women as a recreational drug, not only by men who experience sexual dysfunction.

**Michael Crichton:** It's not possible to have a drug that won't be abused by some portion of the population. Antibiotics are abused. Food is abused. It's inevitable. Part of the problem with things like this is how much they're chattered about. We have a real chattering class now. Along with the explosion of lawyers, there's been an explosion of pundits. We ought to prune them. We could do with about ten percent of what we have. Each new change in society is instantly greeted by ten billion opinions. I remember the immortal words of my first therapist, who used to nod quietly and say, "Time will tell." Time will tell.

**Playboy:** Along with therapy, you have said that becoming a parent changed you, that you no longer take the risks you took when you were younger. What risks were you talking about?

**Michael Crichton:** I behaved ridiculously when I was younger. I was living in Hollywood at a time when a variety of substances were available and I was certainly part of that world. I was very willing to take risks. In retrospect, deep-sea diving to 250 feet on compressed air is not daring, it's stupid. I look back on some of those incidents and think it's a miracle I survived. It's the luck of the draw. I had a passion for Porsches and I used to drive them really fast. I had a new Porsche and was driving on Mulholland Drive, a twisty road. I had locked something in my glove compartment, so I took the key out of the ignition and unlocked the glove compartment to get it. I didn't realize that on the new car, when you take the key out of the ignition, you lock the steering wheel. Fortunately, the wheels were pointing to the upward side of the cliff and I simply drove into the wall. If they had been pointing the other way, I would have gone right over. Just stupid. You play those things back in your mind.

**Playboy:** Do you miss the extremes?

**Michael Crichton:** I don't feel the need to test myself in that way. I feel responsible. It's very important that I be around for my kid. Kids who don't have parents are at a disadvantage. I have an obligation to be there and I take it seriously. Being a parent teaches you other things, too. Kids make you alive in a certain way that adults tend not to, and they bring in a phenomenal amount of chaos, which is beneficial once you get used to it. To me, being a parent is that weird balance of indulgence and discipline. It's also true that there are some unique factors about being an older parent. I am of the age where I could be my daughter's grandfather, and there are certain grandfatherly things about me that are part of our relationship. I'm no longer completely wound up in my career, trying to make it, for instance. I have done all that. If I had wanted to take time off when she was younger, I could have. And I did. I'm not struggling for financial resources in the same way that I might have been when I was younger.

**Playboy:** Have you thought about what you will tell your daughter about boys when she comes of age?
**Michael Crichton:** I watched a lot of my friends with their daughters. The kid would be in a stroller, gurgling, and the father would be saying, "Those goddamn boys. I know what those guys are going to want to do to her!" My reaction is to actually feel sorry for the guys. Look out for this one. She's going to cut a wide swath. There will be a trail of bleeding hearts behind her.

**Playboy:** What lessons have you learned about marriage?
**Michael Crichton:** I really don't consider myself a master in this area. I'm lucky to have the relationship that I have. I am also aware that relationships are breaking up around me all the time. It would be foolish for me to think that mine is less at risk than anybody else's. We live in a world of change, whether we like it or not. I have learned that marriage is really good for me. It is hard, but it's good for me. I've also learned that both people need to have a commitment; the minute one person doesn't want to be there, it gets difficult. You should want to spend a lot of your leisure time together, sharing the same interests. You may not see the person all week, but when Saturday rolls around, if she wants to go shopping and you want to go hiking, you may have a problem. There are also important basics: Are you substantially in agreement on child rearing? How do you approach religion? How important is education? Do you share those things that are often so deep that they're not even conscious? If not, it's tough.

**Playboy:** You contend that everyone has a range of skills, and we hear, for example, you're an excellent cook. Are you the best cook in your house?
**Michael Crichton:** In the early stages, what I most enjoyed was that I was

able to do it at all. Also, I spend a lot of time in my head, and you can kind of float off into a purely fantasy existence. So I found it really beneficial to go to the supermarket and go, "Oh, my God, look what they're charging me for lettuce. Can you believe that? And it looks terrible, too—where are they getting this lettuce?" It was regular life.

**Playboy:** You've said you're a workaholic. Do you enjoy working nonstop?
**Michael Crichton:** Actually, I'm happiest with a lot of time off. It's not like I can't handle it. Years ago I would do a project every three years. Now the market is such that they want a novel every year. Since *Jurassic Park* I've done a novel every eighteen months or so, which is the best I can do. But I do much better with periods of time off. I don't like how it is now—this back-to-back frenzy.

**Playboy:** Do you get your best ideas when you're working or when you're goofing off?
**Michael Crichton:** Definitely when I'm off. In fact, I'm concerned now that I don't have enough fallow time. I'm happier and my mind works in a different way when I don't have to do anything, when I can boogieboard in Hawaii or go hiking or just sit for weeks on end. When I work, I work compulsively. I always have. When I'm writing, I write seven days a week. I'll take a break only when my family rebels. "We haven't seen you for ten days. We need a day." The periods when I'm writing or making a movie are intense. I have no time to read and explore and let ideas drift in and out of my thoughts. I miss it and I'm very happy doing it for long periods of time.

**Playboy:** What's your workday like?
**Michael Crichton:** There is no normal day. My preferred time to work is in the morning. I find that being kind of sleepy is beneficial. It has always been true that my energy and my alertness peak in the morning.

**Playboy:** You wrote *Twister* with your wife. Would you collaborate again?
**Michael Crichton:** Yes—we talk about doing it again, but there is a danger. One needs the freedom to argue with a collaborator—to have strong disagreements. That can be difficult if you're going to see the person at dinner.

**Playboy:** You were sued for infringing on someone else's copyright with *Twister*. You won the lawsuit, but was it a difficult experience for you?
**Michael Crichton:** It was one of the most interesting and awful experiences

I've ever had. I was talking to my wife about it afterward and we agreed that it was engaging, tense, dramatic, and demanding. I'm sure it would have been a lot less interesting if we had lost, but as we looked back, we were just amazed by it. It was interesting to watch a court case like that go forward, far different from TV and the movies. It was like a verbal tennis match: If you hit this stroke, what will be hit back? We handily won the suit, but the media stuck with a theme it created at the beginning even when the theme no longer applied. They originally presented it as a David and Goliath story: The big guns, Crichton and Spielberg, have stolen from some poor little guy. At a certain point in the trial—not very far in—one of the local columnists asked, "What kind of a story is this if it's David versus Goliath and Goliath is going to win and deserves to?" It was a completely meritless case, but the media had this David and Goliath angle to deal with. They were disappointed that that angle had been taken away. It turned out that the plaintiff was a local fellow who was simply wrong and his attorneys were wrong. But no one wanted the angle to change, so the case continued to be reported as a David and Goliath story. Reporters wrote, "The big guys got away with it."

**Playboy:** Are there other downsides to your level of success?
**Michael Crichton:** Well, everything has a downside. But the significant question is, would you want to magically go back to a time when it wasn't there? No. Whatever the downsides are, they are not sufficient to make you regret what has happened.

**Playboy:** It has been written that you are the most highly remunerated writer ever.
**Michael Crichton:** I'm almost certain that that's not true.

**Playboy:** How do you spend your money? Has wealth changed you?
**Michael Crichton:** It has given me the freedom to choose the kinds of projects I want to work on. It's also given me the freedom to be unpopular. For example, I was aware I could get blasted for writing *Rising Sun.* But if I got blasted, if I were murdered, it would be OK because the previous book was *Jurassic Park* and it had done well. There is a freedom that comes from the successes, and I feel obliged to exercise it. Similarly, if you have worldly success, part of your obligation is to spread it around. It's interesting to see where you can have an impact. I'm certainly not a person of enormous resources, but I'm trying to find the things that I think are important that

aren't getting funded and maybe won't get funded because they're not on other people's agendas. I'm very interested in education.

**Playboy:** Do you have a prescription for improving public education in the U.S.?

**Michael Crichton:** I'm a product of public education. I went to public schools until college, and I was very much an advocate of that system. But a few years ago, I went back to my high school. It's still a good high school. But on reflection, I realize that I actually attended a private school. My parents moved to a community where the taxes were higher because that's where the good schools were. We moved there to attend the schools. My parents paid additional money for me to go to those schools, and they felt they had a voice in them. If there was a bad teacher, that teacher was gone. There was no way the damn union was going to keep that from happening. It was a true community-based school. That's gone for the most part, but that's what is needed. It's human nature for parents to want a strong say in the education of their children. They should feel strongly about it. There are very good private schools, including those that are public schools in certain communities, and there are terrible schools about which people have no choice. I support vouchers for that reason. Competition makes schools better. The single largest obligation I have as a parent is to educate my child. That's the biggest thing I can do.

**Playboy:** You still hold some high school basketball records: most rebounds in a game, highest rebound average per game, highest shooting percentage in a season. Are those important to you?

**Michael Crichton:** One of the good things about sports—why kids ought to play sports and why we all like sports—is that sports aren't political or open to interpretation. You either perform or you don't. You win the match or you don't. It's not open to spin.

**Playboy:** While your books and movies certainly are. Have you become immune to criticism by now?

**Michael Crichton:** Pretty much. At least I don't read the critics. If I get praise, it doesn't make me feel very good. If I get criticism, I feel terrible. I just sink like a rock. These days the reviews don't tend to be about the work. They often seem to be about me; about me as a person. So I don't read them, though it takes a certain discipline not to read them.

**Playboy:** Are you aware of the criticisms, however? A common criticism of your writing is that it's formulaic.

**Michael Crichton:** It was always formula; I'm interested in formulas. From my earliest writing, I was interested in taking well-defined genres and doing something else with them—retaining the quality of the genre, whether a detective story, science fiction story, disaster story. That aspect of working within a defined framework has always been a challenge to me. Has it become more formula? I don't know. I do sometimes wish that I could publish a book under a pseudonym just to see how much of the reaction is to the text and how much of the reaction is to me as a known entity.

**Playboy:** Another criticism is that your characters are much less developed than your stories.

**Michael Crichton:** I hope that will change. When I was younger, I was interested in situations in which individual personality didn't matter. Once an oil spill starts, I don't think it matters who the president of Exxon is, whether he's a good or bad guy. The truth is, he can't do anything about it. I was interested in the oil spill itself. Like in *The Andromeda Strain*, the only thing to do about a disaster is never to have it happen. Once it happens, almost everything you do is going to make it worse. In such stories, the personalities of the people don't matter. They tend to be stories about individuals who are powerless, who are caught up in the system in some way. They're kind of pessimistic, which is how I was for a long time. I don't necessarily want to do those stories anymore. First of all, I've done a lot of them. Second, I've become more interested in stories that seem to offer alternatives of action, depending on what kind of a person you're dealing with. They tend to be much smaller stories.

A lot of what I've done in the past has been misunderstood—at least from my standpoint. When I was writing *Jurassic Park*, I was in a tremendous panic. I thought, "It's one thing to try to do a persuasive story about a satellite that comes down—we know there are satellites and one could theoretically come down." But in the case of *Jurassic Park*, I was going to try to convince readers and then viewers that dinosaurs reappear in the contemporary world. I was panicked that people would start to read it and go, "Forget it! No way!" All of my focus was there. Then I write the thing and everybody buys it without discussion. They buy that science brought back dinosaurs. And then they say, "Yeah, but the characters are no good." What do you mean the characters aren't good? This is a story in which dinosaurs are in the real world! Now you want believable characters? To complain about characters meant that they already bought the absurd premise.

**Playboy:** Who are your favorite writers?
**Michael Crichton:** When you're in this business there's a point after which you no longer read for pleasure. I don't read books or go to movies freely anymore. On one hand, there's some competitive sense. On the other, there's a professional interest in the technique or technical specifics, how an effect was achieved. It's just not possible for me to read a book or watch a movie without those things impinging.

**Playboy:** *Travels* was a completely different style of writing—personal, even confessional. Do you plan to do more of that type?
**Michael Crichton:** Yeah, because it was a great experience. It's a little more difficult now. In the past, if I wrote about relationships, they were relationships that were over. If I write about them now, they're going to be current relationships. I have to think: What is my wife going to think about this particular story? How is my daughter going to feel? Kids in her school are going to read this. Am I invading her privacy? Or can I even be responsive to those concerns? Isn't it my job to say the hell with it and just write what happened? It's a problem I have.

**Playboy:** What's your answer?
**Michael Crichton:** The answer is I don't know.

**Playboy:** In *Travels*, you visit alternative healers. Have you had any more psychic experiences?
**Michael Crichton:** No. When I'm finished with a particular problem, I'm finished with it for a while. Beyond the sense of completion, there's a kind of exhaustion, even revulsion. It's why it's tough to talk about novels after I've completed them; I've moved on.

**Playboy:** You once said that you feel like killing yourself after you complete a film. Now that you're in postproduction for your most recent movie, *The 13th Warrior*, are you feeling suicidal?
**Michael Crichton:** No, though I can feel that way after a project. While you're working on a movie there's something wonderful about it that's not yet defined. There are all these fantastic possibilities. When you see it all

together, it's just a movie. Whether it's a good movie, a bad movie, or a medium movie, it's just a movie. In the end, people will sit for a couple of hours, watch it, and go home. I sit and work and write and direct and edit and agonize, but in the end it is what it is: just a movie, just a book.

# An Interview with Michael Crichton

## Charlie Rose/1999

From *The Charlie Rose Show*, November 16, 1999. Reprinted by permission of Charlie Rose Inc.

**Rose:** Michael Crichton has sold more than 100 million copies of his books. He was, at one time, the owner of the number one bestseller, the number one television show, and the number one movie in the country. He went to Harvard as a medical student, always wanting to write. Since then, he has turned writing into gold. His newest book is called *Timeline*. Once again, I am pleased to have him on this program to talk about the book and so many other things that are part of his world. I'm pleased to have him back—welcome back.
**Crichton:** Thank you.

**Rose:** It's good to see you. You now are a New Yorker, too—living upstate. That goes well?
**Crichton:** Excellent.

**Rose:** You moved here primarily because you wanted your daughter to have access to a different kind of school system?
**Crichton:** That's right. I'm an easterner.

**Rose:** Roslyn, Long Island, as I remember.
**Crichton:** That's right. I still think an eastern education has a different quality.

**Rose:** That's a company town out there, primarily, isn't it?
**Crichton:** Los Angeles? It is, yes. They even call it "The Company Town."

**Rose:** Some company. [Laughs] I was thinking about all the things you do,

**165**

and all of your interests in history and science. But in the end, when push comes to shove—as they say in the often-quoted cliché—you are a story-teller.

**Crichton:** That's right.

**Rose:** It's what you do.
**Crichton:** Yes. It's what I like to do.

**Rose:** Where does that come from?
**Crichton:** I don't know, because my daughter has it, too. It started at an ear-ly age when I would tell her fairy tales. She'd stop me and go, "No, Dad. He doesn't come out of the warehouse. He stays in there until the giant leaves." I'd think, "Wait a minute, you're editing Grimm's." So there's some kind of an impulse about what makes a suitable story and what's right. There may also be—it sounds funny—but there may also be some kind of a sadistic impulse in there, too.

**Rose:** Sadistic?
**Crichton:** What you're really doing in a narrative is paying out information bit by bit, which also means you're holding back—trying to make people worried about something. You know how it's going to turn out but you want the reader to have this feeling intermediately, and in that kind of manip-ulation—which is very pleasurable to experience if it's done well—there's something like sadism. That's what Hitchcock was accused of, too.

**Rose:** I know. Do you like the isolated quality of writing?
**Crichton:** Usually, when I'm writing I wish I weren't; when I'm working on a movie I wish I was writing. So it's some way to be perpetually dissatisfied. But yes, the answer is: I do.

**Rose:** It's been a long time since you've directed.
**Crichton:** Yes.

**Rose:** Why haven't you directed more? *Westworld* was the last thing I re-member. Was there something after that?
**Crichton:** There were things after that, but primarily what's happened is that this has been a good writing time for me.

**Rose:** The '90s?

**Crichton:** Yes. So every time I think about directing something or writing something else I think, "I'll keep writing." It's that sort of moment-by-moment decision.

**Rose:** We have talked about this before, but everybody's curious about this: How is it you have this uncanny sense of choosing a serious subject that fascinates us—this having to be physics and going back to a previous time—quantum teleportation, which is what? What is that?
**Crichton:** Quantum teleportation?

**Rose:** Yes.
**Crichton:** It's very interesting. It's something that has been demonstrated—just last year—in several laboratories around the world. It's talked about as if it were beam-me-up-Scottie—it's not really, exactly. It's a transfer of a certain kind of information from one photon to another. It implies instantaneous transportation of information across distances—doesn't matter how far—across the entire universe. It's a very curious thing.

**Rose:** You have to understand how time works, don't you—and how the speed of light works, and all of that?
**Crichton:** It's pushing at some of those notions. In other words, before quantum teleportation was demonstrated, there was a lot of thought among physicists that it might or might not actually be a real phenomenon—there was speculation. Now it turns out it is real.

**Rose:** What's real?
**Crichton:** That this kind of transfer can occur instantaneously with nothing in between—no carrier mechanism.

**Rose:** This book is about an archeologist from Yale going back to 1357, the fourteenth century. [His students] travel back to rescue one of their own to bring [him] back to 1999. That's not real.
**Crichton:** Not as far as I'm aware. [Laughs]

**Rose:** [Laughs] But that is part of the idea of quantum physics and teleportation, yes? Does it draw on that, or not?
**Crichton:** It does.

**Rose:** You've taken a liberal imagination here.

**Crichton:** Yes. I don't want to say that quantum technology is going to lead to time travel—I don't think that's a fair thing to say.

**Rose:** But, do you believe it will?
**Crichton:** I don't know.

**Rose:** Ah! That's even more interesting. You don't know? Do you believe it's highly unlikely, or do you believe it's possible?
**Crichton:** I believe it's possible. If I had to guess, if you asked me to bet, I would bet against it.

**Rose:** What makes you think it's even remotely possible that somebody could travel back to the fourteenth century?
**Crichton:** It's not clearly contradicted by theory. You know what I mean?

**Rose:** I really don't know what you mean because I know nothing about physics, but go ahead.
**Crichton:** If you have an accepted theory, then it has certain consequences that follow from that. A simple one is it does seem to be very unlikely that you can travel faster than light. One of the issues about quantum teleportation is it seems to be nudging at that a little, potentially causing a problem. But, in general, we believe you can't travel faster than light, so if you write a story where someone travels faster than light—that's an impossible story, according to what we believe now. I try and stay within the boundaries of what's not understood to be impossible, even though there's dispute about it.

**Rose:** Alright. Let me frame this this way, because this is interesting—you and the idea is interesting: Knowing what you did in so many other books that grabbed our attention, because you're on the cutting edge of what people talk about—whether it's sexual harassment and *Disclosure*, whether it had to do with the rise of Japan in *Rising Sun* and so many more, having especially to do with dinosaurs and all that came out of that—where did you first get the idea? When did you say, Michael, there's a book here?
**Crichton:** I don't know.

**Rose:** Okay, but about when? What started the process for you? You're reading a magazine and there's a story?
**Crichton:** No, this was an odd one in a way, because for a long time I had

wanted to do a time travel story. One reason is that I'm attracted to the challenge of trying to write a story that will be persuasive, even for a few hours, on some subject that's impossible or highly, highly unlikely. All the time I was writing *Jurassic Park* I kept thinking, "This is a dinosaur story. Is anybody going to go for this?"

**Rose:** But that's your commercial sense, too. Some would say it's a story about biogenetics and you're saying, "No, it's a dinosaur story," which shows your instinct for what sells, as does your ability to make people keep turning the pages. That's an instinct for what sells, the way you write. You'll give me that?
**Crichton:** But I don't know how I do this.

**Rose:** You know it's there?
**Crichton:** Yes.

**Rose:** And you know it's a story about dinosaurs, rather than some highfalutin idea of biogenetics.
**Crichton:** That's right. That's right. That's what carried it. It was not obvious to me when I was writing it that I could get away with this, that I could carry it off, that people would say, "Oh, yeah." The first people who read it, quite by accident, were people in bioengineering fields. I was watching them just gulp it right down and I thought, "Wow. We did it."

**Rose:** "We got something here." [Laughs]
**Crichton:** And another equally challenging kind of a story is time travel.

**Rose:** Ray Bradbury—*Distant Thunder*. What was that about?
**Crichton:** Is that the one about the dinosaur?

**Rose:** Time travel, I think.
**Crichton:** People go back in time and someone steps on a butterfly.

**Rose:** Right. That's exactly right.
**Crichton:** Changes the world.

**Rose:** Changes what happens in the future. Right.
**Crichton:** There's actually a really interesting book by a physicist named Paul Nahin about time machines. He summarizes all the writing that's oc-

curred in the past; which is, in a way, very discouraging, because what you realize is that all the changes have been wrung—in fact, most had been wrung by the 1920s—so there isn't really any new thing to do there.

**Rose:** If someone says to you, "You're marrying thriller with science fiction," you say—not so much fiction?
**Crichton:** I hope, yes.

**Rose:** Yes, a thriller. Yes, a novel. But less science fiction than you might imagine.
**Crichton:** That's always my intent in my effort.

**Rose:** Your calling card.
**Crichton:** Yes, because, for example, quantum physics is very, very difficult, and I'm hardly a person to really be knowledgeable. When I'm looking at this, it's so hard to describe it at all. I recognize that there's a certain level where a physicist would say, "Yes, that's the correct way to state it," but no one would get it at all; no reader would understand it. Then there's another way, which is pretty easy to understand, but the physicist would say, "No, no, no. That's completely wrong." Somewhere in the middle is a way of putting this information that's okay to read for a reader and the physicist will say, "Well, okay." That's what I'm trying to get—some balance between what's technically accurate and what's understandable if you're not in that field.

**Rose:** We know at some point you got interested in this and you figured out some kind of storyline. You have to have characters. Tell me the story—guy goes to France and he's doing a little research . . .
**Crichton:** It's a group of people doing research in France; they're historical archaeologists—medieval archaeologists—they're excavating a site.

**Rose:** Let me interrupt this one second before you pick it up. Have you always been interested in things medieval?
**Crichton:** No.

**Rose:** So the fourteenth century didn't have any special appeal to you?
**Crichton:** Not when I began.

**Rose:** Not knights and battles and Hundred Year War and all that?
**Crichton:** Knights.

**Rose:** Knights did?
**Crichton:** Yes, because knights are a cliché. Everybody thinks they know what knights are.

**Rose:** Shining Knight, Camelot, and all that—roundtable.
**Crichton:** Yes, right. Roundtable.

**Rose:** [Slaps his table and laughs]
**Crichton:** There it is—round. I always thought, "What was the reality? What was actually going on? What was knighthood, really? All this idea of courtly love doesn't sound like how the world worked if you're very young." So I would have these sorts of thoughts but I didn't know anything. One of the pleasures of working on this book was that I got to find out.

**Rose:** About all your books—you get to find out.
**Crichton:** Yes.

**Rose:** So you have to have characters—you have these archaeologists, historical archaeologists, doing some investigations in France.
**Crichton:** Right.

**Rose:** What happens?
**Crichton:** The company that's funding them, that they see as a sort of benign patron, sends a vice president over who says, "We really want to start reconstructing this village." They say, "No, no, we're not ready." And they say, "Yeah, we should. You can at least build the castle wall from here to here and then over to the round tower in the woods." One of them says, "Wait a minute. What round tower?" Nobody knows it's there. So they go out into the woods and start looking and indeed there is the remains of a round tower. This vice president knows more about their site than they do, and they want to know why. That's the initial impulse. So the leader of this group, who is a senior professor, goes back to the company headquarters—essentially vanishes.

**Rose:** All of a sudden he's in 1357.
**Crichton:** What happens is—we shouldn't go through the whole book.

**Rose:** I'm not going to [give] anything away, but we have to get at it—you want people to be interested.

**Crichton:** He's been gone for several days. They're continuing their excavations and they find a set of documents from some earlier time; they've been buried; they uncover them. When they open them up and look at them, there's a letter in the professor's handwriting that says, "Help me."

**Rose:** So the race is on. We have a thriller and we're going to have our fabulous Yale graduate students in battle with all the knights they find in 1357, who are our bad guys. So we have our good guys—our Yalies—and bad guys. We have a corporate billionaire who's behind some of this, right? Sounds a little like *Jurassic Park*.
**Crichton:** It certainly bothered me when I did it. I finally concluded that there isn't another form. In other words, if you abstract the form enough, then everything looks like everything—Bambi looks like the life of Hitler.

**Rose:** [Laughs]
**Crichton:** Trouble with the father . . .

**Rose:** Bambi wanted to be a painter, that whole thing. [Laughs] Go ahead.
**Crichton:** I just couldn't think of another way to do it. In other words, what they share in common is that these are technologies that are being pushed that are phenomenally expensive. So if you're going to try and tell a story that in some way rationalizes them, or speaks about them as if they were real, one of your problems is, in each case: who's going to pay for this? A stunning amount of money—where does it come from? It can come from someone rich.

**Rose:** Alright. We know what you have to do now. So where do you go do your research? Why do you choose the fourteenth century? 1357, right?
**Crichton:** 1357.

**Rose:** Why then, at the end of the Hundred Years War?
**Crichton:** No, it's actually earlier.

**Rose:** Earlier than the Hundred Years War.
**Crichton:** Yes.

**Rose:** The Hundred Years War was from what to what?
**Crichton:** 1331 to 1450 or '60.

**Rose:** Okay, it's at the same time.
**Crichton:** Right.

**Rose:** So it's during the Hundred Years War?
**Crichton:** Right.

**Rose:** Why then?
**Crichton:** A couple of reasons. I wanted a period of warfare in which ordinary life is very chaotic. There was this element of civil war in all this.
There's an element of war between France and England. It's very confused,
it's very bloody, you never know what's going to happen next. I wanted that
kind of a really chaotic time—it suited that. Then there was an event that I
couldn't get out of my mind, which was in 1356. The year before the Battle of
Poitiers, which the English won against the French, the English captured the
French King and took him back to England where he was ransomed for an
enormous amount of money. This notion that your king could be captured
by the enemy and then, of course, treated in this courtly fashion.

**Rose:** A pawn.
**Crichton:** Yes, but also welcomed with all the ceremony, because the nobil-
ity cuts across all these national boundaries. I couldn't stop thinking about
this—this notion that the king of a country was gone, and what that would
mean to the remnants of that place which is not yet a nation-state. England
at this time is pretty much England, but France is not France.

**Rose:** You've pointed out, I've seen you say this, that this is an interesting
time because also it's an enlightened period. This is the time that [the] Ox-
ford and Cambridge seeds were planted.
**Crichton:** That's right.

**Rose:** This was the time that nation-states were being formed, so a lot of
interesting things are happening. It's not so far back that you can't find interesting things that are taking place.
**Crichton:** Right. It's also the time, not the moment, but the immediate period of the decline of the knights, because the English longbowmen have
become supreme over everything else and mounted shock cavalry, which
is really the justification for all the knights—great charging men on horse-
back with lances—doesn't work anymore. The French still do it; the English

dismount their knights to fight; but the French still charge and they're just slaughtered.

**Rose:** It's not a smart thing to do.
**Crichton:** There's a rain of arrows; they shoot twenty arrows a minute.

**Rose:** Twenty arrows a minute.
**Crichton:** They can shoot them two hundred yards and be accurate.

**Rose:** It's over for the guys on the horses.
**Crichton:** It's over. If they don't die, the horses do.

**Rose:** Did you fancy yourself as being a knight?
**Crichton:** No.

**Rose:** You never thought about that?
**Crichton:** I didn't have that because when you're doing something like this you're going to identify with the contemporary people.

**Rose:** Right. Some might say, "How do contemporary people, academicians—no put down of academicians or archaeologists—but all of a sudden they're transported back and they're going to be going hand-to-hand with all these bad guys who are inhabitants of the fourteenth century."
**Crichton:** How can they do it?

**Rose:** How can they do it?
**Crichton:** You'd better justify it before you start. [Laughs]

**Rose:** Exactly. So that's part of the novelist's challenge?
**Crichton:** Right. Fortunately for me there's this area which is called various things. One thing you call it is experimental archaeology—in which people try and recreate conditions of living in order to understand what it must have been like. One of the characters is one of these people who's really interested in learning how to use a broadsword and fight in a joust and is acquiring all these skills in his capacity as an historian, but it turns out he has use for them.

**Rose:** Here comes one aspect that's interesting to me: You think about historical novelists, you think about Tolstoy and *War and Peace*, you think

about Victor Hugo, you think about so many historical novelists—they, the argument could be made, were essentially interested in character and love and passion and relationships and all that. It just so happened they put it in an historical background. Character disfunctionality was key. You seem to be less interested in character—tell me if I'm right or wrong.
**Crichton:** That's true.

**Rose:** And more interested in science, events, some big idea.
**Crichton:** Yes. It's also true.

**Rose:** Of course, we're not arguing with one hundred million books sold either.
**Crichton:** I think in a very weird way this isn't an historical novel.

**Rose:** No, but it looks forward because it's quantum teleportation, and it's also going back to understand the past.
**Crichton:** Right, but you're telling the past through the eyes of the present, which prevents you from only residing in the past. The structure is much more "behind enemy lines" than it is a conventional historical novel. But the answer to your question is: From the beginning I've been interested in people caught in circumstances, and often those circumstances don't really have that much to do with who they are. In the same way that people on an assembly line, we now understand, can't improve quality; they're stuck on the assembly line. If you're going to improve quality in an automobile, it has to be done from the design all the way through.

**Rose:** Nothing's come along to make you obsessive about character.
**Crichton:** Actually, I've been thinking more and more about this because I have very odd ideas about this. For example, I think it is really not knowable why people do what they do.

**Rose:** Motivation is something that can't be comprehended.
**Crichton:** Right. And you can't ask the person, either, because it's very clear they will give you a sort of after-the-fact explanation, and they will also give a different explanation to someone else. They will tailor their explanation.

**Rose:** You and I are mirror images of each other. Just let me be personal for thirty seconds. I'm more interested in why Michael Crichton is interested in these things than I am the things he's interested in. I'm really interested in what motivates you, why you're interested in these things. I may not be able to determine it, but I'll make an effort. More than the science, more than the dinosaurs, more than whatever it is that you find you want to light on—I'm interested in what led you there and what're you going through and what motivates you and all of that stuff. It is different than you.

**Crichton:** Yes, and I'm telling you stories about that because I don't really know. [Laughs]

**Rose:** [Laughs]
**Crichton:** I don't know! Where do I get my ideas? I call an 800-number.

**Rose:** You don't know?
**Crichton:** I don't know where they come from.

**Rose:** Read a lot?
**Crichton:** Yes.

**Rose:** A lot?
**Crichton:** A lot.

**Rose:** Historical things or popular press, or what?
**Crichton:** Actually a lot of academic press.

**Rose:** Really?
**Crichton:** Yes.

**Rose:** How do you access it?
**Crichton:** Usually through other kinds of journals. For example, my primary interest in the *New York Review of Books* is the ads. I just go through and circle all these books.

**Rose:** That's great! That's just great! [Laughs]
**Crichton:** I'll order all these different books—if it looks like an interesting title I'll get it. Ten percent of the time it's really interesting, ten percent of the time it's ridiculous, and the rest of the time it's in the middle.

**Rose:** You don't think much of the internet?
**Crichton:** No.

**Rose:** You think what—bad information?
**Crichton:** That's one thing, and it's also the "Home Shopping Channel," let's face it.

**Rose:** Be careful.
**Crichton:** Well, it is. The one thing I really do like about it is that in the course of my day I don't feel that I really see enough ads, so now I can get online looking for information and I can have these.

**Rose:** You have your web page there now.
**Crichton:** It doesn't have any ads, though.

**Rose:** I know, but maybe people know about it; they can get into you real quick.
**Crichton:** The reason I started the webpage was to handle all the misinformation.

**Rose:** That was coming about you?
**Crichton:** Yes; from all over the place.

**Rose:** Like what?
**Crichton:** I have cancer.

**Rose:** There was a story you had cancer?
**Crichton:** My mother called up in tears. My agent said, "Michael, is everything all right?" I said, "I had no idea. What are you talking about?" "There's this report; it was on these various websites."

**Rose:** Price of freedom. Price of an open system. Price of no editorial.
**Crichton:** That's what it is: no editorial.

**Rose:** Right. I mean no editor.
**Crichton:** Right. I think we are going to learn. To me, we are in the greatest era of snake-oil salesmen baloney in the history of mankind. P. T. Barnum is rolling over in his grave not to be here now when there are so many suckers and you can get them instantly on the internet. I think we're not clear that edited information is the only real information. Everything unedited is data or gossip.

**Rose:** Yes. And nobody has time to check it or has time to, as you say, edit. You're also not thrilled about all the pornography on the internet, either.

**Crichton:** Who is? I have a ten-year-old now who's logging on. Just seeing the kinds of things that my assistant runs into when I ask her to get this or that piece of information—suddenly up pops a picture that we can't even describe here. I had in mind to go talk to a group of computer manufacturers because they're all very much into First Amendment, First Amendment—and I am as well—but what I was going to do was give a speech but then just pop up these images continuously that I have come across in the internet because it is a genuine problem.

**Rose:** They are probably like me. I have no idea what you're talking about because I'm just not out there—not because I'm any less interested in anything like that than anyone else is, it's just that because of the schedule and everything I don't have any idea what you're talking about. It's out there. I know that pornography [exists], and I hear about stuff that's going on, but I really haven't seen it, and I suspect I'd be shocked if you popped those images up.

**Crichton:** I bet you would be, yes.

**Rose:** Shocked that it's there.

**Crichton:** Yes. In this way, I'm really surprised that, for example, we can make voluntary agreements to keep liquor and cigarette advertising off television, and that's how we've gotten around the First Amendment. I don't know why, for example, we don't have similar agreements about political advertising. I don't know why we don't say, "Take all the ads you want, as long as you stand up as a candidate and say whatever you want to say. But we're not going to have all these dissolves, and all these banners, and all this music, and we're not going to sell people like soap." That's not good for the electorate, it's not informative, it's part of what's turning people off.

**Rose:** Part of the problem is who has access; having to do with how much it costs and who has access to media. That's another First Amendment issue.

**Crichton:** Right, but we're not going to do anything about campaign finance, that's clear. It's a bipartisan agreement.

**Rose:** There are some fighting the lonely battle—Feingold and McCain and others.

**Crichton:** McCain, right.

**Rose:** Pop culture today, entertainment culture—too much of it? Are we obsessed by it? Is it in some way doing something demeaning to the soul of a country? World?

**Crichton:** If I make any kind of critical comment I'm seen as hypocritical.

**Rose:** Because you're benefitting from it, because they buy your books and watch your movies.

**Crichton:** I was watching television the other day—I don't always see too much TV—and one character in a sitcom said to another, "Well let's face it mom, everyone knows you're full of crap!" I was kind of: "Hello. I've been out of touch."

**Rose:** But you have to be in touch to write *ER*. I guess one of the characters is based on your life as a young medical student, right?

**Crichton:** Yes.

**Rose:** So you have to be in touch. You used to write a lot—you wrote how much of it?

**Crichton:** I actually only wrote the pilot.

**Rose:** Did the pilot, that's it?

**Crichton:** Yes.

**Rose:** You stay in touch?

**Crichton:** No, I've stopped.

**Rose:** You sold it.

**Crichton:** No. You pass it on, and in terms of the people who are really running the show it's really into its third generation of, in that sense, owners, because you can only do it for some period of time.

**Rose:** Do you have any more television shows in you?

**Crichton:** Maybe. [Laughs]

**Rose:** [Laughs]

**Crichton:** It's hard to know now, because it's a funny time in television.

**Rose:** Paramount has bought *Timeline*.

**Crichton:** Yes.

**Rose:** For a lot of money.
**Crichton:** Well, actually, it's a complicated deal but Paramount is developing it.

**Rose:** Ovitz did well for you, though, I'm sure.
**Crichton:** He did. He did. He's good at what he does.

**Rose:** He's good at what he does. Why don't you direct this?
**Crichton:** This is a big directing job.

**Rose:** So, you're not up to it?
**Crichton:** Here's what you do—you look at this and you say, "Okay, this is somewhere between one and two years out of my life—only thinking about this. I've already spent three years on the book. I don't know that I'm the person to . . . "

**Rose:** You'd rather go direct somebody else's material? Other characters that you don't quite have as great a sense about as you do this? Or you want to direct some small little love story somewhere?
**Crichton:** Or at least something that I wrote as an original screenplay so that I hadn't been with it for such a long time. And I've wanted to do a picture with Dick Donner for a long time.

**Rose:** He's pretty good. He's going to direct this?
**Crichton:** He's going to direct it. So I'm happy.

**Rose:** He has a sure instinct like you. This is like Midas meets Midas.
**Crichton:** [Laughs]

**Rose:** It is. Didn't he do all the *Lethal Weapons*?
**Crichton:** *Superman.*

**Rose:** *Superman.* He's done a lot of stuff. He's a $10 million man—Mr. Donner.
**Crichton:** It's true.

**Rose:** He's going to direct it?
**Crichton:** He's going to direct it.

**Rose:** Steven turned it down, accordingly, with this response: "I'm into the twentieth century now, and I'm not that interested in the fourteenth century."
**Crichton:** Yes. He also said, "I am committed four pictures ahead." I don't know if that's accurate or not, but I think he's got his work schedule.

**Rose:** He did *Jurassic Park*.
**Crichton:** He did; did it great.

**Rose:** More than a billion dollars probably in the end, wasn't it?
**Crichton:** Don't know.

**Rose:** I saw $912 million. If you got that close, you probably. . . . You don't know?
**Crichton:** I have no idea.

**Rose:** Don't you really?
**Crichton:** No.

**Rose:** I bet you Ovitz knows.
**Crichton:** [Laughs] Maybe he does!

**Rose:** Are you still in therapy?
**Crichton:** In a way. A little bit, yes.

**Rose:** You get something out of it? You think it helps your creative powers?
**Crichton:** No. For me, it's much more to do with mundane things.

**Rose:** Like what?
**Crichton:** I have a big tendency to take on too many projects because I imagine I can do them more quickly than I can.

**Rose:** Tell me about it. [Laughs] Or as my mother would say, "Boy, your eyes are bigger than your stomach."
**Crichton:** That's right. Exactly. So I have somebody who says, "Can you really do this? Because it seems like you can't." And that's helpful.

**Rose:** Yes, it is. Is it Freudian?
**Crichton:** No. I've never had a Freudian.

**Rose:** Jungian?
**Crichton:** No.

**Rose:** Just a listener?
**Crichton:** Yes. I've always had a lot of trouble with Freudian thought and I'm having more as time goes on.

**Rose:** Really?
**Crichton:** It's becoming clear that he is the greatest novelist of the twentieth century—Sigmund Freud. He is. If you define the impact of a novelist as the ability to impose a fictional view of the world—their personal and fictional view of the world—and to make it real and persuasive to other people, which I suppose is a good description of Tolstoy or Dostoyevsky, Freud beats everybody hands down. He has these elaborate fantasies, libido, death wish. . . . It's all based on no clinical studies, examination of eight patients in some cases, nothing is double-blinded, nothing is verified, and off comes this entire movement and this whole way of thinking. Psychoanalytic criticism in academia, based on. . . . In other words, today if you were to say I have this new therapy and it's efficacious and if it were required to be demonstrated in the same way the FDA requires the efficacy of a drug, it would fail without any question.

**Rose:** [Laughs]
**Crichton:** It would.

**Rose:** Then how did he get to be so . . .
**Crichton:** That's a very interesting question. Wittgenstein, who was another Viennese and who knew him, said in the '40s or '50s about Freud, he said, "It's going to take a very long time to undo this." He didn't explain why.

**Rose:** That it would take hold.
**Crichton:** It was already taking hold. He was saying it was going to take a long time to unravel it. There's something phenomenally appealing about it—Freudian ideas. And I, at least, read those books just avidly. They're tremendously exciting to read; wonderful writer. But I think, for example, the notion that there's a secret about you, that there's a whole secret existence in this unconscious that by penetrating we can find out what's really behind it; the notion that what happened to you very early, that this kind of seed grows or festers or flowers, or whatever it does, and that we can walk backward to

that time. The idea that we can know—that we can really know why you like to be on television, you're drawn to that. And I say I'm not drawn to it but here I am. [Laughs]

**Rose:** That's a whole other story we can talk about. It's not so much "like to be on television," it's "like to do what you're doing," and it so happens that you also would like to do it in front of all the world's people.
**Crichton:** That's right.

**Rose:** The idea is however you can communicate it. If I can get them all in an arena I would be happy to do it there.
**Crichton:** Right.

**Rose:** It is the driving curiosity about the impact individuals have and what shapes them and how they move an idea; what we just talked about with respect to Sigmund Freud fascinates me—motivation.
**Crichton:** Motivation? Oh, it's enormously fascinating.

**Rose:** You were just saying, "My boy, you can learn less about it than you think. You're overly optimistic in terms of what we can know and understand about motivation, whether it is going back to some relationship in your childhood, or something that happened to you in your childhood, or whether it is choices you make. It may be unknowable. It may be just some combination of brain chemistry and something else."
**Crichton:** Or whether, in fact, our brains have weather. We have gloom, we have excitement.

**Rose:** We know that's related to chemistry.
**Crichton:** Yes.

**Rose:** We know that.
**Crichton:** But what we understand about weather is it comes and goes. We don't say, "It's rainy today because it was rainy in 1950." We just say, "Well, today a combination of events occurred and it's rainy."

**Rose:** What do you think about the whole pharmaceutical thing, from Prozac to Lithium to Viagra.
**Crichton:** It's here. It's here. I don't have any objection to it.

**Rose:** When you latched onto quantum teleportation, what was in second place as an area of exploration—as an area of great curiosity for you—something that you might have stepped up to if this let you down?
**Crichton:** Sigmund Freud. [Laughs]

**Rose:** [Laughs] There's an element of truth there.
**Crichton:** Absolutely. No, he's waiting in the wings because the things you were talking about before—having to do with character—I have these ideas that you can't know these things. A lot of twentieth-century fiction has elaborated this internal psychic landscape which characters are thought to move through and have feelings for these reasons, and I don't believe any of it. I'm, in that causative sense, much closer to Hemingway, who says, "The Rain fell. It was cold. The leaves were blowing. I had a cup of coffee."—with nothing that connects and says this is because of that; but I think I have to explain that; probably have to write something.

**Rose:** Will it be a book, or will it be something else?
**Crichton:** No, it'll be a book.

**Rose:** I remind you, you did a book on Jasper Johns, right?
**Crichton:** Yes.

**Rose:** You have been known to go off and investigate the lives and talents and contradictions of interesting people. Jasper Johns happens to be alive.
**Crichton:** Yes.

**Rose:** So it would be in the course of events for you to do that. It wouldn't be that much of a departure for you.
**Crichton:** No, but when I was working on the Johns book, at a certain point I really began to wonder whether the things that I was writing were descriptive of him or of me. It's an odd problem. It's akin to the problem of whether or not you can ever write history that's not contemporary history. Can you ever describe another person and not be saying more about yourself?

**Rose:** Picasso used to say, "Every portrait's more about the painter than the sitter."
**Crichton:** Yes, although I think it's probably halfway in between; but yes, I think that's right.

**Rose:** Picasso said about Gertrude Stein—she said, "It doesn't look like me." He said, "It will." [Laughs]
**Crichton:** That's nice. [Laughs]

**Rose:** And it was true, it did. As she got older, she came to realize it was true. Travel—you wrote that wonderful thing about travel; Kilimanjaro, all that stuff. Don't you yearn to do that? Why can't we just take off some time and not be so obsessive about work?
**Crichton:** For me, it had to do with the thought that, if I were going to do a trek of the sort I used to do, about the fastest that I could do it would be five weeks. And I just didn't want to be away from home that long.

**Rose:** Really?
**Crichton:** But now, as time goes on, my daughter is less interested in having me around sometimes.

**Rose:** How does that catch you?
**Crichton:** Adolescence is adolescence.

**Rose:** "Oh, dad, you're no longer interesting. I used to love those conversations but I'd rather be with Bill—he's so much more fun than you are."
**Crichton:** Yes, "and so much more interesting, and much more hip, too."

**Rose:** Exactly. "He and I like the same music."
**Crichton:** I'll drive her to school and she'll say, "Don't get out of the car."

**Rose:** Does she really? [Laughs]
**Crichton:** [Laughs] So I'm seeing the possibility that I might be able to do that again.

**Rose:** When she leaves the nest, you may be able to escape again.
**Crichton:** But for the moment, no; not for that duration.

**Rose:** Anne-Marie worked on one of your projects, I've forgotten which one it was.
**Crichton:** A movie called *Runaway*.

**Rose:** Did she have something to do with *Rising Sun* or not?
**Crichton:** We wrote . . . [hesitates]

**Rose:** It's good for you to get this, I'm telling you. If you don't . . .
**Crichton:** *Twister* together.

**Rose:** You're in trouble.
**Crichton:** That's exactly right—I'm sorry, honey!

**Rose:** Can you describe her contribution?
**Crichton:** Yes, I can. Actually, there was a lawsuit about this.

**Rose:** Somebody accused you of having gotten this idea from them. You had to go to court to prove otherwise.
**Crichton:** Right; very interesting experience for me.

**Rose:** Really? In what way?
**Crichton:** It's a gigantic chess game. I am going to write about it. It's this thing where I would say to the attorneys, "Well, why don't you just say this?" They'd say, "Well, if we say this, and he says that, then we have to say this, or we don't want to say this." It's like a chess game where you're playing several moves ahead, and it's all verbal. I just thought it was phenomenally interesting.

**Rose:** This is easy. All you have to do is figure out how to set a novel in the court.
**Crichton:** I'm going to do nonfiction. I'm going to describe what happened.

**Rose:** Oh, you're going to describe this particular event?
**Crichton:** I'm going to do it.

**Rose:** How much of that is simply a little bit of getting back?
**Crichton:** Revenge? [Laughs]

**Rose:** Yes. [Laughs]
**Crichton:** Hey, you want to take on a novelist, there is that risk.

**Rose:** Or a filmmaker, or whatever.
**Crichton:** No, I think it's to get it out of my mind; to put it to rest. And also because there's this way where almost everybody has heard that the accusation was made and many people have never heard that we won.

**Rose:** Exactly.
**Crichton:** There was a huge article in the *New York Times* when the trial started and none when we won it. None.

**Rose:** Now you can work these things into novels, too. You take *Airframe*. You took your swipe at the media right there.
**Crichton:** Yes, back when it wasn't so clear where so much of it was going on.

**Rose:** Did I miss something? Has that already been made into a movie?
**Crichton:** No.

**Rose:** I didn't think so.
**Crichton:** We stopped it.

**Rose:** You stopped it?
**Crichton:** We got what I thought was a very good script by Frank Pierson. We started budgeting it and it was just phenomenally expensive so we began to work. Joe Roth at Disney was great about it. We started trying to find ways to get it down to a reasonable level and we never could. It's just inherently costly because you have to have two major airplane events and film them—have to do them great.

**Rose:** But it's so timely. Look at today's headline. Can I tell you what today's headline is? "FBI May Be Asked to Take Over Case of EgyptAir Crash; Cryptic Words on Tape; After Review of Voice Recorder, Safety Board Is Concerned about Intent of Pilot." There's a novel right there.
**Crichton:** Would not be the first time. I think there have been at least two other crashes where they believe the pilot was committing suicide. I believe that's the question here.

**Rose:** I don't know. I haven't read beyond the front page—I assume it was either that or something else. That's very sick—to take that many people with you.
**Crichton:** It is difficult, isn't it? It's worse than Columbine.

**Rose:** By far. Now, does that interest you—Columbine, and all the sense of America and violence?
**Crichton:** I got very interested at the time that it happened—did a lot of re-

search about media and violence at that time, because I try to limit violence in what I do.

**Rose:** Or you put it in the fourteenth century.
**Crichton:** That's beheadings with swords. What I mean is I try to keep handgun shootings out of what I do. I try not to have that happen any more than I have to. What I found is this very unpopular thing but it seems to be quite true—the correlations are difficult or impossible—all the time that we're having these discussions about the increasing media violence and rise of video games and so on, the murder rate is dropping in this country; it's been falling for six or seven consecutive years.

**Rose:** I asked someone about that last night. I said, "Why is the crime rate dropping?" This was broader than just murder. They said, "It has a lot to do [with] science and technology and how they report stuff and how they demand accountability and a lot of other stuff, as well as police on the ground and all that stuff." What do you think?
**Crichton:** I'm sure that's true and I'm sure there's some kind of demographics involved where there are fewer juvenile males in this period.

**Rose:** That's part of it.
**Crichton:** There are about to be many more. But I don't think there's any question that—it's unfortunate—a lot of the increasing incarceration has had an effect and a lot of the police focus has had an effect. The notion of what's happened in New York where you're really going after petty crime and cleaning up the environment seems to have an effect that I think is counter-intuitive.

**Rose:** Sends a message. If you're cleaning up squeegee guys, you're sending a message that this is just a small example. If we're going to take care of this, we're going to take care of the big stuff, too.
**Crichton:** I think it does more than that because when you're now in a cleaned-up environment you behave differently. The behavior that might have seemed not so aberrant now seems aberrant.

**Rose:** It's interesting. Not relevant to that, but I've been frantically searching to find a place to live. I'm literally homeless now—an apartment, right. I was

talking to a friend of mine the other day who said, "The first thing you have to do is find an apartment with a lot of light. You have to find an apartment with a lot of light because I have essentially lived most of my life in the dark. I went to work when it was dark, I sat in an office all day, and I came home." And he said, "I think it had terrible impact on me."
**Crichton:** I can imagine.

**Rose:** Yes.
**Crichton:** [Gestures around studio] Here we are.

**Rose:** Here we are in the dark studio. What am I doing? Couple things before we go. What does it mean that in 1998, *Forbes* magazine, one of those great surveys of the richest people in entertainment, had you like eighth or ninth or something like that? Does huge wealth mean much to you other than freedom?
**Crichton:** No—the short form of the answer. I think Galbraith was right. He said: "There is a big difference between not having enough money and having enough. And there's very little difference between having enough and having more than enough."

**Rose:** Is that right?
**Crichton:** Something like that.

**Rose:** But do you think, because you're in this range now, about how you can use it?
**Crichton:** Yes.

**Rose:** You do?
**Crichton:** Sure. Of course.

**Rose:** Because you're such a consumer and connoisseur of ideas and frontiers that you know how to make a difference.
**Crichton:** Actually, I just look for situations where funding isn't going to come from other sources; certain kinds of publications that are having difficulty or certain kinds of educational programs need scholarships. I'm drawn to that.

**Rose:** This book is called *Timeline*; 1.5 million copies. It's a Knopf book. Michael Crichton. It's another great story and it is always good to have Michael here. I thank you for coming.
**Crichton:** Thank you, Charlie.

**Rose:** Michael Crichton for the hour. Thank you for joining us. See you tomorrow night.

# The Next Step in the Evolution of Crichton's Fiction

### James Cowan/2002

From the *National Post*, December 10, 2002. Courtesy of *National Post*.

Since the publication of *Jurassic Park* in 1990, Michael Crichton's name has been inextricably linked to the image of a rampaging Tyrannosaurus Rex. However, the sixty-year-old novelist's career extends far beyond velociraptors. He's a graduate of the Harvard Medical School, one of *People*'s 50 Beautiful People and an Emmy Award–winner for his work on *ER*.

In his latest book, *Prey*, Crichton moves from telling stories of giant lizards to tiny robots. *Prey* follows a battle between a swarm of deadly microscopic nanites and the scientists who created them. Crichton spoke to the *National Post*'s James Cowan about his new book, the science that inspired it, and his life as a doctor-turned-novelist-turned-blockbuster-creator.

**Cowan:** Many of your books—most notably *Jurassic Park*—have evolution as a central theme, but in *Prey* the evolution is non-biological. Has science's understanding of evolution evolved?

**Crichton:** Yes. Twenty years ago, the only concept of evolution was the evolution of living creatures, but there's now another way in which evolutionary ideas are being used. The notion of evolutionary programming is becoming more and more powerful. I saw a demonstration of a solar collector that was "evolved" inside a computer by having different solutions to a problem "mate" with each other and having the solutions' "offspring" survive to produce ever more sophisticated solutions to how to make a solar energy device. A great deal of genetic research is now done with genetic algorithms in a computer. They get the molecules to evolve themselves.

What I was pointing to in *Prey* is that because you can do these things inside a computer, it may be easy to say, well, let's evolve a population of

**191**

robots. We can't fix this problem—let's see if they can evolve and find a solution on their own. And that's how we get the mess that the story is about.

**Cowan:** *Prey* is one of the few novels I've read that includes a bibliography outlining the author's source material. What's the relationship in your novels between real-world science and science fiction?
**Crichton:** I'm not exactly sure how the science transforms into fiction. In my own mind, it's a process of excretion, like a coral reef. Very small things get added over time and then eventually the whole thing sticks above the water.

This book started with two separate things that I combined. One was an image that kept coming to my mind of this well-dressed businesswoman coming home after a long day of work and slapping her child in the nursery.

The other idea derived from a speech I gave to the American Association for the Advancement of Science. It was about the image of science and scientists in the media, and one of the core images I encountered was Frankenstein. It is one of the fundamental mythic images we have, and I realized what most people think about when you say "Frankenstein" is Boris Karloff with bolts in his neck. That image is now getting to be eighty years old, which is an eternity in science. So I began to think about what Frankenstein's monster would look like in the twenty-first century. And my feeling is that it wouldn't look anything like Boris Karloff. It would be entirely different.

**Cowan:** *Frankenstein* is a morality tale about the dangers of playing God. Are your novels morality tales as well?
**Crichton:** I certainly see them as cautionary tales. I'm not sure that I would call what they deal with morality, exactly. I write to start a process of thought for people who haven't thought about something before.

**Cowan:** *Prey* not only offers insight into nanotechnology, but a host of other science-related tangents as well. At various points you tackle the science behind animal herds, human physiology, and the stock market. Did these diverse ideas all come up when you were researching nanotechnology?
**Crichton:** I think most of those ideas came from my research. In terms of writing fiction, one of the important reasons for research is that reality is always stranger than what you imagine. When I was writing *Prey*, I would think, "What would a nanotechnology assembly line look like?" and then I'd

make something up and decide it's not very persuasive. So I hunt to see who has already envisioned such an assembly line and what their conception of one would be. And it's usually much more interesting than mine.

I think that's part of what interests people about my novels. The last book I wrote, *Timeline*, was about life in the fourteenth century. And I would be searching for specific details that were often very hard to obtain. How did they clean their armour? What did they have for breakfast? Did they have breakfast at all? How were the rooms furnished? And so on. But whenever I found answers, they weren't what I expected them to be. That notion that the world isn't what you imagine makes it something that readers pick up on.

**Cowan:** Your critics often allege that your books are specifically designed to become summer blockbusters. True?

**Crichton:** At this point, so many of my books have been made into films that it's possible to have that thought. But if you ever talk to any of the people who adapt my books, they'll tell you it's very difficult. I've tried it myself and it's a pain in the neck.

If you take a screenplay and rewrite it as a short story, it's going to be forty pages long. So generally speaking, you're taking a four hundred–page book and condensing it into forty pages. That means a tremendous amount of material has to be excised, and the story still has to make sense with all that material missing.

Books are very forgiving. You can write a dialogue scene that really rambles, and it's OK when you read it. It's not OK when you watch it on the screen.

**Cowan:** I can think of a bunch of lawyers, such as Scott Turow or John Grisham, who have become novelists, but you're one of the few doctors I can think of that writes fiction.

**Crichton:** There was a belief when I started that the technical training needed for science and the humanistic background that leads you to write fiction are not usually found in the same person. I don't know why. It seems to me that we live in societies that are really influenced by technology. We're dependent on the technology, we're under pressure from the technology, and we're constantly trying to understand the social pressures that arise from the technology.

One could argue you couldn't have the feminist movement without convenient birth control. That's a social movement of tremendous importance that came after an enabling technology. So there are powerful technological influences driving individuals and societies, and it doesn't enter fiction as often as you would expect. I think that's odd.

**Cowan:** You've now written eighteen books. Do you ever go back and read your old work?

**Crichton:** I did actually look at *The Andromeda Strain* before I wrote *Prey*, and I did it for a very specific reason. I felt that, bit by bit, my books were getting a little windy. It's not my natural inclination to write a very long book, and I'd started to do it. I thought I'd like to go back to a crisper style. So I was really interested to look at *The Andromeda Strain*. It's very quick and tense. It manages to be tense without making itself obvious. But I don't think I can write like that anymore. It's as if it was written by a different person.

# Author Crichton Ponders Fear, Real and Imagined

## John Marshall/2002

From the *Seattle Post-Intelligencer*, December 16, 2002. Reprinted by permission of The Hearst Corporation.

The master of the techno-thriller has been scaring millions for years with his fictional tales, but fright of a far scarier sort arrived recently for Michael Crichton.

First came September 11, 2001, that morning when Crichton was aboard a jetliner heading from the East Coast to his home on the West Coast, that morning when other West Coast–bound jetliners crashed into the World Trade Center and the Pentagon and a field in Pennsylvania. The plane bearing Crichton was diverted to Indianapolis and grounded there, with one of the world's most popular writers left to ponder his brush with fate and what-if.

"I went through a personal . . . well, what can you say," remarked Crichton in Seattle last Thursday. "Let's just say it was something to absorb, to digest. I can say that I was not going through what everybody else did that day."

Then came September of this year when Crichton was asleep in his Santa Monica home during predawn hours when he was suddenly awakened with a gun to his head. Two men in ski masks gave him orders, then tied up and gagged the writer and his twelve-year-old daughter and ransacked the house where the writer had been living since his separation from his fourth wife. The two Crichtons suffered no more physical harm from the armed robbers, but what they went through then and afterward made the rampaging dinosaurs of the novelist's *Jurassic Park* seem like overblown fantasy.

"What was interesting to me after all the frightening parts were over," Crichton recalled, "was how the media attention afterward was far more traumatic than the event itself. With all the TV cameras encamped outside, with reporters on the lawn and others filming the house, I became so paranoid. I was sneaking around, trying to avoid attention, entering the house from the alley.

"And the second interesting thing to me was what I heard later from friends and acquaintances. It turned out that a lot of people had had violent encounters like that, although they usually don't speak about it. I must say I'm about to become that way myself. But I now know that such violent encounters are more common than anyone might expect."

These reflections, offered with carefully considered pauses, provided a rare glimpse of the personal side of a writer famous for his zealous protection of his privacy. And, as he suggested, likely to become even more that way because of what he's been through.

But Crichton was not a reluctant interview subject during the last city stop on a national book tour to promote his latest resident at the pinnacle of the bestseller list, *Prey*. It's his first book in three years, half of a two-book contract with a new publisher that will pay him a reported $30 million, plus $5 million for the inevitable film rights.

Crichton was polite and reserved, in a gentlemanly way, but also thoughtful and erudite, as befits his Harvard education (summa cum laude undergraduate degree, medical degree as well) and his year of teaching anthropology at Cambridge. Shifting his 6-foot-9 frame from one chair to another in a hotel suite, doffing the coat of his dark Polo suit and installing on a straight-back chair, the sixty-year-old author came across more as shy than standoffish, a reluctant giant who might well have preferred to inhabit a far less noticeable frame.

Discomfort is usually the posture of Crichton's readers when they confront another of his irresistible page-turners of science gone terribly wrong. *Prey* delivers that expected Crichton charge, this time focused on the emerging field of nanotechnology, where manufactured micro-particles are invested with such functions as mobility, photography, computing.

That these machines are 1,000 times smaller than the diameter of human hair is just one of the revelations about nanotechnology for the lay reader, as Crichton relates in his straightforward introduction to the novel. That the U.S. government has spent more than $1 billion in the past two years in developing nanotechnology is another.

In *Prey*, Crichton spins out a chilling worst-case scenario for nanotechnology, which focuses on unscrupulous techies, under a military contract for camera-born nanoparticles, who release them outside their supersecret Nevada plant where the self-replicating little monsters form ever-increasing attack swarms that devour any life forms in their path, from jackrabbits to scientists.

Called to the rescue is an unlikely hero, Jack Forman, an unemployed Silicon Valley research analyst who has been playing house-husband for six months after blowing the ethical whistle on the leadership of his previous employer. Julia Forman, Jack's career-obsessed wife and mother of their children, just happens to be an exec in the nanotechnology startup whose plant is the site of the nefarious doings. She also has been not quite herself in recent weeks, prone to snappish outbursts, as if some strange she-devil were inhabiting her skin.

Jack Forman, aided by a comely field biologist, is soon battling evil outside the plant and inside, too, including the apparent plottings of his wife and the plant manager. *Prey* thus becomes a race against destruction, with permutations on a theme expounded in the novel's opening line: "Things never turn out the way you think they will."

That statement happens to summarize Crichton's thoughts about emerging technologies. *Prey*, as he has done in many bestsellers, has twisted the plausible into the nightmarish. It's popular entertainment with red flags waving about future perils. Whether what happens in *Prey* will happen is less important to the author than it could happen.

Crichton likens nanotechnology to biotechnology awhile back: "When biotech began, a lot of those involved in the field said it was just an extension of the breeding that humans have been doing for thousands of years. It was just better breeding, that's all. Now, no one would dare say that with a straight face. Whatever biotech is, it's not just breeding. That analogy has proven to be unwise. So that's why I often focus on potentially problematic developments so that people have some level of awareness."

Matters of awareness are important to Crichton, the awareness of his readers, his own awareness as well. The writer was much disheartened when his thorough analysis revealed that the plots of his novels seem to follow a similar plot pattern that he describes as "slow, then fast, then tapering off." He applied the same analytical approach to his use of time when he was trying to answer that midlife quandary of what to do with the rest of his life.

"I believe," he said, "in that Ben Franklinesque attribute—keeping track of how you're behaving and how you're using your time."

It would seem that the creator of *The Andromeda Strain*, *The Terminal Man*, *Disclosure*, and the TV medical series *ER* would be using less of his time for work and more for relaxation. After all, his huge success landed him amid the world's 100 most powerful celebrities in the 1999 rankings of *Forbes* magazine, listed at No. 8 right after Michael Jordan and immediately preceding Harrison Ford and the Rolling Stones, and the only writer included in the top ten.

But Crichton has discovered that he simply cannot stop. Without writing, he finds himself feeling achy and twitchy and out of sorts. He used to cure that with meditation, but found that the true cure was the writing.

As he admitted, "If I'm not writing, or if I go for a long time without writing, then I get weird. I have to keep writing so I don't get weird."

Crichton's writing has seldom earned many plaudits from critics. Characterization and writing style are not his forte. It's his acknowledged ability to generate and orchestrate gripping plot lines that has placed him in the stratosphere of popularity occupied by only a few writers (Stephen King, Danielle Steel, Tom Clancy, John Grisham).

The surprise, given his phenomenal success, is that Crichton seems quite aware of his abilities as a writer. He concedes that his work often is not "technically polished."

"I do not have too many illusions about what I do," he emphasized. ". . . I talk to a limited number of readers and listen to them. I always hope they'll say, 'It's great! Don't change a word!' They don't usually say that.

"That's why I've always believed what a friend told me—that all writers should have tattooed on their foreheads, backwards so they could read it when they looked in the mirror every morning, these words: 'Everybody needs an editor.' I've always remembered that. When a writer says, 'No one can edit me,' that's the beginning of the gas bag decline."

No such decline seems likely soon for Crichton. The Chicago native has the second novel of his new contract to write, a television series to create for Fox, a new contract with the video game giant, Sega.

Crichton's greatest talent may be his ability to master many trades at the highest levels. He has been a book writer, a screenwriter, a producer, a film director, a software company director, a creator of video games.

That is why he is sometimes approached by others interested in emulating his success in one or the other of the fields where he has prospered, others wondering just what it takes to achieve what he has.

"I've known a few geniuses who wanted to become writers or film directors and they've asked for my assistance," Crichton recounted. "It soon becomes clear that most of them do not want to work hard enough. There's just some way that I'm not afraid of trying things. . . . I don't think my light opera will surface any time soon, but if somebody asks me to do a play, I don't automatically decline. I'm just not scared because I always like to do new things. And I also know it's just hard work to put your fanny in the chair and pound it out. And if it's not right, you just do it again."

# Interview with Michael Crichton

## Beth Anderson/2004

From *Audible.com*, December 13, 2004. Reprinted by permission of Audible, Inc.

**Anderson:** I'm very pleased to introduce Michael Crichton—author, screenwriter, film director, and TV series creator. He's here today to talk about his latest book, *State of Fear.* Michael, *State of Fear* challenges most of our assumptions about global warming and the environmental movement. For our listeners who haven't yet read or listened to your book, could you give them a sense of your argument?

**Crichton:** The easiest way to tell them about it is to tell them what happened. I was reading an article in a science journal and it was one of those front of the book things—it was very short and didn't make a lot of sense. I kept reading it trying to understand what the problem was. Finally, I concluded that when somebody writes a one-page piece that doesn't hold together it's because they want to say something they don't feel they can say. I thought, "Well, the only thing this guy would want to say is that global warming isn't real and that's ridiculous." At the next opportunity between books I decided to go online and look at the temperature records because I hadn't paid a lot of attention. When I started this my views were highly conventional, they were pretty much like everyone else's. All the temperature records are online—you can easily see what the situation is. It wasn't very long before I began to have substantial reservations. It simply wasn't clear to me why the last thirty years in which temperature has gone up in association with carbon dioxide should be considered more relevant than the previous thirty years where temperatures went down even though carbon dioxide went up. I just assumed that I must not understand—there must be some other factor here I wasn't getting because it didn't make a lot of sense to me. So I looked with ever more attention to detail and, for better or worse, the more detail I got into the less persuaded I was.

**Anderson:** As your reader or listener is going through your book, you're really leading them through the same discovery you went through as you were going through the research. You're posing assumptions and then offering countering evidence and countering facts.

**Crichton:** That's exactly right. The only thing that's different, or the only challenge in this sense for me in doing the novel, was that I took the better part of three years to very slowly come to the conclusion that, in this particular area, the conventional wisdom wasn't satisfactory. I knew from my own experience that my immediate reaction to exposure to this was to say, "No. I don't accept it. I'm staying with the conventional views." So, in order to do a book in which readers might accept this or just take it tentatively for a little while was a challenge to structure.

**Anderson:** That's been my exact reaction as I've been listening to your book. I say, "No! That can't be true!" In the next moment you have a character ask that question and get an answer. So it's as if we're having a dialogue as I'm listening along in my car.

**Crichton:** One of the things that's difficult in this particular one is that there are a lot of graphs that can't be shown in audio. They have to be described, and sometimes that's not as easy as it might be.

**Anderson:** At what point in your research did you decide there was a book in this—that you could make this into a novel?

**Crichton:** I talked to a few—actually, very few—climate scientists because this is a very, very politicized area and I didn't really want to have anybody influencing me. I thought, "I'm an outsider; I'm not sided; I'm a political agnostic and I think what's valuable is that I have come to my own conclusion here." But it was clear in the brief conversations I had with the people who were doing the modeling that where we part company is—I think what they're doing is terrific; the climate research is, in many ways, dazzling; an extraordinarily ambitious undertaking; this is a multi-generational computer modeling activity that's being done, and it's fabulous—it's simply not good enough to set policy on. Whereas they, of course, think it is. That was the essential difference. But to the extent that there's controversy about my views, I must say it's really amazing to me because I never thought the idea that you can't predict the future would be controversial. When I talk to audiences, I get up and say, "Can we agree that you can't predict the future, unless you guys think you're all psychic? But if you're not psychic, then we really have to face some cold realities about how unpredictable the future is." I talk to them about, for example, what a person in the year 1900 would predict for the year 2000. The big problem that a person in the year 1900 would see was: Where will they get all the horses for the year 2000 and what will we do with all the horseshit? There's a very interesting picture floating around on the internet which is said to be from the 1954 issue of *Popular Mechanics* showing the Rand Corporation's mockup of a home computer. It's really silly and very amusing, and unfortunately it's a fake; it's great, but it's a fake. I was sufficiently intrigued by this that I went back to *Popular Mechanics* to look at what they did actually say about the home computer. Do you know what they said?

**Anderson:** No.
**Crichton:** Nothing at all. Do you know why?

**Anderson:** They hadn't imagined it.
**Crichton:** That's right. No one thought it was possible.

**Anderson:** What sort of reactions are you getting from academics, researchers, environmentalists, activists—who's saying what?
**Crichton:** I'm quite interested in the number of people who have responded by raising their level of skepticism, and I'm pleased by the number of people who think it's a fun ride to take, that it's an exciting story, which always makes me happy. Unfortunately, and it's one of the things I criticize in the novel itself, a lot of environmental thinking has taken on a fundamentalist tinge, as if it were religious. That's bad for a number of reasons. The biggest one is that we really do need a good environmental movement. We really do have an environment that needs our attention. It really is not as good as it could be and should be. There are huge areas where we just don't have information—not the areas that are usually talked about, because I think the environmental movement is not doing what it really needs to do.

**Anderson:** What should it be doing?
**Crichton:** The first area of concern I have, looking toward the future—because I like to hike, I like to be out in nature—it's become clear to me that we don't know how to preserve what we call "wilderness." We don't know how to do it. The test case of this—the poster child—is Yellowstone National Park, the first national park. It's been a national park for more than one hundred years and our management of it has been disastrous. There is now raw sewage coming out of the ground. But it isn't only Yellowstone and it

isn't really only America. In parks in Africa, in parks in India, in wherever there are such parks, it turns out the difficulty of being a good steward is vastly greater than anybody imagined. The core that I've come to conclude is that we don't know how to do this. We don't know how to manage. The environment is a complex system and what we know now about how you interact with complex systems tells us that we can't really be sure what the effect is of any of our actions. We have to be constantly monitoring, constantly probing, constantly reexamining what we've been doing—even to say, "I don't know." All of that behavior is not suited to a fundamentalist philosophy. Fundamentalists are really good at saying, "I know the answer and you don't." But when nobody knows the answer, then we better get into a more scientific headset and out of a more religious headset.

**Anderson:** Do you think it's an area of science that money will be devoted to—to allow this kind of research to answer some of these questions?
**Crichton:** No, I don't think so. I'm very, very disheartened as I think about the future because if you look at the behavior of every generation in this area, every generation says, "Well, the last generation, what a bunch of idiots they were. Look at the stupid mistakes they made. They got all the wolves out of Yellowstone because they thought they were preserving elk, because they thought the elk were becoming extinct, which was wrong. It was wrong to get the wolves out and it was wrong to move the grizzly bears. But this is a new generation. We see all their mistakes and we're not going to make those mistakes. We know what we're doing." Unfortunately, what they don't seem to realize is that the past generation thought it knew what it was doing, too. Every generation thinks they know what they're doing. The only real change that's going to happen is when somebody gets up and says, "Folks, we don't know. We better go learn." There are some people, very few, doing fundamental research in this area. I've identified some in the book. There's a psychologist named Dietrich Dorner who got academic colleagues to work on computer simulations of different kinds of environments—one was a town in Maine, one was a desert community in the Sahara. What he found almost immediately was that the great majority of people who set out to manage these environments ran them into the ground. They made everything much worse, which is, of course, the ordinary human experience. He then studied the relatively few people who did the job well. What did they do? How did they interact with this environment? The answer was: They didn't have a philosophy that they were too attached to going in. They monitored their behavior very carefully. They looked for unexpected consequences and

when they saw them they acted immediately. The summary of his thinking was that people who are dogmatic would come in and say, "This is the way to do it." Then, as time went on—and of course that didn't turn out to be the way—they made fewer and fewer interactions until finally it all went bad and they blamed something. The people who were successful started out with less of a philosophical conviction and, as time went on, they made more and more interactions; they kept modifying, kept revising, kept trying to refine and they didn't blame anybody. They were successful. We're setting aside more wilderness area, which is fabulous. I'm entirely in favor of it. It would be even greater if we knew how to take care of it, which we don't.

**Anderson:** What about the rest of the world? Are they responding to the problem better than the U.S.? Is there more research going on in Europe or in Asia?
**Crichton:** No, and one of my criticisms of having a focus on the year 2100 . . .

**Anderson:** By that, you mean the Kyoto Protocol?
**Crichton:** Yes, all of that intense future orientation; the notion of the long-range view, which has never been successful. Look at the predictions of the Club of Rome, a group that did the early computer projections in 1973. They said we would run out of all sorts of raw resources by 1993. We didn't run out of anything, which is not to say that we may not eventually, but it is to say that those predictions were significantly, significantly in error. They also predicted that by the year 2020 we'd have a world population of fourteen billion, and there isn't anybody who believes we're going to get anywhere near that.

**Anderson:** In *State of Fear* you have a character—an academic, a professor emeritus—who describes something that he calls the political-legal-media complex, and he asserts that it's replaced the Cold War as an organizing principle for modern society. Is that something you believe, or was that a fictional device? Can you talk a little bit about that?
**Crichton:** I do believe it. My way of thinking about this is: The United States was organized as a government by a bunch of really smart people, and one of the core principles of the way they organized it was checks and balances. They had institutions that were really either opposed to one another or in some way monitoring and tolerating a certain level of conflict. When I look at modern society today, I see politicians and media and lawyers. Don't for-

get, we have three-quarters of all the lawyers in the entire planet—they're a phenomenally powerful group. These three really have a stake in the promotion of ongoing fears and crises. There is no countervailing institution that has as its purpose, or has a reason to stand up and say, "No, don't be afraid of that one. No, that one's fake. No, don't be buying into that." The poster child for false fears is, of course, Y2K, which is recent enough that most people can still remember it. For months—years, really—we heard fears expressed about what terrible things were going to happen: airplanes were going to drop out of the sky, financial markets were going to collapse. People sold their houses, they withdrew all their money, they moved to higher ground, they bought guns. Nothing happened.

**Anderson:** So your title, *State of Fear*, is really a broad statement about our condition now.
**Crichton:** Yes, about how our societies function or are arranged. Absolutely.

**Anderson:** What should we be afraid of? Is there anything that scares you now?
**Crichton:** I'm really afraid of people who are certain about a lot of things. I'm really afraid of people who can't listen to opposing views. In general, I'm not against religion, but I'm against fundamentalism. I actually feel sadness that as our societies become more secular—which is fine with me—there is a religious feeling that tends to be inherent in human beings and if that religious feeling isn't in a church or a synagogue or a mosque, if it doesn't have its place there, floats off and attaches to other things. One of the things it's tended to attach to is our feelings about the environment and about the world. That's too bad, because that's an area where we really need to be detached. From my point of view, we're not doing that well. We need to do a lot better, and I don't think you can learn new information from inside a fundamentalist perspective. People who are fundamentalists think they already know.

**Anderson:** Has your research and writing on this environmental issue affected your political beliefs at all?
**Crichton:** No. It's a long time since I've been enthusiastic about an American administration, unfortunately—by which I mean decades. What has changed, which is really interesting, is that it was such a large adjustment for

me to look at this material and say, "You know what, I wish I could believe it better but I don't." As a result of that I began to look at how many new fears are being fomented every day. The most recent one I've seen: I've just come back from London where they're all atwitter about laptops causing infertility in men. But there's a new one tomorrow or the next day. What has happened to me as a lasting change is that I've gotten phenomenally skeptical about everything I see in the mass media—everything.

**Anderson:** You must have felt during the election, when day after day after day a new fear was raised to try to sway the electorate one way or the other, you must have felt like saying, "I told you so!"
**Crichton:** In a way, and even about the conduct of the election. People would call me and say, "Oh my God! The Democrats are registering Mary Poppins!" And I'd go, "Maybe." Then they go, "Oh, the Republicans are keeping black people from voting!" "Maybe." That's kind of how I feel: "We'll see."

**Anderson:** Who do you like to read, Michael? Who are your favorite authors?
**Crichton:** It's interesting. I almost entirely read nonfiction, and it changes. In other words, I've read environmental material now for the better part of three years—which has gone from being phenomenally interesting to being a real puzzlement to something I'm now ready to stop reading. So I've moved on to new areas of interest and I'm reading intensively in those areas—which have to do with the 1930s in the United States, and also ideas about psychology and how psychology is applied in the courtroom in the post-Freudian era. That's my new area of interest.

**Anderson:** Should we expect to see a book on that theme in a couple years?
**Crichton:** Yes, I think so. [Laughs] At least, I would be surprised if we didn't.

**Anderson:** Wonderful, wonderful. What's coming up between then and now? Any new movies? TV projects?
**Crichton:** The film version of *Prey* has been slowly percolating along and I hope that will start up soon; other than that, no. I'm just doing this writing and having really a terrific time with it.

**Anderson:** Thank you, very much. This is obviously an area you've given a great deal of thought to and I think you're going to encourage all of us to give it a lot more thought than we normally have, so I thank you for that.

**Crichton:** You're very welcome. [I hope] people come away with a new, less pat attitude toward things and also with a greater focus on the present. We live in a world where, every single day, ten to twenty thousand people die of waterborne illnesses. We have it in our capacity, we can easily accomplish it, we know how to do it, and we have plenty of money to see that all these people get clean water. I would argue strongly that what we should be doing is dealing with problems that exist in the present and worrying a little less about problems that may or may not arise in the year 2100.

**Anderson:** Thank you, Michael Crichton.
**Crichton:** Thank you.

# Reflections on Careers
# in Entertainment

## Students & Leaders Program/2005

Transcribed from the C-SPAN *Students & Leaders* program with Michael Crichton on March 16, 2005. Copyright © by C-SPAN. Used by permission.

**Levenworth:** Good morning. I'm Deane Leavenworth and I'm with Time Warner Cable. I want to thank you students and the faculty and staff here at Cleveland High and the Los Angeles Unified School District and its board for hosting these events—the Students and Leaders event. This is something we feel is very important. For more than twenty-five years the cable industry and C-SPAN have worked to not only educate and inform, but to engage our viewers. When we have events like this, we feel it helps us accomplish those goals by engaging the leaders of today with the leaders of tomorrow. So we want to thank you very much for taking part in this. I want to introduce one of the leaders of tomorrow, the student body president at Cleveland High, Harvard-bound, Ji Eun Baek.

**Baek:** I am so excited. Good morning. Cleveland High School has been an amazing place for me for the past four years as I'm sure it has for you guys. My job is to introduce the very internationally renowned celebrity guest we have today. He went to Harvard Medical School—he's a doctor. I'm sure you know he wrote *Jurassic Park*, in addition to other very, very well known novels. Without further ado, I'd like to introduce Dr. Michael Crichton.

**Crichton:** Thank you, Ji Eun. Hi. What I'd like to do today is talk very briefly about myself—I can actually talk for a long time about myself. One of the formative experiences for me when I was in college was Edward Albee, the famous playwright, came to my school. I hurried off to see him because I wanted to get a look at what a real writer was. Albee got up and gave a speech and then left. It was like a professor's speech—he was a pretend professor except he wasn't very good. I was disappointed. I wanted to talk to him about what I wanted to talk about. So today I'm going to talk about what you want to talk about. Let me tell you a little bit: I grew up in a suburb of New York City—a town called Roslyn. I went to high school there and I was the first kid in my high school to go to Harvard. I was terrified. It turned out okay. I was in the English Department but they didn't like the way I wrote. I had always been very interested in writing—I was one of those kids who, at a very young age, had a feeling about what I wanted to do. In the third grade I was writing and when I was in high school I wrote for the school paper and for the town paper—covered local sports and stuff like that. I was pretty proud of my writing and since they didn't like it I switched departments and studied anthropology. From there I went to medical school. In the course of being a medical student I had to pay some of my tuition, so I began to write books because that was the only thing I knew how to do. I thought, "Maybe I can earn some money by writing books." At that time, the James Bond books were very popular—this was the late 1960s—so I began to write sort of James Bond thrillers. They were original paperbacks and I found I could eventually do them in about ten days. Christmas vacation would come and I would write a book. It was great, great training for a writer because the whole idea of it was that I should write something that was not original, that was not an expression of me. I wrote under a pseudonym—it had nothing to do with me personally. It was just intended to be a thing people would want to read and that the publishers would take and print and never send back to me for any changes, because by then Christmas vacation was over and I was back in the hospital. I didn't have any time to change things. It was fabulous. I did six or seven of those books. By the time I started to write under my own name I had none of the anxieties that writers usually have because it was just another book. I retired from medicine. It's hard to describe now what that was like. That was a huge deal; it happened in 1969. In the late 1960s doctors were revered only slightly below Supreme Court Justices. It's gone now. People don't feel that way about doctors. So for me to quit medicine and go to Hollywood was like quitting the Supreme Court to become a bail bondsman. It was an inconceivable transition but it was what I wanted to do, so I did it. Why don't I stop there and let you guys ask me some questions.

**Question:** Hi, my name is Camille. I'm a freshman here and my question for you is: What motivated you to speak to the students here at Cleveland High School?

**Crichton:** I was asked to do it. [Laughs] It's a funny thing about writing—

you don't get to see an audience ever. Sometimes I'll be on an airplane and somebody's reading my book. I'll look at their face—they're smiling or they're frowning or they slam it shut. But usually you don't get that chance. When I first started directing movies, it was amazing to sit in the audience and think, "Wow. Look at how all these people are reacting to what I've done." I'd never had that experience so it's really helpful to me—it's also why I do book signings. I like to see what everybody's thinking about. This is for my benefit, in other words, not yours.

**Question:** Hi. [I'm] Alexandria—I'm also a freshman here. Many kids my age view college as extremely important. In fact, our student body president was accepted to Harvard and we're all very, very proud of her. How did your dreams and aspirations differ from when you entered Harvard and when you left?

**Crichton:** There were two things that were really great about Harvard for me: One was that they basically left you alone and you could kind of do what you wanted. The other thing was that there was a great variety of things going on—it was a true university. I'd always had an interest in astronomy. A friend of mine was studying astronomy. We went to the observatory one night and saw how all that worked. I decided I didn't want to stay up late at night freezing myself to death, but that was great. It's great to have the ability to explore these different alternatives. When I went into college at seventeen, if someone had said, "When you come out you're going to go to medical school," I would have said, "Absolutely not." But slowly over that four-year period I really changed my goals enormously. The idea about being left alone was also, in a sense, an accident. Harvard at that time had a tutorial system where one of your classes, as a junior or senior, was with a single teacher and you would write papers. My teacher was a professor named William Howells and he was very interested in popular writing. He himself was a popular writer of anthropology books. I would meet with him once a month and he would say, "What would you like to write a paper on?" I'd say, "Well, I'm interested in Neanderthals." He'd say, "Okay, here are some references. Look here, look here, look here to begin, and I'll see you in a month." My job over the next month was to do all this research, write a twenty-five-page paper, turn it in. He'd read it. The next week we'd meet, he'd discuss my paper, mark it all up, explain what was wrong, and then say, "What would you like to write about?" I'd say, "Well, I'm kind of interested in what happened to the Indians in the southwest of the United States— why some of these groups disappeared." "Okay. Start with this reference, this reference, this reference. I'll see you in a month." That was how I spent, basically, the last two years of college and it's kind of how I spent the rest of my life.

**Question:** I'm Jennell—I'm also a freshman here. You stated in your remarks to the Commonwealth Club in San Francisco that one of the most powerful religions in the western world is environmentalism. Can you explain why you refer to environmentalism as a religion?

**Crichton:** Because I have training in anthropology. The idea that anthropologists have about what constitutes a religion, or what functions a religion serves, are a little bit different from how you think about it if you categorize religions as Christian, Muslim, Hindu . . . something like that. From the standpoint of an anthropological view, a religion is a collective set of beliefs; there is a leader or leaders who promote the beliefs among the followers; followers make some kind of contribution or change in their lifestyle based on the religious belief. The religious belief gives them a total view of the world—in terms of how the world is structured, what's right, what's wrong, what's good action, what's bad action. That all fits perfectly onto environmentalism. The other thing environmentalism does, which I said to this group, is rather precisely map a lot of Judeo-Christian beliefs about the origin of the world and so on. In environmental thinking there is a view that there used to be a sort of Eden, and then people came and ruined that Eden. We are therefore sort of original sinners because we're destroying this planet. What we can do, however, is get salvation through sustainability. If you're a good person you will seek salvation and if you're a bad person you'll drive SUVs. That is a kind of religious belief. That was my argument.

**Question:** What brought you your greatest joy—the success of your books or the success of your directing, *ER*, movies, and television?

**Crichton:** It's really weird. I knew a guy who had been in the movie business for most of his life. He vanished for a long time and then he came back. He had been a Buddhist monk in Nepal. He returned, he said, because his son was on drugs and he wanted to be there to help raise his kid. He had this completely different perspective. He said, "Show business doesn't make people happy." It's a very strange thing—it's exciting, you're working with tremendously talented people, it's glamorous from the outside—movie stars, red carpets, and all this stuff. But there's something about collaborative work that drains a lot of the pleasure away. I don't know why it happens—we talk about it sometimes. So my answer to you is working on books is great. You do the book; it's all your own effort. What's good about it is yours, what's bad about it is yours. When I'm done, I can hold the book in my hand and say, "I did that." I can't say that about a movie or about *ER*; a lot of people did it.

**Question:** Hello, I'm Jasmine—freshman here also. My question is: Would you ever consider going back to medicine as a full-time job?
**Crichton:** Would I consider going back? I would not, Jasmine. I think it's my personality; I don't know why. Somebody once described what I do as cud-chewing behavior. It's like a cow; my life is like a cow. The cow sees one clump of grass so it eats that clump, and then it sees the next clump so it eats that clump, and then it sees the next clump. The cow is just going from clump to clump. After a while you see the cow has gone across the whole field, but the cow doesn't have that kind of goal; the cow just eats the next clump. For me to go back I'd have to do all my training again. But I feel in a certain way I never left it. When we started *ER*, we were in the hospital all the time. I thought, "I've been trying my entire life to get out of the hospital and here I am again." And I'm not a good doctor. I'm a terrible doctor. People would come to me and say, "Doctor, I have these pains and they're worse after I eat and so on." They obviously had an ulcer. I would think, "I wonder what kind of disease I can dream up that would explain these symptoms?" It took me a long time to realize they weren't coming to me for an imaginary disease; they were actually coming for help. It was not my job to make up stories. So it was good that I got out. When I got calls in the middle of the night, they'd say, "Jimmy has a fever." I thought, "Well, just give him a Tylenol." I was very unsympathetic. [Laughs]

**Question:** Hello, I'm Samir. I would like to ask about a common theme in your books being technology gone askew. Does this theme have any relation to how you feel about technology?
**Crichton:** It does in the sense that I feel we live in a society where technology has just phenomenal boosterism from the corporations that are making the technology and the people who are buying it. With each new technology there are these fantastic claims made and these fantastic hopes that people have for it; it never really turns out. I'm old enough so that when I was not much younger than you, television was introduced. For the first ten years of my life there was no TV. I remember a world without television and I remember what people said when television came in—about how it was going to be this wonderful universal education and everyone was going to know

all the plays of the western world. In reality, it turns out to be shows about people sticking their faces in plates full of bugs and eating them. One of the early founders of television who worked all through the beginning said, "We had these great hopes for this medium and what we've actually invented is the biggest waste of time in the history of mankind." There's a way in which all that's true. The automobile offers universal freedom and transportation for everybody but we all sit in traffic jams. So there is this, I don't mean to say it too strongly, self-defeating aspect of technology. I always look at the other side of things.

**Question:** Hello, my name is Jennifer—I'm also a freshman. While at Harvard Medical School it is said that you nearly passed out many times at the sight of blood. What persuaded you into staying at the school year after year?

**Crichton:** It's true. I couldn't draw blood—I would just get dizzy. My first rotation was in the Boston City Hospital. The job of the medical student was to come in every morning before rounds and draw blood from thirty patients. Usually you just went boom, boom, boom, boom—you know how fast you can draw blood. Well, it took me half an hour. I would start to draw the blood, I'd feel sick, I'd run to the window, I'd stick my head out the window—it was January in Boston—it was cold. I'd settle down, wipe the sweat off, and I'd go to the next patient. It was a fortunate thing that some of the people on the ward were drug addicts. They saw me coming; they'd go, "No, no. You're not touching my veins." I would give them the needle and the stuff—they would draw the blood for me. [Laughs] I'd come back and collect it, but it still took me a long time. What's odd is that by the time I got to the emergency room I could do anything because there was no time to indulge this emotional reaction or whatever I was having. Everything was rushed, you were on the line, you had to sew people up. It didn't matter if the little baby was screaming and moving—you had to somehow hold them down and get the cut sewn up. That was an interesting experience to realize that these terrible, terrible fears or emotional responses could be taken away quickly if something else was more important.

**Question:** Hello, my name is Scott and my question is: How often do you apply your anthropology knowledge to your books or your writings?

**Crichton:** A lot. Anthropology, in my way of thinking, is a way of looking at the world. It's a combination field of many different disciplines. It involves everything from psychology to medicine. I studied physical anthropology, which was sort of CSI stuff. For example, one of the things we had to do was identify bone specimens. We would have these quizzes where they'd hand around little bits of wrist bone and you were supposed to say whether it was male or female, left or right, all that stuff. We were trained to identify physical remains that you would find at an archaeological site. That's one part of anthropology. Another part of anthropology is social behavior and how people interact. It's not always widely shared knowledge. When I wrote, about fourteen years ago, a book called *Rising Sun*, it talked about the differences between Japanese in Japanese society and in the United States. It caused a lot of furor here because people claimed it was racist. In fact, I was just doing anthropological thinking. My publisher, who's been my longest publisher—thirty-five years we've been together—taught me all these things about how to behave and how to have a meal in a Japanese way. For example, you have to pour Saki for the other person. You can't pour it for yourself. You can't pour Shōchū for yourself. That means you have to be watching other people. Sometimes somebody will say, "Can I give you some more?" Your cup is full. What you're supposed to do is drink a little bit, let them pour, and realize they're pouring for you because you're so neglectful—their Saki cup is empty and they need it refilled. It's really different from how we think about things, which is: "You want some food? Get it in the refrigerator." It's very different.

**Question:** Hi, my name is Adam. I'm a junior here. My question is: You said the greatest joy you get is from writing and not necessarily from producing. When you write a book and it gets made into a movie—such as *Jurassic Park*, *The Lost World*, *Rising Sun*—how do you feel when somebody reads the book then sees the movie and says, "They left this out, they left that out?" How do you feel when [directors] leave things out? How does that make you feel or what are your thoughts on that?
**Crichton:** I've done it myself. I did the first draft of *Jurassic Park* and I've done the screenplays of some of the other books I've worked on. What I know is the average book will be four hundred pages. A screenplay is 120 pages, but it's in a particular format—most of you have probably seen a screenplay. If you convert it to text it'll be forty pages. What that means is ninety percent of your book is gone. That's just how it is. You may be able to make a reference to some idea if you can find a visual thing, or stick something in at the end of a scene to try and beat the fact that ninety percent of your story is out. But, in the end, that's how it works. I'm okay with that. I actually feel fortunate. I'm happier with the movies that have been made

from my books than a lot of people are. I think a couple of them turned out really well, so that's great.

**Question:** Hi, my name is Brian and my question is: How would you feel if technology was used more violently than in a helpful way?
**Crichton:** Here's the thing about technology, Brian. It is always, in a certain sense, neutral in terms of use. You can die from an overdose of water. Every single thing you might invent can be used positively or negatively or neutrally, and that's just how things are. A car can save you or a car can kill you. It's hard to think of any technology which is either totally good and can't have any negative aspect or totally bad and can't have any positive aspect. Even the most toxic poisons from spiders now are sometimes converted into drugs because they have anti-coagulant effects. How we use technology is the important question; whether we're able to decide how to use it well, not anything about what's inherent in the technology. It's neutral.

**Question:** Hello, my name is Hanu. When you were in college it is said you wrote thrillers under a different name. How would you do that?
**Crichton:** I wrote really fast. I can't do more than one thing at a time. There are people who can talk on the telephone and write things. A friend of mine is a Buddhist philosopher named Ken Wilber. He's running this whole new school and website; he gets up at two o'clock in the morning and starts writing. I couldn't do that. I can only do one thing. So when I was writing I would actually drop out of school, but only for a short time. In second year of medical school they have these one-week instructional courses, so to this day I know almost nothing about the kidney because that was a week I stopped and wrote a book. [Laughs]

**Question:** Hi, my name is Cameron. You stated there was nothing wrong with DDT and it shouldn't have been taken off the market. What is your reasoning for that?
**Crichton:** I don't know if I stated there was nothing wrong; I said it was not a carcinogen. DDT was the subject of hysteria in the early 1960s. There are a few things to say about it: One is that it is actually quite safe—you can eat it. The reason why we know that is there was an experiment in which they fed it to prisoners for a couple of years; they ate a certain amount of the powder every day and were okay. There was also, at one time, a very unusual and much un-discussed study which seemed to suggest that DDT exposure decreased your risk of cancer. But the short version is: it was heavily used, it

was clearly overused. The extent to which it remained in the environment, the extent to which it became concentrated going up the food chain, the extent to which it was deleterious to birds, the extent to which it thinned eggshells—those are all things people were terrified about. The information they had—if you go back and look at, for example, Rachel Carson and the evidence she cites—that kind of evidence is completely unacceptable forty years later. The guy who was doing the eggshell studies—it turned out he was not giving the birds enough calcium. The final outcome, as I understand it, is that some birds of prey are absolutely susceptible; peregrine falcons, for example, are absolutely susceptible to DDT. DDT, arguably, has certain other effects. It has never been demonstrated to be carcinogenic. The reason why any of this is a point of discussion is that by eliminating DDT, malaria worldwide exploded. Malaria had been the great scourge of mankind in the twentieth century. One by one, illnesses like Yellow Fever were dampened down—most of these diseases were in the United States in 1900. The United States had malaria in the south, for example, and it was gone. DDT took the total number of malaria cases in India down to fifty thousand a year. It was a true miracle—not that it wasn't also coming into situations where there were malaria-resistant mosquitoes and so on. Nevertheless, across the globe it was a powerful, powerful way to save lives. When it was banned by Ruckelshaus in '72 or '73 in this country, he specifically excluded medical uses from the ban so that it could be used abroad. Environmental groups, eager to make a name for themselves, pushed hard. The ban was really made final around the world in 2001. By then people knew the ban was lethal in terms of the number of people who died. Something like thirty million people died as a result of banning this substance and I think it's one of the great scandals. That's more people than Hitler and Stalin together killed. I'm sorry, but we don't have malaria in the United States, they don't have it in Sweden, they don't have it in France—so we don't care. We can ban DDT and use something else on our crops. People of color, people in Asia or in Africa—they're the ones who are dying. I'm sorry, a lot of people in this country just don't care, and that's really wrong. I'm getting riled up—you can see I feel very strongly. We have an obligation as a rich society, a rich nation, to be positively acting in the rest of the world and this is not a good example for us.

**Question:** Knowing that kids see what you create, does that change how you write?

**Crichton:** I operate on the assumption that kids are smarter than adults, because that's my experience. It's not only that the world is now filled with adults who are turning to their kids, going, "How do I get online and do this?" But the answer is no. I'm very trusting of my audience. People always say, "Aren't you afraid that you're going to do this?" The first book I did, *The Andromeda Strain*, people said, "Aren't you afraid you're going to be enhancing biological warfare and giving the government ideas?" I thought, "If the government has to get ideas from novels, we're in terrible trouble." But my answer is no. I think people read my books and understand.

**Question:** In your novel, *State of Fear*, you were very negative toward environmentalism. What caused you to be so prejudiced towards this religion?
**Crichton:** I don't think it should be a religion. It's interesting that you said I was "prejudiced." It's a disagreement; I would argue it's not a prejudice—it's a different way of seeing things. The core of my argument is that the environment is always changing, and [we must] understand that the environment is always changing if we are to do better than we do now. I would tell you that at this moment we have raw sewage seeping out of Yellowstone National Park, so we're not doing a great job. I mention the parks because the parks are unlike land-use where there are conflicts about "should we build a house." The parks are set aside. The parks are there for us to preserve. It turns out we don't know how to preserve them and we won't admit that we don't know how to preserve them. It's been a disaster—what we've done. When I look at how we treat the environment, I think we have to be flexible, we have to try things and see how they turn out, we have to be ready to change course, we have to be able to adapt, we have to say, "We're wrong and let's do it right," we have to do research. This is all stuff that fundamentalist religions can't do. If environmentalism is a fundamentalist religion, then that's not a good way to manage the environment. We need a scientific approach, we need a nonreligious approach, we need a way to look at this and do better than we've done. A lot better. It's essential; it's essential for you guys and for your children.

**Question:** Mr. Crichton, hi. If more aspects of anthropological studies were incorporated in standard high school curricula, like we do here at Cleveland, do you think it would have an impact on social issues or awareness? If you do, what kind of influence do you think it would have on such?
**Crichton:** What anthropology gives you is a perspective outside your own culture. We're all culture-bound in ways we never think about—that's why we're bound. How many meals should you have every day? How are they organized? What do you call the first meal, the second meal, the third meal?

What is the proper way to sleep? Do you sleep on the floor? Do you sleep off the floor? How do you interact with your family? What is your relationship to your mother, to your father? Do you have specific relationships with their brothers and sisters? In some societies, mother's brother's sister, or father's mother's brother has a specific kind of relationship and is required to do particular things for a child. A child will grow up knowing that if it's a question about sex—obviously you don't want to talk to your mother or father—you go talk to this person. And that perspective, that people really do organize their lives and their societies differently, is very liberating. We don't often have it—I'm glad it's here.

**Question:** Hi, Mr. Crichton. My name is Vin. This is a question from both me and my friend John, who's a big fan of your work: In several of your books it seems as if you are implying that big-time corporations, industries, and monopolies are a negative factor. Why is that, and what are your opinions on the matter?

**Crichton:** I love things that are really challenging. Some of you may know the reason why Japanese automobiles became so phenomenally successful globally in the 1980s was because of the Japanese interest in an American named W. Edwards Deming, who was a quality control guy. He was the one who helped them to understand—he's dead now, but he's a revered person there—to understand that to get quality control you have to do it all the way through manufacturing. It's not something you just slap on the bumper. I finally met Deming and we were talking about this. I said something negative about monopolies and he said, "What's wrong with monopolies? Monopolies are good." I thought, "Ew. I'm an American and I think monopolies are bad." "Aren't monopolies bad? Shouldn't we have competition?" He said, "What's so good about competition? We had this wonderful telephone company that was the best in the world and now we don't"—this was before cell phones. So I can have my mind changed. In the novels what I was trying to talk about is: sometimes there are large, monolithic organizations that may be making decisions about what technology will be available to us. Our range of choices has exploded. For example, a lot of companies now make thirty kinds of toothpaste; Crest—there are thirty kinds of Crest; there are little strips and there are tubes and there are bottles that stand up and bottles that lie down. For what? It's a kind of fake choice—it's toothpaste. In other ways, corporations may not be giving us the range of choices we'd like.

**Question:** Hi, my name's Brian. I'm a junior here at Cleveland. I was wondering: As a writer yourself, how do you respond to the critiques of other journalists, or do you even care or read about your books?

**Crichton:** I tend not to read reviews at all. A person who was very influential in my life is a painter named Jasper Johns, who you may know for his paintings of American flags. He's twelve years older than I am, so he's kind of a mentor. He said once in passing, "I always read these reviews hoping to learn something that's interesting about my work, but I never do." I thought, "Well, that's curious, because I haven't either." It seems as though in the end I always know more about my book, including its faults, than the reviewer. I'm only left with my emotional reaction and I'm constituted in such a way that if the review is good, I don't really get a boost; but if it's bad, I feel terrible. So, by and large, I don't read them. That's been true for a long time, not just this last book.

**Question:** You stated earlier that when you used to draw blood you felt sick. Did you feel sick at all when you were writing books as graphic as *Congo*?

**Crichton:** No, it's fantasy. When *Jurassic Park* was published there was a large—it seems silly now—but there was a large controversy about whether the book was anti-scientific; whether it was going to hurt science. My books are often seen as anti-something-or-other. I used to go around and say to people, "Guys, it's a dinosaur story." As Hitchcock used to say, "It's just a movie." So I don't get upset—it's fun to write them. I used to get up very early and write. One day my assistant came in and she thought I was having a seizure because I was sitting at my desk going [Turns his head and bites several times] and I was completely unaware. I was imitating a raptor in order to write about how the raptor did this biting. I act things out, but no, I don't get upset about what I write.

**Question:** Do you think you could have done as well with books like *The Andromeda Strain* if you didn't have an MD degree or any knowledge of medical sciences and workings?

**Crichton:** No. The problem for a young writer is: What do you write about? Before I went to medical school I wrote what a lot of young writers write: "She wouldn't go out with me," and "We went to the party and had an argument; she talked with this other guy instead." It was what was on my mind at that time, but it wasn't really of wide interest, especially to older people who just looked at it and went, "Another adolescent." Medical school was great because it gave me something to write about. It gave me something from the real world. In that sense, it's fantastic training. You see people who are severely ill; you see life in a raw and inherently dramatic way. I came out of there four years later with a subject matter. In that sense it was fabulous.

**Question:** Hi, my name is Diane. Is there anything you're working on right now or plan to in the near future?
**Crichton:** I just finished a book that's pretty controversial in a lot of circles, so I'd like to do something that isn't. It took me three years to do this last book, which is a lot of research and I'd kind of like to do something that isn't that intensive. I've also been married more times than I care to admit, although not as many as Mickey Rooney. So I thought I would write about a marriage and it would end, of course, in a murder. The other thing is that all my life people have said, "You write in a very external way. It's as if, when I read your books, I'm watching a movie. You're not inside the characters heads." I would always say, "Because I don't think that's possible." I think when somebody writes what the person is thinking, that's just a fantasy, it's artificial, it's not really what's going on. I think people don't have any idea why they do what they do. So I thought I would write a book that would explain that point of view. Maybe that'll be controversial, too.

**Question:** Hi, my name is Dwija. What advice would you give for people who want to become writers?
**Crichton:** Write. It's a funny thing, I never thought about it, but Stanley Kubrick was asked that question: "How do I become a movie director?" He said, "Go make a movie. Get a camera. Go and do something." I think it's the same. There are two reasons: The first is that if you are interested in writing, which I think of as a kind of physical occupation—I know you're just sitting there, but it feels like it's physical—you learn to do it in a way like you would learn to pole-vault. You've have to go do it. You have to fall on your face a lot. Eventually you learn: "Okay, stick the poll in the slot this way, and you go up this way," and it's complicated. That's the first thing. You learn a little bit about how to do it. The second thing, which is probably more important, is you learn if you really want to live your life that way. It's an unusual life. You're alone a lot and you're a self-starter. When I get up in the morning, if I don't sit down and work, nothing happens. I don't have a boss. I don't have somebody saying, "Punch the clock." It's not a lifestyle for everyone.

**Question:** Have you ever noticed people over-interpreting your work? How does that make you feel?
**Crichton:** Not long after I wrote *The Andromeda Strain*, I got a letter from

a sixteen-year-old girl who said, "I've read this book and it's all based on the human hand. There are six scientists, and then there are five, and those are the five fingers. This one is this, this one is this, the person who didn't come was named Kirk and Kirk is church, so the religious aspect is being set aside. I read this, and this is all the symbolism that's in the book. I want to know if that's what you intended?" It was a fantastic essay. I read it and thought, "Wow. Isn't this incredible," because it made complete sense. I had to, unfortunately, write her back and say, "None of this was in my mind." I could see that it all worked out. The character whose name was Kirk—I wasn't really thinking of church. I was actually thinking of Kierkegaard, but I didn't want to say Kierkegaard, so I shortened it. I had different ideas. It doesn't mean that her interpretation was not right. I actually think my books are usually under-interpreted. People go, "Oh, well, he's just doing that." A lot of people do that.

**Question:** Hi, my name is Jessica and I'm a senior. I'm in creative writing right now, so we started writing plays and books and poetry. I had a really hard time trying to get started and getting in a state of writing. What advice would you give me and other students in my creative writing class?

**Crichton:** I learned only two or three things about how to write. The first thing is that it's a state, as you said, and the way to get yourself in the state is to follow a ritual. If you look at how writers behave, most of them have rituals. Hemingway used to sharpen all his pencils every day. A lot of writers—Jack London, Hemingway, and others—would insist that they did a certain number of words; five hundred words or fifteen hundred words. If Hemingway was going fishing the next day he'd do double the number of words so he could take the next day off. This kind of formal structure is really useful. For most of my life—I'm embarrassed to admit it—but my way of getting into it was I would go in and make a cup of instant coffee and have a cigarette. By the time I had done that I was ready to go. Now, of course, all that's left is the instant coffee. Anything you do repeatedly will get you there. The other thing I discovered, which is really weird—I used to have writer's block a lot in my life—I discovered that the real reason why I was blocked was that I didn't know what I wanted to say. If you sit down before you know what you want to say, that's worse because now you're staring at the paper or the computer going, "I don't know what to say." So I learned it was easier to decide what you wanted to say before you actually did it. I don't sit down until I've really thought through things, and I'll think about something to write for a couple of years. You don't have that luxury in this class, but it's nice to really make a plan and then sit down and execute it—that helps.

**Question:** Hi, my name's Aradi and I was wondering: You said that when you write books it causes a lot of controversy. After you publish, do you have any doubts that it may cause more?

**Crichton:** What's unfortunate about controversy is that generally you can predict in advance exactly how it'll go and exactly who will say what—who'll like it, who won't like it. It's as if everybody's decided their position on everything and you're just feeding the hopper in some way. I mentioned earlier Jasper Johns, and I did a book about him in the 1970s. He was having a large retrospective at a museum in New York. After I'd worked on this book for nine months and gotten all the pictures, and it was such an intense thing, I said to him, "I wonder what the reaction will be when the book comes out, and when the show comes out?" He and a couple of other people who worked with him were there and they just stared at me, like, "What do you mean? This one will say this, this one will say this, this one will say this, this one will like it, this one will think it's stupid, this one will think it's overrated." The entire art world knew everyone's response before the show came out. No one was having a fresh response. I think in controversial areas, like the last book—which is in the environmental area—people have their positions and they hold them. Since the idea of the book is to try and encourage people to take a fresh perspective, a lot of people won't like that.

**Question:** Hi, my name is Jonathan. As a writer, what type of books do you read for inspiration or just for leisure?

**Crichton:** It's funny. I practically don't read any fiction and I don't know why that is. Maybe I don't have time. I'm usually researching something and I'm often trying to answer a question that may be very ill-formed. Right now, for example—and I don't know why—I'm interested in two things: What is it that makes people really want to tell other people how to behave? Like, "Let me tell you." You guys are in school, that's different. But in the wider world there are people who really feel they know how everybody ought to be. Whereas my feeling is always: I have my hands full just taking care of myself; other people, as long as they stop at the stoplights and so on, can make their own decisions. I'm interested in what psychologically makes somebody have that confidence. The other part of that is I think there's a deep and secret human impulse to live in a totalitarian state. We all say, "Oh, no. We wouldn't want that." But it's amazing, the extent to which there's a conformist desire among people. I don't understand that and I'm not even sure what I said is true, but I'm reading a lot to try and get a perspective.

**Question:** Hi, my name is Lindsey. If you had not begun your career in writing, what career would you have chosen?

**Crichton:** I guess I would still be a doctor and still telling people, "Why are you calling me in the middle of the night?" I was interested in being an architect—I liked that. I liked the idea of something that would combine engineering and some kind of artistic aspect. But the truth is I don't think I can imagine myself doing anything else. I feel phenomenally fortunate to do what I do. I get to ask some question: What was going on in the United States in the late 1930s when Hitler was establishing this Nazi society in Germany? How were the Americans reacting? I know some Americans admired Hitler; some famous ones: Charles Lindbergh, Joseph Kennedy—who was John Kennedy's father—a lot of people. But how did Americans feel? What was anti-Semitism like at that time? That was before I was born, although not long before I was born. I feel really privileged that I can take a few months out of my life and research that.

**Question:** This will be the last question: What led you to believe that the facts proving the hazards of secondhand smoke are misleading and false?

**Crichton:** Secondhand smoke is an amazing story. The short version is that the EPA investigated it in, I think, 1991–92, and was not able to demonstrate that there was a carcinogenic effect. By "not able to demonstrate it" means, according to the EPA guidelines, you have to have ninety-five percent confidence intervals; there has to be statistically strong evidence. They couldn't get it. They did six studies; they combined all the studies. They still couldn't get it. They dropped their thing to ninety percent. To go from ninety-five percent to ninety percent—it's hard unless you know statistics—ninety percent means it may or may not be there. You want ninety-five percent or ninety-nine percent. They didn't have it. They nevertheless classified it as a Class-A carcinogen. California was the first state to pass anti–secondhand smoke ordinances—all of which I'm in favor of. I don't like people smoking next to me. I don't feel good in places like Germany and France where they smoke right next to you. I don't want people smoking—smoking causes cancer. But secondhand smoke does not cause cancer. Part of how I got to it was my daughter and her friends were going down the street pulling their shirts up as they passed some poor schlump out smoking a cigarette. I said,

"What are you doing?" They said, "Oh, it's cancer." It's not. In '98 a federal judge said to the EPA, "You can't do this. You haven't made the case. You've broken your own guidelines. This is not demonstrated. It has never been demonstrated." Believe me, there are physicians and groups dying to show it, and it has never been brought to a level of significance. It may have other effects. It's certainly unpleasant, but I'm opposed to passing laws based on phony science. I think it's a bad precedent. Thank you.

CPSIA information can be obtained
at www.ICGtesting.com
Printed in the USA
LVHW090338191221
706242LV00001B/57

9 781617 030